The pioneers of jet aviation believed a daemon lived in the sky, behind an invisible wall called the 'sound barrier'. These early pilots said anyone who challenged the barrier in the quest for more speed was confronted by the daemon, who would shake your aircraft so violently that your instruments would shatter, your controls would freeze up and you would poop in your flight suit.

This man is funny; he makes me want to dive back into his book every evening faster than a refugee in an airstrike.

Serge has the right stuff, and the wrong stuff, and some stuff that will peel the enamel of your teeth and make your hair stand up. And that's why he's a pilot. God bless aviators.

Paul Carter, author of *Don't Tell Mum I Work on the Rigs . . .*
She Thinks I'm a Piano Player in a Whorehouse

MAC 'SERGE' TUCKER

FIGHTER PILOT

MIS-ADVENTURES
BEYOND THE SOUND BARRIER WITH AN
AUSTRALIAN TOP GUN

ALLEN&UNWIN
SYDNEY · MELBOURNE · AUCKLAND · LONDON

This edition published in 2014
First published in 2012

Allen & Unwin
83 Alexander Street
Crows Nest NSW 2065
Australia
Phone: (61 2) 8425 0100
Email: info@allenandunwin.com
Web: www.allenandunwin.com

Cataloguing-in-Publication details are available
from the National Library of Australia
www.trove.nla.gov.au

ISBN 978 1 74331 870 6

Maps by Darian Causby
Set in 12/17 pt Minion Pro by Midland Typesetters, Australia
Printed in Australia by McPherson's Printing Group

10 9 8 7 6 5 4 3 2 1

MIX
Paper from
responsible sources
FSC® C001695

The paper in this book is FSC® certified.
FSC® promotes environmentally responsible,
socially beneficial and economically viable
management of the world's forests.

*To JP—A true gentleman, mentor, friend and leader;
and my fellow brothers in arms with whom I have served.
YKYMF!*

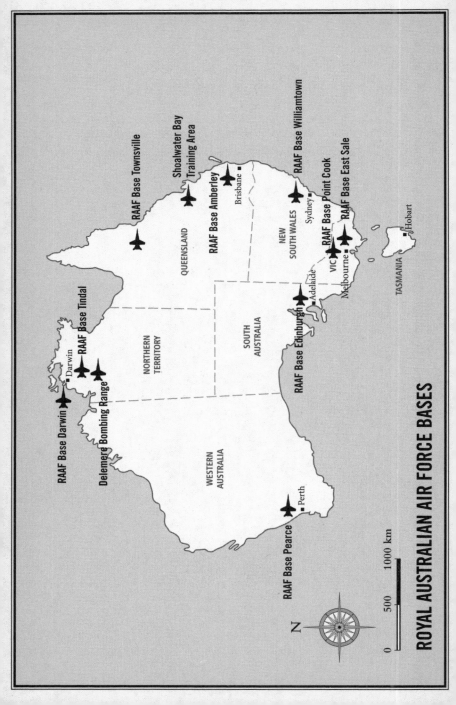

ROYAL AUSTRALIAN AIR FORCE BASES

RAAF Base Darwin
RAAF Base Tindal
Delamere Bombing Range
RAAF Base Townsville
Shoalwater Bay Training Area
RAAF Base Amberley
RAAF Base Williamtown
RAAF Base Point Cook
RAAF Base East Sale
RAAF Base Edinburgh
RAAF Base Pearce

Darwin
Brisbane
Sydney
Melbourne
Adelaide
Perth
Hobart

NORTHERN TERRITORY
QUEENSLAND
NEW SOUTH WALES
SOUTH AUSTRALIA
WESTERN AUSTRALIA
VIC
TASMANIA

N

0   500   1000 km

Contents

Introduction

WHY DID I write this book? A number of reasons I guess—although I'm unsure of the relevant weighting on each of them. Six years ago, when I first started writing, I think it was largely to prevent my brain atrophying as I watched a jumbo's autopilot fly me around the world while fantasising that I was still a pilot. For those of you who find this statement hard to understand, I hope this book provides you with some insight as to why most fighter pilots detest their airline jobs as they become enslaved to their wallets.

As a fighter pilot I always felt guilty about the undeserved notoriety attached to the job. From the first time a girl said to me, 'Yeah, right,' when I told her what I did for a job, until now where I am still considered, in ever decreasingly small circles, some sort of superhuman for what I did ten years ago—thanks, Grandma. I hope this book lifts the veil on the profession and shows it for what it truly is rather than the Hollywood version. We never played half-naked volleyball like Maverick and Goose in *Top Gun*—although streaking on Friday nights was fairly common.

I hope I have provided an honest account of one of the best jobs on, and off, the planet. I'm constantly being asked what it was like, and can I have a chat to Johnny who is thinking of joining the air force. The intricacies of the job make it hard to describe in any way that does it justice; the personalities, the psychology, the risk, the sacrifice and the rewards. It is a complex mosaic that cannot easily be answered at a dinner party without railroading the conversation for the entire evening—something fighter pilots are actually very good at doing . . . especially if their hands are not tied together.

This is probably the number-one reason that there aren't more books on fighter flying—it is almost impossible to describe the dynamics without using both your hands, your watch, two stubbies and a couple of beer coasters. This limitation is also why I have minimised the number of flying sequences throughout the book and maximised the fart lighting and beer swilling.

I am proud of what I achieved within this elite organisation and the men I served alongside. It is not a force that is easily used in the villages of Afghanistan, nor in the streets of Baghdad. It is an incredibly expensive insurance policy against a worst-case national defence scenario—which is why it's so easily handballed around during peacetime budget estimates. It is not a force that can be used to win hearts and minds, even though Western nations are still trying. It is a force to be unleashed when your country is backed against a wall and the politicians no longer care about their next election cycle. This is the mentality of those who fly fighters—the majority take it very seriously and dedicate their all to the cause. Unfortunately for Australia, few fighter pilots make it into senior military positions due to their uncompromising dedication to the mission—something most senior officers trade in for a comfortable life and fat pension.

While fighter pilots are some of our nation's most capable individuals, they are also fallible and stupid like any other human being; they get scared, make mistakes, embarrass themselves and get paper cuts on their arse. I have tried to show the human side to fighter flying as much as shooting MiGs and dropping bombs.

I sincerely hope you enjoy the book.

Serge

The GOAT— Glossary Of Acronyms and Terms

1FTS No. 1 Flying Training School—basic flying training which was conducted on the CT-4 air trainer at RAAF Base Point Cook, Victoria

2FTS No. 2 Flying Training School—advanced flying training which was conducted on the Macchi MB-326H jet trainer at RAAF Base Pearce, Western Australia

81 Wing the entire operational fighter force of the RAAF consisting of No. 3, No. 75 and No. 77 Squadrons

AA-11 Russian heat-seeking missile—codenamed 'Archer'

AC-130 C-130 Hercules that shoots three big guns sidewards . . . the Taliban's worst nightmare

AAR air-to-air refuelling—or 'plugging'

ADF Australian Defence Force

ADFA Australian Defence Force Academy. Where 'ACWACS' (Academy Wackers) go to get a degree before starting pilots course

ADI attitude display indicator . . . your best friend when flying supersonic at low level in a thunderstorm at night

AGL above ground level—the most important number in the HUD when flying near the ground; although most low flying is done with eyeballs alone

AIM-7 F-18 semi-active radar—guided missile—also known as the Sparrow; was replaced by the AMRAAM in the late 90s

AIM-9 F-18 heat-seeking missile—also known as the Sidewinder due to the path flown by early versions of this missile

alert fighters are maintained at high levels of readiness depending on the

alert state e.g. alert 3 (three minutes to take-off); alert 60 (60 minutes to take-off)

AMRAAM Advanced Medium Range Air-to-Air Missile. The most advanced radar guided air to air missile in the world—a MiG's worst nightmare

AMSL above mean sea level—sea level is often used as our altitude reference datum; 6076 feet (1850 metres) AMSL equates to the Mile High Club, something few fighter pilots ever get to join in their single-seat aircraft

afterburner AB—maximum power selection which the pilot achieves by pouring fuel directly into the hot jet exhaust at a rate of 19000 litres per hour; nothing more than a controlled explosion under your arse

angle of attack the angle between the waterline of the wing and the free stream airflow—nose-high attitudes equate to high angles of attack or high alpha

APU auxiliary power unit—a little jet engine that is used to start the bigger ones

AVMED aviation medicine—a bunch of guys in white lab coats who like exploding things under fighter pilots' arses and exploding their sinuses

bandit an enemy aircraft during training—replaced by the term 'hostile' during operations

BFM basic fighter manoeuvres, or dogfighting—there is nothing basic about it at all (I'd hate to find out what advanced fighter manoeuvres are all about)

Blue Death BDU-33 (bomb, dummy, unit, 33 pounds) practice bomb—while used predominately for practice, the effectiveness of these weapons was once proven on a fire truck at Beecroft Range which was misidentified as the bombing target (it never drove again)

blunt derogatory term used by pilots to describe any ADF personnel at the bottom of the pyramid, such as cooks and bottle washers. More commonly, the term is used to describe anyone, including pilots, who display a lack of focus on the operational aspects of the force

Bograt junior fighter pilot—generally equates to a D-category fighter pilot who is not yet qualified to lead a pair

C-130 Hercules transport aircraft, also known as Fat Albert—after flying to the east coast of the USA and back again in one of these aircraft I'll be happy if I never see one again

CAP combat air patrol—a specific search pattern flown by fighters that optimises their sensors to detect enemy aircraft

CASA Civil Aviation Safety Authority

chaff fine hairs of aluminium that are released to confuse an enemy radar

CFI chief flying instructor

CFS Central Flying School—RAAF flying school at RAAF Base East Sale for flying instructors (non-FCI) and navigator instructors. Also home to the Roulettes—the RAAF's aerobatic team

clean a jet configured with no external stores such as fuel and ordnance—absolutely useless in a real shooting match, this configuration is always preferred during training so that fighter pilots can fantasise about being Luke Skywalker

CO commanding officer—the boss of a fighter squadron and holds the rank of wing commander (doesn't make sense to me either)

cons contrails, or vapour trails—generated by jet aircraft at high altitude where temperature and moisture levels are appropriate; generally avoided in modern combat but can sometimes be used for 'spoofing' the enemy

CT-4 CT-4 air trainer—a single engine, low wing, side-by-side seating RAAF training aircraft; affectionately known as the Parrot

Datalink a radio connection between aircraft over which information such as location, radar mode, weapons and fuel state is continually passed. This removes the requirement to use the radio for this information

DIO Defence Intelligence Organisation—an oxymoron used to describe the organisation that is supposed to manage the intelligence associated with foreign military equipment

dogfight the classic test of a fighter pilot's mettle—one aircraft against another where each aircraft attempts to manoeuvre behind the other in order to employ the gun (see also BFM)

DSTO Defence Science Technology Organisation—a bunch of really smart boffins trying to find better ways for the ADF to do business

E2B compass a $50 ball of fluid fitted to all military aircraft (once saved my bacon)

EMCON emission control—no-emission tactics where fighters inhibit the use of their radar, radar altimeter, TACAN, IFF, Datalink and jammer

ESM electronic support measures—detecting enemy radio emissions

F-22 Raptor the best manned fighter aircraft that will ever be built—balancing kinematics with stealth, this aircraft can out-shoot and out-bomb most enemy aircraft or SAMs purely through its kinematics; the joint strike fighter, which the RAAF have bought, however, is a flying guppy totally dependent on stealth for survival and which has difficulty out-shooting or out-bombing an F-18

F-111 'the Pig'—a high-speed, straight-line, missile-absorbing, bullet-attracting, taxpayer's-money-soaking aircraft that did a great job of lighting its own farts at airshows and convincing people it would last more than 30 seconds in a real shooting match

FCI fighter combat instructor—a RAAF weapons instructor who is qualified to train fighter pilots in all sequences of flight, including advanced tactics; the qualification is approximated by that held by a Jedi knight; FCIs are often referred to as 'Charlies' (which is the phonetic letter for 'C', which is short for cunt)

fight's on radio transmission used to commence a dogfight

FL290 flight level 290 equates to 29 000 feet—aviation units are totally screwed up (metres for visibility, feet for altitude, nautical miles per hour for speed, milliradians for angles in the HUD, degrees for attitude, the confusion goes on and on . . .). In this book I've tried to standardise so those of you without a fighter pilot's brain for numbers can get a feel for the action, but accept no responsibility for the fist-shaking of other pilots out there. Where radio calls in fighter-speak have been reproduced I've included metric units as well

FLA four-letter abbreviation

FLIR forward-looking infra red—targeting pod that can see at night

flying suit Nomex fireproof suit worn by pilots

four-ship four-aircraft formation

Fox 1 code word used to announce the launch of a semi-active radar homing missile such as the AIM-7 Sparrow

Fox 2 code word used to announce the launch of a heat-seeking missile such as the AIM-9 Sidewinder

Fox 3 code word used to announce the launch of an active radar homing missile such as the AIM-120 AMRAAM

freezer code word used when reducing the heat signature of an aircraft by reducing thrust and launching flares to deceive any heat-seeking missiles. At least one pilot has inadvertently shut down both engines when overzealously applying this tactic

G force the force of gravity—sitting there reading this, you are experiencing 1G such that you weigh whatever your scales read in the morning or you tell your boyfriend when he asks you; when a body turns a corner it accelerates such that the force it experiences is greater than 1G (this is how water stays in a bucket when you swing it up over your head—it is pushed into the bucket with centrifugal force); at 8G the body experiences eight times its own weight

GAF government aircraft factory; or, gives a fuck?

gate go code word used when selecting afterburner. Requires the pilot to manually push the throttles through a physical gate

GF general flying—flying techniques where the pilot does not use instruments but looks out the window

gin barge navy boat (definitely not a ship)

go-around an aborted landing where the aircraft applies full power prior to touchdown

gouge information that is very useful for fighter pilots (such as your XO's mobile number on a Friday night in Singapore)—an ounce of gouge equates to a pound of knowledge

GPS global positioning system

hard deck imaginary ground level of 1500 metres above ground, used for training purposes so pilots do not fly into the real ground

hot bunking also known as 'hot racking' or 'hot bedding', when more than one crew member is assigned to the same bed or 'rack' to reduce sleeping space. Two or even three people might end up sharing the same bed, depending on the shift rotation. Unfortunately for the few straight guys in the Navy, the term does not get its name from the fact that you might be sharing your bed with a hot woman but rather that your bunk might be 'hot' (or at least warm) from the sweaty fat guy with crutch rot who dribbled all over your pillow before you

FIGHTER PILOT

HUD heads-up display—an electronic display projected onto a pane of glass through which a pilot looks; the HUD imagery is focused at infinity which allows a pilot to simultaneously look for bandits, sight-in a ground target, and read his flight and weapon instrumentation

IF instrument flying—flying techniques where the pilot uses instruments to fly the aircraft at night or in cloud

IFF Identification of Friend or Foe. A transponder that is fitted to all fighters that transmits a friendly radio signal in order to identify the friendly when beyond visual range

INS inertial navigation system—stabilised platform that utilises accelerometers to determine acceleration, velocity and location; may be augmented by GPS

intakes air inlets for the jet engine

knucklehead term of endearment for fighter pilots that aptly describes their lack of common sense

LEX leading edge extensions—wing root extensions that run forwards down each side of the cockpit; very useful for falling off, putting used 'pisser packs' on, and directing highly disturbed air flow down the intake at extreme angles of attack

LGB laser-guided bomb—fighter pilots' weapon of choice for air-to-ground missions, LGB deliveries create extremely high workloads which result in high levels of satisfaction when the mission goes well (slowly being replaced by GPS-guided bombs, where the bomb has the high workload and the pilot just goes brain dead at 12 000 metres . . . nothing hard about it)

LGTR laser-guided training round—a practice LGB; they still do a lot of damage when you get it wrong

LOAC Law of Armed Conflict—a seriously flawed concept that most countries signed up for after World War II which outlines the moral ways to kill, as opposed to the immoral ways; by abiding to the moral code, while our enemies do not, we ensure that conflict lasts longer, ultimately increasing the cost on civilian life that the protocols portend to protect

LOWFA low-flying area

mach a measure of fighter speed as a proportion of the speed of sound—Mach 1 equates to the speed of sound (1236 kilometres per hour) while Mach 2 equates to twice the speed of sound and more than likely a near-death experience in the F-18 (as flight-tested by my USMC mate Spook)

Macchi MB-326H RAAF jet trainer—a tandem seat, constant thrust, variable noise Italian sportscar

MiG any aircraft designed by the Mikoyan-Gurevich Design Bureau—MiG is often used as a generic term to describe bandits during training—a hangover from the cold war

Mk 82 Mark 82—500-pound high-explosive bomb; can also be used as an aerial laid mine, or for fishing when you're in a hurry

MRE meal ready to eat—awesome US ration packs that include some voodoo magic; you can piss in the bag in the snow and it will boil the contents . . . just make sure you piss in the right bag

MSA minimum safe altitude—a number in the HUD that provides you safe separation from the cumulus concretus below you

NAVO navigation officer—responsible for making maps, data cards and electronic data files to load into the jet

NCO non-commissioned officers—the mature guys who drag the drunk knuckleheads home and put them into bed when they've been asleep on a park bench. Think twice next time you see a relatively young homeless guy

NOCOM no communications—no-radio tactics used to avoid detection by enemy listening posts

Nomad Australia's last attempt to make an aircraft—rebranded the Widow-maker (the RAAF sold them to the Indonesian air force—smartest strategic move the RAAF ever made)

NOTAM notice to airmen—the memos pilots must read before flying that outline safety-related matters such as airspace, navigation aids and runway works

NVG night vision goggles—the RAAF delayed the acquisition of NVGs beyond that of our regional neighbours as 'goggs' were deemed to be 'too dangerous' (the guy who 'deemed' it had never used them)

OLA ordnance loading areas

OPSO operations officer—manages the day-to-day aspects of the flying schedule including weather, weapon configurations and airspace

OTS officer training school—a three-month course in how to use a knife and fork politely for pilots who don't want a degree but just want to fly

PACAF US Pacific Air Force—winners of WWII and the US command under which the RAAF will fight regionally if there is a US-led coalition

P-3 Lockheed P-3 Orion—used to hunt for submarines while its occupants consume a serious number of prepared frozen meals; personnel assigned to these aircraft are called 'fish heads' as they spend most of their time at sea

Parrot term of endearment for the CT-4 air trainer basic training aircraft

PRF Pulse Repetition Frequency—a radar setting that can be modified by the pilot to optimise the range of detection

RAAF Royal Australian Air Force

rack to sleep, or a bed—not to be confused with a Mae West

RAN Royal Australian Navy

ROE rules of engagement—the rules by which we're allowed to 'play' with an enemy (Can we use our radar? Can we lock him up? Where can we lock him up? When can we shoot? etc.); the ROE were usually written by a bunch of lawyers who had little idea WTF they were talking about and inevitably required rewriting by an FCI

rpm revolutions per minute

RV rendezvous

RWR radar warning receiver—a magic box that deafens you if an enemy radar locks you up

RTB return to base

RWY runway

SAM surface-to-air missile—the number-one threat for fighter pilots (there's a shitload of them on the planet, they're easy to use, hard to defeat and we don't always know where they all are), as opposed to enemy fighters (which are rare on the planet, difficult to use, relatively easy to defeat and can usually be found parked near bitumen runways). Sad thing is the RAAF has no ability to train in a SAM environment as it is more 'fun' training for the Battle of Britain

SAR search and rescue

SAS Special Air Service—members of which we affectionately called 'chicken stranglers'

Secumar life vest used by pilots when they bail out over water—the nickname 'Mae West' originated because someone wearing the inflated life-preserver often appears to be as physically endowed as the actress, and it's also rhyming slang for breast

scramble order for jets to conduct an immediate take-off

sidewinder nickname for the AIM-9 heat-seeking missile carried by the F-18

SM-1 SAM a big flying telephone pole that the RAN would practise shooting at us—it turned about as well as a telephone pole and did little more than reassure the gin bargers

SOCO social club officer—the worst secondary duty that a fighter pilot could be given; responsible for seating plans, stocking the fridge, social functions and ensuring the weekly curry is delivered on time

speed jeans G suit

speed of sound the speed of sound equates to 1236 kilometres per hour

SQN squadron

spoofing tricking the enemy into believing something that is untrue—generally achieved by electronic warfare or cyber warfare; tactics can also be used to hide the friendly's intentions

STBY standby

SUU-5003 combined four-shot rocket launcher and six-round practice-bomb dispenser

tally I can visually see the enemy

TACAN tactical air navigation system—a system invented for the United States Air Force in Vietnam which is used to measure the distance between fighters; largely superseded by Datalink

TACP tactical air control party, or 'tactical place'—RAAF officers embedded in army headquarters for the purposes of winning the war

TIMESO times officer—second worst secondary duty in a fighter squadron; responsible for logging every flying minute and ensuring the squadron does not under-fly or over-fly their allocated hours (I once forgot a trailing zero in my calculations which resulted in us flying across Australia and back again on the last day of the financial year to use up our hours . . . yet the RAAF would not pay for a sandwich if we over-flew the mess lunch hour)

USAF United States Air Force

USMC United States Marine Corp—joint service that incorporates air, land and sea elements including F-18s; unlike the ADF and its 50 000 personnel, the USMC is able to focus 250 000 personnel on the same mission, in which they perform extraordinarily well (just don't ask them to conduct peace-keeping operations)

VB Victoria Bitter

vector kill heading that is used to control fighters

VSI vertical speed indicator—tells you how long you have until you hit the ground; usually measured in seconds

WEAPO weapons officer—secondary duty in a fighter squadron; responsible for logging all weapon releases to ensure each jet remains 'sighted in' and can accurately lay down ordnance

WMD weapons of mass destruction

WOFF warrant officer—senior rank of non-commissioned ranks; usually very crusty and short in patience with junior fighter pilots who think the world revolves around them . . . which it usually does

WTF What the fuck?

XO executive officer—second in charge of the squadron and the last true flying job before issues such as DUI, Skype and sexual harassment start to take over from the flying

YGTBSM You've got to be shitting me

zoom bag flying suit

1

When I grow up I want to be a fighter pilot

'Unfortunately, son, you can't do both.'

Dad

Off the coast of Newcastle, Australia, early 2000

'Hunter 1, inwards turn—fight's on.'

'Hunter 2, fight's on.'

I eased the jet into a turn to point directly at Matty, who was 200 kilometres north and simultaneously turning directly towards me. At 15 000 metres, even in full afterburner, the jet was a dog, the air too thin to produce the thrust I needed. We were closing at three times the speed of sound, or about 3600 kilometres per hour, and would cover the 200 kilometres in a little over three minutes. The smallest error, the slightest miscalculation, and we'd both be pink mist. Even after all my years of flying fighters, the adrenaline was still spiking through my veins, causing my right knee to shake uncontrollably—like some sort of supersonic Elvis move. Somewhere inside I knew this much adrenaline in my body wasn't good for me but, like a hopeless junkie, I couldn't stop—nothing else made me feel so alive.

I rarely felt emotional during a dogfight but today was different. This was my last ride, my very last time doing the one thing that I loved most in life—the thing that I had given everything to for so long. Up here on the edge of space, it was just Matty and me, in two 'clean' jets. No external stores, no pylons, no excess weight nor drag—just maximum available performance. It was the most amazing feeling. Better than drugs, better than sex—pure, unbridled speed.

I had just finished running a fighter combat instructor course, which Matt had duxed. He was the new swinging dick in town and I was the old neutered dog. Thirty years old. That was pretty much the use-by date for fighter pilots. Was I making the right decision leaving the air force now? I was about to find out.

I turned to centre the radar lock in my heads-up display (HUD) in order to gain tally of Matty's jet. It wasn't totally necessary at our altitude as we had both been able to see each other's condensation trails, or 'cons', from 160 kilometres away.

'Hunter 1, tally,' I transmitted.

'Hunter 2, tally,' Matty replied, and the dot on the horizon started to take shape; two wings, two fins then the intakes.

Despite the 3600 kilometre per hour closing speed, our brains were working overtime—calculating distance and speed, getting used to the time compression—and seemingly slowing down the events for us. Matt was positioning to pass down my left side and rolled onto his left wingtip in order to pull directly towards me. I matched his manoeuvre and gently pulled the jet into a 3G turn so it wouldn't bleed all my airspeed away. At this altitude the jet was extremely unforgiving. If you ham-fisted it, you could lose 150 kilometres per hour of speed in the blink of an eye. Fighter pilots have a saying— 'Speed is life'. And right now, I needed all the speed I could get.

We both pulled towards each other, both in lefthand turns, both looking through the tops of our canopies to keep sight of each other—I could see Matty's dark visor fixed on me like a laser dot sight. Then we merged . . . and suddenly things no longer seemed slow—at a few hundred metres 3600 kilometres per hour is brutally fucking fast.

The fight of my career was just beginning. But whether I won or lost this fight, leaving fighters would be my loss.

Aviation is almost unique in its ability to stir passion into the hearts of men—particularly young men. From the great fifteenth-century inventor Leonardo Da Vinci, to the now-infamous bicycle mechanics Wilbur and Orville Wright, who built and flew the first aircraft in 1903, man's journey to 'break the surly bonds'[1] is full of tales of bravery, ingenuity, tragedy and stupidity—the latter appearing just a little too frequently in this book (unfortunately for me). For some, their passion for aviation is an obsession—an illness—which they cannot control. They are the ones you see standing at the end of a runway with stiff necks watching aircraft take off and land—the 'planespotters' or 'airshow nerds'. You may see one stop mid-stride as he attempts to hone in on the almost inaudible sound of an airliner flying overhead at high altitude. They are everywhere and, as nerdy as they may seem, I must confess, I am one of them.

Where my obsession with flight comes from, I'm not sure, but with a father like mine I was doomed from the start.

When I was a young child, and much to my mother's horror, my father launched himself off the top of London Bridge in Victoria with a homemade hang-glider. You see, Dad was an electrician, and was able to source the electrical conduit at a good price. Together with some aluminium pipe and a tarpaulin, Dad was able to MacGyver up a pretty cool looking hang-glider designed around a Rogallo wing. The trouble for Mum was not so much that her bird-brained husband had converted his excess trade supplies into an aircraft, but that he was jumping off with her four-year-old son—me—strapped onto his back.

My dad still proudly produces photos of this event to anyone who can survive the first three hours it takes to make it through the entry foyer of his apartment, which is wallpapered with aviation memorabilia. The hang-gliding photos are particularly memorable, featuring my dad and his friends looking like 70s porn stars in their skin-tight flares and Mexican-bandit moustaches, with their cigarettes perfectly balanced on their bottom lips.

I wish I could remember more about it, but all I can recall of this momentous day is Mum and Dad fighting, Mum storming off to the landing site with the idea she could somehow catch me, Dad handing me the picnic basket that Mum had thrown down in a tantrum, Dad launching off into space and then . . . freedom.

I don't know whether the fascination for flight originates from the same place for all airheads, but I'm pretty sure that man's unending pursuit of freedom has a lot to do with it. An aircraft is a teenager's ultimate fast car—a passport to anywhere in the world you want to go, to freedom. I remember the first time my teenage brain took a moment to forget about girls and work out that a fast car would take me to that wild town called freedom a lot quicker than a slow car.

The year was 1986 and I was sixteen years old. The F-18 Hornet had just been introduced into service with the Royal Australian Air Force (RAAF) and two jets had flown down to RAAF Base East Sale for an airshow so the Australian taxpayers could see the latest weapon in their arsenal. Airshows were a regular feature of life in our family and, with Dad being a complete aviation nut, I don't think I ever missed one as a kid.

The F-18 was like nothing I had ever seen before, except maybe Luke Skywalker's X-Wing fighter. It completely outmanoeuvred its predecessor, the French-built Mirage, and every other aircraft at the show. It was full of computers, had a heads-up display, and with the leading-edge extensions (LEX) and twin tails it looked like no other aircraft on the planet at that time. I was mesmerised by that plane and my career decision was made right there and then, much to my father's disappointment—he'd wanted me to become a doctor. (I quickly realised that Dad's child-like love affair with aviation did not extend past his own social insecurities and the implied elevation that a doctor in the family could bring him.) I quietly wondered if the air force offered a PhD in aerial combat. I didn't know it at the time, but eleven years later I would find out the answer.

That day at the airshow I couldn't wait to have a look at one of the jets up close, and after the show I struggled against the crowd to get to the front barrier rope. The engines cried out in deep howls as they were shut down—as if the jets were protesting against being tethered back to the earth. The pilots stepped down from the cockpits, took off their safety equipment and walked over to the crowd. Signing pictures and T-shirts and handing out stickers, they seemed more like rock stars than military officers. I guess I could put up with a bit of the limelight if I had to, I thought.

I waited for the crowds to die down and then nervously approached a tall, dark-haired pilot who was fit and clearly the focus of most of the women in the crowd.

'Aaah, um, hello, Sir, I just wanted to, um, talk to you about the Hornet.' I was so nervous in the presence of this war-god from the heavens I stumbled over my words like a complete idiot.

But my embarrassingly obvious keenness must have endeared me to the pilot, who introduced himself as Ross Fox, or Foxy, and put me at ease straightaway, showing me around the F-18 and describing what it was like to fly and what life as a fighter pilot involved. My extreme thirst for knowledge would normally have had a fighter pilot like Foxy concerned that hostile intelligence agents were at work, but he saw it for what it was: a boy totally infatuated with flying—just like he had been some twenty years earlier.

He ended up spending two hours teasing me with his tall tales from the other side of the sound barrier, and then he made me an offer no sixteen-year-old airhead could refuse.

'Would you like to come to Williamtown and see what we do up close?' he asked.

I couldn't believe it. He was giving me a chance to go to a fighter base and spend a week doing some work experience with the fighter pilots. I checked with my dad, got the thumbs-up, all the arrangements were made, and a few months later I was off to RAAF Base Williamtown—'The Home of the Hornet'.

Dad drove me through the night from Melbourne to Newcastle, about 160 kilometres north of Sydney, to an address Foxy had given me in East Newcastle. At the time this was a pretty dodgy part of town as it was located close to a lot of bars and beaches—two things I would come to appreciate for myself in just a few years.

Foxy had organised for a fighter pilot named Mookeye to look after me. I looked at the address again to confirm I was at the right place and tentatively knocked on the door. No answer, so I knocked a little louder. Still no answer. Shit, maybe I got the details wrong from Foxy. I knocked one more time and finally heard some creaking floor-boards in response. Then the door opened and the guy in jogging shorts did not look happy about me waking him up at midday.

'Umm, ah, hi,' I stammered, 'I'm Mac. I was meant to be meeting Mookeye here.'

To my relief, his frown dropped away and he smiled. 'G'day, Mac—come in, mate. I'm Mel. Mookeye will be back soon and told me to look after you until then. Here, let me grab your bags.'

It seemed Mel wasn't pissed off after all. He made me feel totally welcome and showed me around, and I discovered I was going to spend a week living with three junior fighter pilots—affectionately known as 'Bograts'. Let me assure you, junior pilots not only fly hard, they party hard. If my father had known then what he knows now, he would never have agreed to me staying there. I'd been a fairly sheltered sixteen-year-old, but this week was an education for me in more ways than one.

The boys were, however, great at looking after me—at home and at work. In Newcastle we ate out, went to the beaches and pilot parties, and had an awesome time. I can handle this lifestyle, I thought. But it was at work where I had the most fun.

I spent the entire week working alongside the fighter pilots of No. 3 Squadron, except when they went flying. The daily rhythm of morning brief, mission brief, mission, debrief, lunch, mission brief, mission, debrief and bar became second nature by the end of the week. When the guys were airborne, Mookeye arranged visits for me around the base. At the air traffic control tower I got to use the radio and clear the jets for take-off and landing. At the Sector Air Defence Centre I got to vector fighters to intercept and kill 'bandits' by telling them what heading to fly over the radio. And finally, the highlight of my trip was the simulator, where I got to practise shooting missiles and dropping bombs. This was years before PlayStations and Xboxes—the only computer I had ever played with before was a Commodore 64.

The week over, I reluctantly said goodbye and thanked Foxy, Mookeye, Mel and all the pilots from No. 3 Squadron. Dad picked me up and we drove home to Melbourne through the night, with me on constant transmit telling him about everything I had done. It was a fantastic opportunity for a sixteen-year-old boy and something I subsequently did for a few kids when I was flying fighters—one is now an F-18 pilot at No. 3 Squadron. In the words of Paul Kelly, 'From little things big things grow.'

Wanting to be a pilot wasn't just about the aircraft or the lifestyle, though—it was about freedom. My teenage years at home hadn't been the easiest. My mum and dad had separated when I was four (not sure how long after the hang-gliding 'issue') and my brother and I went to live with our father.

I saw little of my mother during my childhood except for compulsory Christmases and birthdays. These were always uncomfortable for everyone, with one particular Christmas, 1984, being most uncomfortable for Dad. I was fourteen years old and Dad drove my brother and me to my grandparents' house in Gippsland, as this was deemed to be neutral ground for my parents. My mother's extended family were all in attendance, while Dad sat alone in the corner like he had shit his pants. Until a particularly good-looking blonde arrived at the festivities. Well, this was exactly the opportunity Dad needed to show his ex-wife just how hot he still was—just you watch me work my mojo, bitch. Things went pretty well for Dad and we left the family lunch after the court-ordered mandatory two-hour period.

On the drive back to Melbourne my dad started to brag about his manly exploits. 'Did you see that leggy blonde Vanessa, boys? Gaawhh, I think she was pretty keen on me. What do you think?'

My brother and I could not constrain our smirks and giggles.

'What are you guys finding so funny back there?' my father asked.

'Nothing, Dad,' I lied, while my brother turned lipstick red doing his best to control his laughter.

'I said, what the hell is so bloody funny? If I have to stop this car . . .'

I had to answer him now but was too afraid that the truth would make him stop anyway—it was a lose-lose proposition for me. My brother and I were fucked.

'Vanessa is Uncle Jack,' I blurted out in a mix of laughter and tortured confession.

Since we had all last seen Uncle Jack he had decided he was really a woman and had the chop. The look on Dad's face was priceless. My brother and I spent the next three hours studying the broken form of our father through the rear-vision mirror. He had the look of an Aussie expat who has just found out that the cheap Thai hooker was too cheap to be true. I can only imagine how my mother felt about Dad's mojo.

By the time I was fifteen, I'd lived with three mothers and two fathers, so you can see why I thought the RAAF might be my quickest way out of the domestic ground zero. I know that my mental tenacity was forged over this ten-year period—arguably the most impressionable years of my life.

At the end of high school I went for an overseas holiday with my mother which, sadly, felt very awkward. For all our years living apart I felt emotionally disconnected from her and not 'deserving' of such a gift. That holiday was, however, the first step in re-establishing our relationship, which we are still working on today. When I was still a kid Mum got remarried to a wonderful guy, who has looked after her tremendously well, and we now enjoy each other's company whenever we can.

The highlight of this holiday with my mum was a visit to Topgun in the US. Topgun is the United States Navy Fighter Weapons School that was made famous by Tom Cruise in the movie of the same name in 1986. Before we left Australia, I wrote to Topgun and told them to get ready, because I was on my way. When we arrived at Miramar Naval Air Station in California, a young F-14 pilot met me at the gate to give me a tour of the base and the facilities. I spent the remainder of the holiday sewing the Topgun badges onto my leather jacket, imagining I would give Tom Cruise an arse-whipping as soon as I graduated from fighter training.

When most kids my age were hanging out at the shopping mall, I was hanging out at the Australian Defence Force recruiting office in St Kilda Road, Melbourne—and no, it wasn't just about the hot blonde corporal in the blue dress. I just wanted to make sure that whatever it took, I was going to be out my front door and into the RAAF at the first opportunity.

I had all my paperwork completed, including permission from my parents as I was under eighteen and a stop notice on the mail so I could intercept my Victorian Certificate of Education (VCE) at the Melbourne General Post Office an entire day earlier than my peers. I signed for it at the GPO and excitedly jumped on the tram to the recruiting office. I think they pushed me straight through just to get rid of me (I wasn't the corporal's type apparently—can't imagine why not).

Eventually I got the call to come in for pilot screening. My main worry was the medical screening, as I had asthma. As a child I had suffered a lot of bronchitis, croup and upper respiratory tract infections. This was in the days when doctors would prescribe penicillin for a sneeze and I was forever getting shots in the arse for a runny nose which would hurt for days due to the penicillin being semi-frozen when it came out of the fridge. The end result was that I wasn't the healthiest kid . . . until I got asthma in my early teens.

The first few attacks scared the shit out of my dad and me as we didn't know what was happening. Eventually I was diagnosed and I cried myself to sleep that night, knowing I could never join the air force. I remember this night very clearly as it was one of the few occasions in my life that my father looked on me with compassion and held me while I cried.

The next morning I woke to the healthiest breakfast I had ever seen, with my dad fully convinced that asthma could be overcome: 'We just need to find a way to beat it,' he said.

His confidence was contagious and when I arrived at school that day I joined the cross-country team. I started training twice a week at school and at home as well. I refused to use a Ventolin inhaler and some nights I'd return home dizzy with blue lips. After a few months I couldn't feel any improvement and started to think that Dad's theory might not work—until he booked me in to see the man I came to call 'The Witchdoctor'.

Dad worked for the Melbourne Metropolitan Board of Works as an electrician on their underground tunnel-boring machines. Dad never rated his job very highly but I have wonderful memories of going to work with him as a teenager—descending down the shaft for hundreds of metres in a cage, going into a compressed airlock then travelling for kilometres in underground locomotives. It was like Batman's Cave and I loved every day on the job with him.

One of Dad's work colleagues was an Italian we will call Mario. Dad had been talking to Mario about me and my asthma when Mario, who could hardly speak a word of English, told Dad matter-of-factly that he could fix my asthma. Dad, my newfound supercoach, booked me in straightaway.

That night Dad excitedly told me I needed to come home straight from school the next day as Mario, 'his mate from work', was going to cure my asthma. I was still convinced that Dad knew how to kick this thing and so, just as excitedly, I agreed.

Dad and I headed off as soon as I got home from school and drove over the Westgate Bridge to Mario's house. On the way I thought I heard what sounded like a bird cooing inside the car and turned around to see a box with a towel draped over it in the rear of the stationwagon.

'Dad, what have you got a bird in the car for?'

'Oh, I, um, ah, I'm just minding it for a mate.' He looked shifty but it seemed reasonable to me—I had heard way more weird things from Dad in my life.

When we arrived at Mario's he greeted me with a hydraulic hand-shake and asked Dad if he had the 'thing', upon which Dad handed Mario the towel-covered box and Mario disappeared around the back of his house. I was starting to think that something was up as this guy did not look like any doctor I had seen before, in his Stubby shorts and wife-basher singlet. I was about to ask Dad what the fuck was going on when Mario came back, his hands and singlet covered in blood, like he *really* knew how to work the singlet.

I started to instinctively back away when I felt Dad catch me from behind, and before I could tell Dad that I thought I might have seen his mate in *One Flew Over the Cuckoo's Nest*, Mario had shoved a still-beating, bloody pigeon heart into my mouth, slammed my jaw shut, incanted some weird spell and passed me a glass of water to wash it down. (What, no Pinot? Goes well with pigeon heart, or so I'm told.) Mario went on to say how important it was that we returned the pigeon's body to the water as soon as possible.

I think I was still in shock at being force-fed a live pigeon heart by my father and a giant, psychotic Italian when we got to the top of the Westgate Bridge and Dad veered over to the railing.

'Throw it out now! Quick! Make sure it lands in the water or it won't work.'

What won't work? I thought. I was raised a Christian but I didn't remember any of this from Sunday School. But Dad was so gung-ho I couldn't argue with him—I let the bloody corpse fall into the water and wondered if I would catch something worse than asthma from eating raw pigeon offal.

Dad and I can't be sure what did the trick, but sometime between doing the pigeon-heart shooter and turning up to the RAAF medical twelve months later, my asthma was gone. Whether it was the year of intensive long-distance running without a puffer, or Mario's mumbo-jumbo magic, I was cured. I have never had an attack since and regularly compete in marathons and Ironman triathlons. Trouble with the RAAF was that if I tried the 'I used to have asthma but downed a live pigeon heart and now I'm cured' approach, they would probably have turfed me on both physical and psychological grounds.

Recruitment to the RAAF is a bit different now to what it was back then. In those days, if you had any medical condition known to man, and I mean any, you were out. If you had used drugs at all, you were out. If you were gay—or too happy, for that matter—you were out. If you had tattoos, you were out. If you had anything more than a speeding fine, you were out. If you were overweight, underweight, too tall, too short, too long in the thighs, could not see the woman instead of the vase, saw your mother in an ink blot or could not coordinate yourself on the hand-eye coordination test, you were out. Today you can be a fully-inked, morbidly overweight, gay, kleptomaniac crackhead and still get in. It seems that those from Gen Y onwards have 'commitment issues' with the ten-year Return of Service contract that all pilots are required to sign, and so the net has had to be cast just a little wider to meet the recruitment quota.

So, at my recruitment, I lied about my asthma, zipped my lips about the voodoo, was diagnosed with a sway back, was deemed to be underweight and the doc had some concerns for my psychological health based on a scar I have had across the back of my left hand since I was fifteen. So I had to go for some back scans, which turned out fine, and agree to put on some weight, which I did.

With all my testing completed I only had the final 'Murder Board' to get through. This was a one-hour interview with a board consisting of the psychologist, the doc, a recruitment officer and a senior pilot. My interview went well right up to the last five minutes when the pilot, Wing Commander Col 'Patch' Patching, pushed some papers in front of me and said that the board thought I had 'the right stuff' to go to the Australian Defence Force Academy, where I would have to spend three years getting a degree before going on to the pilot's course. Foxy had prepared me for this moment and I politely declined. To which Patch started threatening me, saying that I might not get a spot on the pilots' course for some time, questioning whether I wanted to be an officer and whether I would be able to make it to be Chief of the Air Force.

'I just want to fly, Sir,' was all I said—over and over until the recruitment chick I had been stalking for the previous two years got the shits and gave in. I thanked them all and headed home, not knowing if I had completely screwed myself or jagged it. It would be an anxious wait until I found out.

2

Do not get 'scrubbed'

ONLY A COUPLE of months after my 'death or glory' recruitment interview I received my letter of acceptance and was sworn into the Royal Australian Air Force as a commissioned officer (under training). The certificate even had a seal from the Queen—shit, that didn't take much, I thought. I guess those knights in England aren't that big a deal after all.

Not long after I was knighted, my dad dropped me and my suitcase off at RAAF Base Point Cook where I was to undergo officer training school (OTS) and basic flying training at the No. 1 Flying Training School (1FTS). Point Cook was on the western side of Melbourne, conveniently located next to the city's sewerage treatment plant. It would be years before I realised that this was a general theme of the air force; they always seemed to draw the short straw when it came to base locations. It seemed that the RAAF had difficulty locating noisy airbases on Sydney Harbour and the Perth beachfront, unlike the navy and army who seemed to score all the blue-chip waterfront in the country.

I arrived at the front gate with my joining instructions and was directed by the guard to the orderly room of the OTS headquarters. I reported to the front office wearing a dorky shirt and tie, and soon met a few of my fellow classmates, who also looked like they had the dress sense of a three-year-old.

They came from all walks of life. A few were straight out of school like me. A couple had been in the military as non-commissioned officers and were now taking up commissions to become officer pilots. Some came from general aviation where they had accumulated significant flying experience. Of the 36 guys and one girl on our OTS course I, without doubt, had the least idea about life. I started to get concerned that I would not have the 'right stuff' to get through the course.

This feeling lasted about a day, until I realised that the course wasn't going to be that demanding: march properly, clean my room well, iron my clothes, be fit and don't get in too much trouble. Really? I had pretty much been doing this for the last eighteen years at home—the only difference now was that the warrant officer of discipline only dished out push-ups or a run when I got in the shit—too easy.

We marched to the supply store where we were issued with uniforms and camping equipment then marched back to our blocks; WWI Heritage-listed buildings that weren't allowed to be renovated. These weatherboard buildings were draughty and poorly heated which made for some sleepless nights in Point Cook during winter— especially when we were only allowed 'one blanket, NATO-standard, mammoth-hair, ultra-coarse, for the use of'.

Next we were loaded onto buses and shipped into Werribee for the mandatory Long Bay Jail hairdo. It was hilarious watching guys who were clearly bogans from the country having to lose their rat's tails and mullets.

'Just a little off the sides and keep the length at the back, thanks, mate,' they would say to the little Greek guy who hardly spoke a word of English.

His reply was the same to all of us—a number-one blade with the clippers.

The bogans were clearly upset by the removal of their manhood and what Charlene was going to say when they got home on their first leave break.

The first Friday night at Point Cook our instructor 'invited' us to the cadets mess, which was an extension of the officers mess dedicated to feeding and watering the officer cadets and trainee pilots. It was also Ground Zero on a Friday night when the instructors would attend and assist the students with their 'extra-curricular' responsibilities, such as sculling (individual beer-drinking race), boat racing (team beer-drinking race) and playing mess rugby (after completing adequate instruction in the previous two). The back bar had relaxed dress standards which meant we could have a beer without looking like we were going fox-hunting with the Queen.

I felt like I was finally entering the holy of holies of the RAAF pilot-training establishment and turned up on that night proudly wearing my leather jacket which I had emblazoned with every badge I had ever collected from every airshow held during my lifetime— and unintentionally made a lot of enemies.

As soon as I stepped foot in the bar I was literally laughed out again by the senior course cadets and quickly branded with the callsign 'Mav', from Maverick (Tom Cruise's character) in the movie *Top Gun*. It was hurled at me with a lot of viciousness for the next two years. The continual mocking was a form of bastardisation designed to bring me down a notch and make me conform to the tribe's customs. Just like a fat kid being teased in the school yard, I felt totally alone. But my previous year in the caravan had prepared me well. Interestingly it was the older cadets who were the most vicious—it seemed a number of them suffered from 'old man syndrome' and did not appreciate an eighteen-year-old getting into the course ten years ahead of them. The pilots' course became a great equaliser.

My first Friday night at the 'cats mess', as the bar was known, started a trend that would stay with me for the next ten years of my career—drink long, drink hard—but only on weekends. I had never been drunk beforehand but after that I don't think I saw a Friday night sober for the next decade. My introduction to drinking came from an OTS instructor, Dog.

Dog was actually a pilot, but he'd been grounded and demoted for a series of shenanigans he committed while flying P-3 Orions. The most famous incident happened when he was the captain of the aircraft on a long-range submarine-hunting mission, flying low level at night on the autopilot with one engine shut down to save fuel. His copilot was having an authorised sleep with his seat reclined when Dog started getting weary himself. With a supremely blatant disregard for all the rules of safe flying, Dog strolled back to one of the airborne electronics analysts and told him to sit in the left seat and wake the copilot if the autopilot disconnect light illuminated, while Dog retired to the rear of the plane to have a kip. Yes, so much for an unwavering focus on the hunt for Red October. The copilot woke to find a white-knuckled 'scope dope' staring fixedly at the autopilot disconnect light as he had been instructed to do. Dog's punishment? He was exiled to Point Cook to instruct student pilots in how to behave as officers. That was my first taste of the ironic posting system that existed within the RAAF and was certainly not my last.

That night I walked into the 'fishbowl', which was an outdoor courtyard surrounded by glass, to see Dog standing on a bar stool on one leg with two cans of VB balanced on his head and senior course students attempting to knock the beer cans off with party pies. Dog was unflappable in his blue uniform as he became covered in mince and the occasional smattering of tomato sauce which made him look like an extra from a zombie movie. All this was for a bet that he subsequently won, then he shouted the bar a second time.

'What the fuck is wrong with you, cadet? Where's your beer?' he yelled at me when he saw me standing with a can of Coke in my hand.

'Oh, I don't drink, Sir,' I responded, a bit panicked and thinking I should fess up and tell him that in fact I had never drunk alcohol before. Ever.

'What sort of poof turns up at the bar on a Friday night in this mess and says "I don't drink"?' he demanded. 'Here, drink this,' and he thrust a warm can of VB, still covered in meat and sauce, into my hand.

Putting on my best 'Solo, the mark of a man' look, I cracked open the can and took a sip.

'Suit your delicate palate does it, you fucking girl? Now drink,' he said, pouring the beer down my throat, neck and all over my Tom Cruise wanker jacket.

And that was that. I woke up with a shocking hangover the next day and pretty much every Saturday for the next ten years. And I've never worn that jacket again.

Officer training school was more about putting up with bullshit than actually learning any life-changing knowledge that would enable me to lead men to war in an aircraft. It was all early morning rises, physical training, inspections, marching, theory, more inspections, and staying up late getting everything ready again for another inspection in the morning. Occasionally we got onto the weapons range, went out bush for some survival training or sat in a RAAF aircraft for a passenger ride. I found the course resembled a mix between my home life when I was a kid and Scouts. The main leadership attribute it built was tenacity, something that Dad had been doing a good job of instructing me in for the last eighteen years. I didn't find it stressful at all, but some did.

My coursemate, Rick, was a little older than me and highly intelligent in a crazy-inventor sort of way. He had converted the windscreen washers on his old Datsun into high-powered, remote-controlled water blasters that could be used to squirt people as you drove by, or even when you weren't in the vehicle. We enjoyed each other's company but I worried that compared to a brain like his I stood no chance of making it through the pilots' course. Unfortunately for Rick, his association with me soon led to him being branded with the callsign 'Goose'—Mav's crewmate in *Top Gun*. I really started to hate the movie and have never watched it since.

Each week cadets would take it in turns to act as the parade adjutant, the guy who yells the commands to the parade such as 'Ah ten ha' and 'Stand at . . . uugh'. By the time my turn came around I had perfected the commands with such precision it became hypnotic . . . in an embarrassing sort of way. Goose was the next parade adjutant; however, things did not go as smoothly for him.

The night before his stint as adjutant something snapped in Goose's head and he convinced himself he could not yell a few commands at his mates to get them to march around a parade ground. I sat up with him late in the night, practising commands around the officers mess using our tennis rackets as swords until we were both exhausted. Despite my best efforts, I watched as this highly capable guy dissolved before me in just a few hours.

I woke early the next morning so I could help Goose get his room ready for inspection and basically provide him with some moral support. Still half-asleep, I walked into the communal showers to find him standing in a puddle of his own blood as he intentionally shaved his neck from side to side along the line of the blade. As blood ran down his body and onto the white tiles, it was obvious he'd been trying to slice his neck open for some time. Sadly, Goose never made it any further towards his fighter career but was medicated and sent off to wherever they sent crazy student pilots. It was done in a way that minimised any impact on the remaining cadets—we got back that afternoon to find his room cleared out and no contact details for him. That Friday night 'Goose is dead' resonated around the cadets bar about as much as 'your shout'. I felt even more alone now that my mate had been 'rendered' off the base with my callsign attached to him.

With OTS out of the way we moved out of the WWI refrigerators and into the cadets mess proper to commence our pilot training at No. 1 Flying Training School. Finally, I was where I had imagined myself to be since I was a kid.

The first month was academics about weather, aircraft engines and checklists for our basic trainer: the CT-4 air trainer, or 'Parrot' as it was more affectionately known, due to its bright yellow livery—a paint scheme deliberately designed to maximise the ability of students to see each other and avoid midair collisions. This single engine, all metal, low wing, side-by-side seating, tricycle undercarriage aircraft was designed and built in New Zealand, and was fantastic for learning to fly in.

I loved flying the Parrot and had a great instructor called Guy Hall, who was a dedicated professional with a real art for motivating his students to succeed. Within two weeks of starting our flying training we had gone solo and then we were on to aerobatics, instrument flying, night flying and cross country. I couldn't get enough, and didn't seem to have too many troubles other than when I attempted to land without a clearance from the air traffic control tower. Once I landed, I was given a bollocking and sent on a 10-kilometre airfield run in my flying suit, life-preserver vest, parachute and helmet, to give me time to 'think about my misdemeanour'. It worked—I have never landed without a clearance since.

One of our subjects was airmanship, which is the theory of how to be safe in the air and on the ground. We sat in a classroom waiting patiently for our instructor to arrive, when who should walk in . . . none other than Dog, the one-man party-pie shooting gallery. Here was the guy who'd made himself famous in the RAAF for being unsafe, now lecturing us on how to be safe—the irony just kept coming.

The first lesson was on the contents and usage of our Secumar life-preserver vest. As its name suggests, this is an essential piece of a pilot's equipment so every member of the class was fully attentive, knowing that in a survival situation everything we were about to learn could mean the difference between life and death. Dog held up the vest, announced the objectives of the lesson and said:

'OK, guys, so you get lost on your first cross-country flight and end up in the middle of Bass Strait when your engine goes "balfang" and you see a couple of pistons depart stage right. You give the "engine restart" checklist some thought and then think, "Fuck it, I'll get more news coverage if I throw the bird away." So you bail out and somehow remember to pull the cord on your chute . . . so things are looking good for you being on the evening news. When you hit the water though, your vest fails to inflate—What do you do? I need a volunteer. Flashdance, get up here . . .' Dog fitted the life preserver to one of my classmates who had made the mistake of turning up at OTS on day one wearing some sort of *Saturday Night Fever* outfit.

'OK, so you've pulled the emergency inflation toggle and inflated your vest. You then open up the survival pouch and all this shit starts floating around you in the water. Don't worry, it should all be tied to the vest. What's it all for and how do we use it?' he asked after emptying the Secumar in a circle around Flashdance.

'The first thing you need to do is inflate your life raft so the Channel 7 chopper can find you and the chicks get to see who the hero was that threw their jet away.' Dog then went on to show us his methods of employment for the entire survival kit that included using the sea anchor as a party hat, the heliograph as a shaving mirror, the razor blade as a shaver—the entire focus of the lecture was about getting us ready to pull chicks when the TV crews finally found us. It was one of the most entertaining lectures I've ever received in my life, but amazingly there was no mention of the RAAF search and rescue chopper or how to actually survive.

The year flew by and suddenly it was only a few months before we were to graduate from Point Cook. We'd lost a few guys along the way, guys like Goose, who were unable to progress at the required rate and were 'scrubbed'. It was sad to say goodbye to each one of them, knowing how much he had put in, how his lifelong dream was over, and most guys always wondered how long it would be before it was their turn—fortunately for me, I never really had the spare brain space to think about it. Other than Friday nights in the bar and Saturday mornings in bed, it was rare that I wasn't studying or preparing for my next flight. My obsessive personality had finally found a home. The scrub rate, however, was about to drastically increase once we started flying jets.

No. 2 Flying Training School (2FTS) was a massive step up for me. I would now be flying a machine that could kill me at the speed of sound (1200 kilometres per hour). Not only that, but being at RAAF Base Pearce in Western Australia, an hour out of Perth, meant I was away from my family, friends, Melbourne and everything I had ever known in my life. It was tough, but made easier by the companion-ship of the 26 mates I had on the pilots' course, who were now as close as brothers.

The Macchi MB-326H jet was an Italian-built, tandem-seat, transonic trainer; a real pilot's aircraft with beautifully harmonised controls that allowed you to fly it accurately with just your fingertips. On my first Friday night in the back bar I gobbed off about how nice I thought the aircraft was to fly and how well I was going to be able to fly it. An instructor overheard me and thought I was being a cocky little shit—which I was. He challenged me to a steep-turn accuracy competition, where he would fly with me and we'd see who could perform the most accurate steep turn with the least variation in altitude. Full of VB, and the pressure of my course mates daring me, I accepted the challenge.

Come Monday morning I had deluded myself into believing that the instructor was bluffing and the school would not be able to reschedule the program to put the two of us in the same cockpit . . . Wrong. I checked the programming board on arrival and, sure enough, there we were together on the flying schedule. Now, if I'd been just a bit older or wiser, or if I'd just had the merest bit of political nous, I would have politely declined his challenge or intentionally lost. But I was still only eighteen and, in my heart of hearts, still Maverick from *Top Gun*, so I did my best to beat the instructor—and did. It was bloody satisfying and did my ego a lot of good, but in hindsight perhaps not the best way to get ahead in the RAAF. My immaturity put me in the sights of every instructor I flew with for the next year.

During the course, the flying became more and more difficult, and subsequently more and more rewarding. The aerobatics became more dynamic, including violent spins and vertical tail slides that could easily end up as violent spins if you ham-fisted them. Formation-flying scared the shit out of me and took me the longest amount of time to feel comfortable with. We had spent the best part of a year learning how to miss aircraft; now we were expected to perform aerobatics within a couple of metres of 3 tonnes of metal at 600 kilometres per hour.

One of the things I liked best was low flying—flying at 250 feet above the ground at 600 kilometres per hour. But it was here that I was almost scrubbed.

I returned from a solo low-flying exercise to be immediately called into my flight commander's office and grilled for being outside the low-flying area (LOWFA). Low flying is inherently dangerous and at jet speeds you can't see powerlines and towers. For this reason all low flying must be completed in surveyed areas that have been cleared of any obstructions. According to my flight commander, another instructor had seen me low flying outside the approved area. I was quizzed about who I was showing off to and told that the chief flying instructor would be deciding whether I would be staying on course or not.

I was shocked—I'd had no idea that I'd been low flying outside the approved area. Obviously I must have strayed, but I couldn't work out how it happened.

I walked back into our course common room to a bunch of jeers about being a 'Maverick' and was the butt of every *Top Gun* quote the guys could think of, including being dangerous. I then started impersonating my flight commander, quoting him in a way that only a smart-arse eighteen-year-old can. Normally my impersonations were fairly well received, but none of the guys even smiled. Instead they all looked through me to the rear of the room. I turned slowly, knowing I wasn't going to like what I saw. I locked eyes with one of the crankier instructors, Vag, who tore into me in front of everyone.

'I was the guy who spotted you outside the LOWFA,' he yelled. 'We'd agreed that because you were only practising authorised manoeuvres you wouldn't be scrubbed. I think that decision will be rescinded once I've had a chat to your flight commander about your poor attitude.'

My heart sank. Sure enough, another five minutes later I was summonsed back to my flight commander's office, where I was officially suspended from the course, and then sent to face the chief flying instructor (CFI).

To cadet pilots the CFI was not human but some sort of mythical being that you avoided in the corridors. He was the one who ultimately decided our fate, the one we would fly with on our final 'wings' test to determine if we'd become RAAF pilots or not. I was seeing him about six months earlier than normal, and was making myself even more famous for the wrong reasons. Waiting outside his office, I looked at the name on the door:

Chief Flying Instructor
Squadron Leader Frank 'Francois' Atkins

'Frank,' I thought, trying to calm my nerves. 'He's just a guy like me. Wipes his arse like me. Gets up in the morning just like . . .'

'Tucker, come in here.' I started shaking like a leaf. My dream was about to end for reasons I wasn't even sure of. To say I was emotional at that point would be a huge understatement.

Francois, stern and authoritative, then gave me my first lesson in good leadership. 'Tell me what happened,' he said.

'Well, Sir, I was low flying in the northern LOWFA when I heard on the area frequency two more aircraft enter the area. I observed one of them enter the area close to me and so moved further north to deconflict myself from them. I guess while I was heading north I missed the border and somehow ended up outside the northern border.'

He then told me to show him on the maps exactly where I was low flying prior to moving.

'What were you using as your visual feature for the northern border?' he asked, as if he knew the answer already.

He was bordering on Jedi status, I thought, maybe he was reading my mind. I immediately stopped visualising him wiping his arse.

'The black bitumen road as described in the flying orders, Sir,' I replied.

'The eastern 2 miles of the road are actually white dirt, which is why you missed it,' he stated. 'Can you prepare a brief for all pilots and ask the navigation officer to update the flying orders? That will be all.'

I couldn't believe it—I was not going to be scrubbed. I saluted, spun on my heel and high-tailed it out of there for fear that he might change his mind. There was no emotion to the guy, just focus—find the problem, fix it and make sure it doesn't happen again. I subsequently gave the brief to all 150 staff and students at 2FTS, which was more nerve-racking than entering Frank's lair.

The days, weeks and months flew past and I enjoyed myself like never before. I kept my head down and worked hard, hoping I wouldn't end up scrubbed, like more and more of my mates. Along the way I met a fantastic Perth girl, Bel, who became my first real girlfriend. Her family was great to me and for the first time I started to see what real families looked like. Her dad owned a big fuck-off boat and on Sundays we would cruise over to Rottnest Island and pick up some crayfish for dinner. Even though the pilots' course was intense, Bel and I managed to keep a great relationship together throughout it all—a real testament to her character.

My final flight at 2FTS was my 'Wings' test with Frank. This final one-and-a-half hours was a test of everything we had learned in two years, including emergencies, acrobatics, navigation, instrument flying and low flying. I passed the flight and together with my coursemates enjoyed a great week of celebrations which included a twenty-aircraft formation fly-past that we called the 'death cloud'—it was a one-hour continuous near-death experience. My family came over from Melbourne for the graduation parade, where we marched off to the theme of *Thunderbirds*, before a tremendous black-tie graduation dinner. Of the 36 guys I started OTS with, only eighteen of us survived to graduate.

I graduated at nineteen years of age and equal-youngest in my course. While I had the skill to fly jets, my instructors at 2FTS recommended I fly a crewed aircraft for my first posting so I didn't kill myself—I was fairly immature and my flight-commander impersonations were not yet fully appreciated. So they sent me to a single-pilot transport aircraft where I could take out myself and fourteen VIP passengers—now that made sense! The ironic RAAF posting cycle was back at work.

While disappointed I didn't get to fly jets straightaway, I wasn't overly concerned—my goal was just going to take a little longer to achieve. I had been given some good advice by my mentor—Wing Commander Ross Fox, who was now the commanding officer of No. 75 Squadron at RAAF Base Tindal, near Katherine in the Northern Territory.

'Mac,' he'd said, 'if you don't get jets, get a posting to Nomads at 75 Squadron—I'll make sure you get jets after that.'

So that's what I did. First choice: jets—denied, too immature. Second choice: Nomads—granted! The 2FTS instructors couldn't believe I had nominated such a lemon of an aircraft . . . but I had a plan.

My first solo in the mighty Parrot—RAAF Base Point Cook, 1988.

Doing my best to stay the right way up over the Werribee shitfarm, 1988.

How the hell can they let kids fly those things? Pilot's course graduation photo—RAAF Base Pearce, 1989.

No. 150 Pilots' Course—RAAF Base Pearce, 1989. The red circles indicate the guys who were sadly 'scrubbed' off the course. White circles indicate the guys who made it to Fighters.

Australia's best effort to build an aircraft—the GAF N24 Nomad, or 'Widowmaker'. Two of my instructors would die before The Tool and I almost followed suit.

After my RAAF instructor was killed I was posted to the Army to fly the Nomad. Completing a Takeoff Data Card at Hobart Airport, 1989.

Caption No. 75 Squadron in 1990, RAAF Base Tindal. Sadly, three good mates from this photo would be dead within a year.

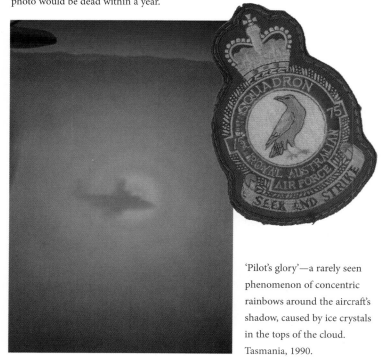

'Pilot's glory'—a rarely seen phenomenon of concentric rainbows around the aircraft's shadow, caused by ice crystals in the tops of the cloud. Tasmania, 1990.

Topcover for Downunder—No. 75 Squadron over the Olgas, 1990.

Foxy's death was a great loss to us all, and I lost a childhood hero. RAAF News, 1990.

Home sweet home for Exercise Talisman Sabre—Townsend Island, Queensland, 1990.
Hint for the inexperienced: do not sleep in your foxhole during the wet season.

'Let us know where you want the pool.' The result of a 0.1-millisecond delay on a Mk 84 high explosive bomb. The CO dropped the bombs to provide a short-term swimming hole for the personnel who were manning the Delamere Air Weapons Range, 1990.

Introductory Fighter Course taught us how to shoot and bomb in the Macchi—as well as how to scare the shit out of fisherman on the beach. East of the Twelve Apostles, 1992.

First solo flight in an F-18—RAAF Base Williamtown, 1992.

Night hang gliding in Newcastle, 1993. Taken from my 'hang gliding pad' by my frustrated girlfriend Kim as the roast dinner burned.

3
Growing up fast

To THIS DAY I still remember arriving at RAAF Base Tindal in the civilian Fokker F-28. The wet-season weather had required the crew to fly an instrument-approach and for ten minutes the aircraft bumped its way through the clouds until it popped out at about 150 metres above the ground. The first impression I had was how beautiful and green the landscape looked—I couldn't reconcile what all that red desert talk had been about. The second impression I had was how good the base looked—it was brand new and I could see condominiums, a golf course, pool and sports fields—all in the middle of nowhere. My heart lifted—this was going to be a great experience for a nineteen-year-old kid.

Monday morning I turned up to my first squadron in my perfectly ironed blues, hat, spit-polished shoes and a single thin stripe on my shoulder—Pilot Officer Tucker. Number 75 Squadron had eighteen F-18 Hornets and two N24 Nomad VIP transport aircraft—the lemon I had been posted to fly. One of the other Nomad pilots, Book, had met me at the mess and driven me to morning brief where we sat waiting for the executives.

'Gentlemen,' someone called, and we all stood to attention as the senior officers filed in past us and took their places in lounge chairs at the front of the room. The morning brief—my first as a real pilot—droned on uneventfully, but towards the end the duty flight commander asked the commanding officer (CO) if he wanted to say any final words.

Wing Commander Ross Fox stood up beaming and immediately locked eyes with me. 'Gents, I would like to introduce our new Nomad pilot, Mac Tucker. Make him feel at home. Come see me in my office after the brief, if you would, please, Mac.'

I felt my face flushing. The idea that the attention of a squadron of steely-eyed killers were at that moment on me was a little unsettling.

After the brief I waited nervously outside the CO's office for him to call me in. He got up from behind his desk and greeted me with a warm smile and handshake—although more than three years had passed, it seemed like only yesterday that he had done the same as an F-18 pilot at the East Sale airshow. He gave me a quick lesson in how to apply myself, fit in, stay out of trouble and, most importantly to me, get to Hornets. No problems, boss—will do!

When not transporting wives to Darwin to go shopping, fighter pilots to Broome for R&R or VIPs around exercise areas, I spent all my time learning about fighter flying. With fifteen Hornet pilots and only three Nomad pilots in the squadron, we were a real minority; however, the fighter pilots made us feel like equals and I soon made lifelong friends.

With the RAAF two-year posting cycle, most guys get very good at forming friendships—or they get very lonely. I was lucky that during my first assignment I became best mates with Tex. One of the fighter pilots, Tex was a great guy with a very dry sense of humour. We were both in lust with the same woman at one stage, which strained the friendship; however, we worked through it to get to the ultimate understanding that junior Nomad pilots just do not compete with fighter pilots. While my posting to Tindal had ended my relationship with Bel, as she had stayed in Perth, I felt there was still some hope for us, and so graciously—and for once, sensibly—bowed out of the cockfight with Tex.

Together, Tex and I trained for triathlons, went rock climbing, four-wheel driving and camping. We completed an around-Australia surfing safari, including Perth, Melbourne, Sydney and Newcastle, and then went to Bali. It was my first real adventure as an adult and I loved it.

Tex was posted to fly F-18s with the United States Marine Corp (USMC) shortly after returning from our surfing trip. This was a highly coveted posting and he had outdone a lot of very capable guys to get it. We wrote and spoke semi-regularly once he arrived in the US and we even planned a surf trip down the Baja Peninsula in Mexico.

But then, we got some unbelievably terrible news. Tex had committed suicide by slashing his throat with a razor blade. His USMC squadron was on deployment away from their home station and he was due to lead a mission in the morning. He completed his mission slides the night before and slid them under his wing-man's door—standard practice for a conscientious leader. He then supposedly drove around all night before going to a hotel and killing himself. I had only spoken to him the weekend before, and he'd sounded excited about our impending surf trip—hardly the state of mind of someone about to top himself. It all seemed so strange and suspicious to me and a few of his closest friends, but nothing we said or did could bring Tex back. I was starting to learn very quickly about the tenuous, fragile nature of life.

Halfway through my tour of Tindal, I was acting as the operations officer (OPSO) and managing the day-to-day minutiae of fighter operations, including aircraft configurations, refuel requirements, pilot changes, cryptographic code loads, weapon loads and weapon range bookings. One of the OPSO duties is also search and rescue (SAR) coordination, which I knew nothing about but was soon to have a quick real-world lesson in.

The crash alarm in fighter squadrons sounds like a World War II air raid siren, and permeates throughout every building when it sounds. I had never heard one before but as I sat at the operations (ops) desk coordinating the flying program the crash alarm rang out.

Wooooooooooo, wooooooooooo. Hell, that doesn't sound good, I thought to myself. Immediately the phone rang.

'Magpie ops, this is Nightcliff. Mayday in progress. Blackbird 3 has ejected,' came an unknown voice over the phone.

'Copied,' was all I could think to say as the administration officer (ADMINO)—thank god—entered the room.

The mission had been a large-force employment mission during Exercise Pitch Black 1990 and all aircraft and pilots were flying in it—except me. We started a log to record all information when I looked at the flying program to find out who was flying in Blackbird 3. My heart sank. It was Foxy.

We confirmed that the search and rescue (SAR) chopper had been launched when the ops radio erupted.

'Magpie ops, this is Magpie 1. Blackbird 3 and 4 have collided. Blackbird 3 has gone down. Blackbird 4 is badly damaged, missing half his wing.' The computerised fly-by-wire system was doing an amazing job keeping the Hornet flying in a situation where most aircraft would be uncontrollable and spin into the ground.

We confirmed that no parachute had been seen where the collision had occurred and were able to give the SAR chopper good coordinates to start its search.

People handle danger and the prospect of death in very different ways. Most people go to pieces, get hysterical. Some can face it, but most can't. Military pilots, in contrast, are trained to methodically think their way out of death's cold embrace. We give little consideration to what *might* happen—we focus instead on what we *want* to happen.

Smitty was the other pilot involved in the accident. He was being helped by the squadron fighter combat instructor (FCI) Crasher, who had watched appalled as the fireball of the collision occurred right in front of him. With little hesitation Crasher calmly started talking Smitty through the emergency checklist. Smitty was losing fuel out of his wing and no-one was sure if the jet could be slowed for landing without entering a spin.

In the meantime, the remaining aircraft still flying started their return to base (RTB) at top speed, in order to land ahead of Smitty without getting in his way. If Smitty crashed on the runway and blocked it, the remaining jets would not have enough fuel to get to the next available runway in Darwin and the pilots would have to eject, leaving their planes to crash—another horrifying prospect.

Once all the other planes had landed, Smitty, guided in by the reassuring voice of Crasher, did a sterling job of landing his jet with only half a wing. It was a testament to a great aircraft and two fine pilots.

We were all massively relieved that Smitty was safe, but tension was still high. We still hadn't seen a chute nor had we been able to identify where Foxy's aircraft had crashed. The SAR chopper was running low on fuel and it would soon be nightfall.

All the pilots started coming into the operations building. They didn't get the luxury of a debrief or counselling session. Instead, they had to quarantine their videotapes for the crash investigation, isolate themselves for fear of recollection contamination, and start to write their witness statements. I could see that the accident affected each guy differently. Some guys went cold, some chatted nervously. I felt sick.

The second in charge of the squadron, Murderer, became the acting CO in the absence of Foxy and ordered me to hand over the ops desk and initiate a search and rescue in the Nomad. Book and I had all the information we needed so we headed straight for our aircraft. I was as nervous as hell jumping into an aircraft knowing that a similar aluminium death tube had just tried to kill my mates but I wanted to make sure that, no matter how slim the chance, if Foxy had somehow lived through the crash he would not be left alone.

With some small-scale maps at hand, and SAR radio frequencies and beacon frequencies selected, we got the Nomad airborne in minimum time and started heading north-west towards the position of the collision. We established communications with the SAR chopper which was coming off station and coordinated our search area to deconflict with where the chopper had already searched. The Nomad didn't have a dedicated SAR fit-out so, using our Aussie ingenuity, we adapted, employing what we had at hand: a pair of handheld binoculars and a night-vision device, which we would need in a couple of hours.

The lack of a SAR beacon was disconcerting for us all. The F-18 ejection seats are fitted with a SAR beacon that is automatically initiated when the seat leaves the aircraft. Without that beacon, the search was becoming less about rescue and more about recovery. Maintaining our optimism as best we could, Book and I methodically searched the area of interest at 150 metres. After about 90 minutes we spotted the wreckage.

Expecting a smoking hole, we were surprised to see that the jet looked like it was completely intact aft of the cockpit, though the entire nose section, including the cockpit, was missing. It had come down perfectly flat on its belly in the middle of a cleared paddock about 100 kilometres north-west of Katherine.

On my 1:500 000 tactical pilot chart I found the cleared area and noted the slight rise in the otherwise flat terrain. The aircraft was smack-bang on the middle of the rise, which had a name that was too much of a coincidence to be real. I checked the date of the map but it had been published six years before. A chill went down my spine—the rise was called Hornet Hill.

The rescue team found Foxy's body still strapped to his seat—he had been killed on impact with Smitty's wing. Thankfully, it had been quick and he had died doing something he loved, but tragically he was leaving behind a lovely wife and children.

After Foxy's death we all spent the first few nights drinking at the officers mess, playing the piano and singing. It occurred to me at the time why the mess halls during the Battle of Britain had been filled with song and cheer—something I had never understood until then. It was a way for young men who had faced their own mortality and narrowly skirted death to quickly forget about the morbid realities of their chosen occupation—so that they could get up in the morning and do it again and again. I'm not sure if the psychologists would approve . . . but it worked for them, and it worked for us.

Since doing my work experience as a teenager with him, I'd kept in touch with Foxy and had met his family a number of times. I wanted to show my respect to the family, but just wasn't sure if I was quite up to it. I thought I would ask the base commander, Group Captain 'Mutt', who'd been a good mate of Foxy's and who I'd met during my week at Williamtown, where he'd been the CO of No. 3 Squadron. Mutt suggested I visit Foxy's wife Vicki.

Having faced very little death in my life before, I had only the barest awareness of how Vicki would feel or what I would say to her. But my teenage idol, the man who had inspired me to join the RAAF, was no longer with us and I felt impelled to go, even if it was only to tell her how much he meant to me.

With my stomach in a knot I knocked on the door. Vicki greeted me in her normal graceful way, with her beautiful smile. She was the ultimate senior officer's wife, gracious and kind. After briefly chatting at the door we walked past the lounge room where dozens of bouquets had been placed. Looking at the flowers, Vicki lost her composure and started to sob. And then we were both crying, holding onto each other. I was a stranger, really, and too young to express any emotional insight, but I choked out all I could.

'I'm so sorry, Vicki. He was my hero since I was a boy and the reason why I'm in the RAAF. I'm going to miss him too.' It seemed totally inadequate, but it was all I had.

The funeral was held in Brisbane's Anglican Cathedral (where I would be married five years later) and it was filled to overflowing—testament to a life well-lived. I was privileged to be asked to be a pallbearer. I did it willingly, even though I'd never carried anything so heavy (nor did I know that this would be the first of three coffins I would help carry and five mates I would bury during my career). The missing-man formation was flown at low altitude over the cathedral. This involves four F-18s flying low and fast in a tight formation, with one of the four pulling up and disappearing into the heavens. Even if you weren't religious, you came close when you saw it.

Foxy's death was particularly hard on Vicki, but I have always remembered her strength of character every time I have attended funerals in the years since.

A couple of weeks after the funeral, Mutt rang me. He told me that I'd done the right thing by paying my respects to Foxy's family, then he said: 'Mac, Vicki wants to have a look at the crash site. She asked if you would drive her out there.'

I thought the hardest part of the grieving process was over—I was wrong.

I drove Vicki and her kids out to Hornet Hill in their family Landcruiser. It was a tremendous honour to be asked to do so, and to this day it remains one of the more emotional moments of my life. I was nineteen years old and acting as the escort officer for a grieving widow and family, taking them to say their final goodbyes. But as difficult and heartbreaking as it was, in truth I would not have had it any other way.

I left them alone to walk around the wrecked aircraft, including the nose section which was eventually found 300 metres from the main fuselage. Foxy was the most-liked CO I ever worked for, and Vicki discovered how respected he was when she saw the beautiful cairn and plaque the 75SQN troops had made for him. I also took the time to thank him for all he had done for me and collected a piece of molten titanium from the wreck. It still sits in my office, together with a photo of Foxy, and has kept me inspired to work towards my goals and remain alert in order to not kill myself nor let someone else kill me. I still wonder if the crash investigation team ever missed that piece of engine.

Foxy remained an inspiration to me for the next ten years as a fighter pilot and I regularly think of him when I consider how it is I have taken the path I have. While I've seen a lot of sudden death in my career as a pilot—more than most, I sometimes think—I still haven't come to terms with it. Death remains a stark, cold wind that blows more often as I age. I'm not sure if I will ever understand death, or even if I'm meant to understand it. I do know this, though: life is precious and temporary—all life. And I will never allow my fear of losing it to prevent me from fully living it.

A month later my Nomad instructor was killed—I started to wonder what sort of career I had gotten myself into. My boyhood dreams of punching holes in the clouds were rapidly vanishing. I was due to travel to Adelaide the following week when I was given the sobering news that the tail of Donno's Nomad had fallen off and the RAAF did not have anyone else who could instruct me. There was no talk of 'Don't worry, it's a one-off'—it was more like 'You feel lucky, kid?'

I started looking into the aircraft a bit more and found out its history was marred with corpses, including the first test pilot, who was Guy Pearce's father. I started feeling like the Nomad was far more dangerous than the F-18.

I soon had my revised travel orders and the RAAF sent me off to the army's 173 Reconnaissance Squadron at Oakey, Queensland, to complete my Nomad training. I was treated like the lowest life-form on the planet by the army instructors because I was a 'Raafy' and I was wearing the lowest rank when they checked out their RAAF rank chart. I didn't mind—I was there for the flying and the flying was fantastic. A lot of the instructors were ex-Vietnam pilots who knew a thing or two about low flying—and I mean low.

My first low-flying flight was with an army captain, Danno, who explained to me how important it was that the authorisation book was filled out with the letters 'AO' so that we knew what our legal altitude limit was.

'What does AO stand for, Danno?' I asked.

'Above obstacles,' he replied, like I was the dumbest pilot ever to step foot in the establishment.

'So why is it so important to know my altitude limit is AO?' I still didn't get it. 'It's not like we can fly below obstacles?'

He grumbled a response which sounded to me like he didn't understand what I was asking. Once we were airborne though, he demonstrated beyond a shadow of a doubt that, in fact, you can fly *below* obstacles.

After we'd completed our upper airwork Danno told me to descend into the low-flying area. I started quacking all the RAAF low-flying checks about clearances, visually clearing the area, making sure all equipment was stowed, to which Danno's response was, 'Can we just go fucking low flying?'

'I am,' I said, as I levelled the aircraft at 150 feet—the lowest altitude I had ever flown at.

'Taking over,' he grunted and then proceeded to pull up to 30 degrees nose-high, roll the aircraft on its back and complete a wingover that had us in a 10-degree descent toward a field of crops. He then continued down through 150 feet, 100 feet, 50 feet, 20 feet, 10 feet and right into the crops. To say I was shitting myself with terror would have been an understatement—my arse was sucking up my seat cushion in fear. A loud '*sssshhhhhh*' sound could be heard through the airframe and then Danno pulled the aircraft back up and into a reversal to show me where he had headed the seed off the crops.

I guess that was the reason for writing AO—you could actually go below them if you were *fucking stupid*!

After completing three months of awesome flying with the army I returned to Tindal to see out another year of 'Top End Tours' at 75 Squadron. By this stage Tool, who had been held back after our pilots' course, turned up at Tindal and we got to spend the next year together exploring northern Australia.

My last flight in the Nomad was never meant to be my last. Tool and I were conducting some training, during which he wore a hood over his helmet so he could only see the captain's instruments and I flew what we called 'eyes-out' to make sure we did not run into anything. We were about an hour into the flight and Tool was completing an instrument approach to the runway at Tindal. At about 150 metres he selected full flap to land, after which there was a violent shaking of the aircraft between zero and 4 Gs. We were thrown around in our seats and then into the ceiling with such force that I started to worry about the aircraft breaking up in flight.

Tool commenced a go-around to abort the landing, but the oscillations only became more violent. I politely suggested he immediately land wherever he could—as in, 'Just put it down right fucking now!'—as it really felt like the aircraft was falling apart. After about four cycles of the oscillation we selected the flaps up and the oscillations stopped. Tool and I were shitting ourselves, though we did pull ourselves together for an ice-cool mayday call. Tool did a great job of putting the Nomad down and we pulled up just before the end of the runway.

By the time we'd taxied back in and shut down, the engineers were already running out of the hut towards us.

'G'day, guys,' Tool said. 'Sorry about the mayday but we had some weird vibrations. You might want to check the controls out.'

The engineers, who were facing the back of the aircraft, started pointing and going pale. Tool and I spun around to see what they were looking at, and I instantly felt sick. The Nomad was a wreck; each engine was hanging by a single engine mount, the right flaperon was hanging loose and there was giant wrinkle in the upper skin of the wing where the wings had bent up and almost separated from the aircraft. The flaperon was a critical flight control on the wing, and together with the damage to the wings this meant we were lucky to be alive.

That was the last time that particular Nomad ever flew. Because of the damage to the aircraft, a board of enquiry was convened. After an exhaustive investigation, the board still had no definitive cause for the accident, but found the most likely cause to be Tool overspeeding the flaps and both of us lying about it to cover our arses. This allegation hung over our heads for nearly two years before the truth came out.

Aircraft engineers use a '1.5 design load factor' in all their calculations, which essentially means that if the wing snaps at 300 kilometres per hour then the maximum speed allowed is 200 kilometres per hour (this is not exactly how it works because of force being proportional to the square of the airspeed, but it's close enough for the sake of the story). It turned out that the government aircraft factory (GAF) engineer who designed the flaperons had forgotten to add the 0.5 to the 1.0 on his slide rule. This meant that the global fleet of Nomads had been flying around for years with their flaperons about to fall off and nobody knew. Needless to say, I wasn't disappointed that I never flew Nomads again.

4

Morning death

By 1991 I had been recommended for fighters and arrived at RAAF Base Williamtown to commence the Introductory Fighter Course on the Macchi jet trainer. This six-month course was designed to teach me how to dogfight in aerial combat and drop bombs in air-to-ground combat. I was nervous—I was now on the base officially known as 'The Home of the Hornet' and operating alongside the F-18. This was my greatest challenge yet—I had arrived at base camp and the summit was casting a daunting shadow over me. Before I would get the chance to master the art of aerial warfare, however, I would first have to master the art of the nodding dog—convincing senior officers that I was awake and in agreement with their daily dose of verbal valium.

Morning brief in a fighter squadron can be one of the more incredibly frustrating events in a fighter pilot's inhumanly busy day—even for experienced knuckleheads with at least half a clue about how to not fly into the ground, run out of fuel or run into their wingman. Originally designed to provide morning 'battle orders' during WWII, the modern morning brief has morphed into *War and Peace* on everything other than the most important thing for fighter pilots—that is, how to kill the enemy. Fighter pilots are extremely motivated, outcome-focused individuals—that's how they get through the two-year screening process. For a fighter pilot to pay attention during morning brief the information needs to be concise and relevant.

But the morning brief was a test for the soul. Mind-numbing subjects included: bafflingly obvious risk management (don't hit the ground, run out of fuel or hit your wingman); weather conditions in the Northern Territory during the dry season (it is highly likely the dry-season weather will be fine, as it's been fine for the last million years and will be fine for the next million); notices to airmen (NOTAMS) that inform pilots of the status of airfield equipment and services for the base that they have operated from for the last year (which change about as often as the dry-season weather); and the critical flight safety implications of the social club officer (SOCO) not unpacking the orange juice containers from their individual plastic wrapping, thereby forcing the commanding officer (CO) to do it himself, a distraction that was deemed likely to cause him to crash (most of us snickered at this one, knowing that the poppers would have little to do with the CO creaming himself into a mountain, and his mental instability was in fact the thing he should be more concerned about). We called this kind of useless information 'common dog fuck' (CDF) and it bored the life out of most of us—Welcome to Morning Death.

For anyone other than the most junior pilots (Bograts), the morning brief just soaked up valuable time that we would rather have devoted to mission preparation. The only comparable time-waster was our secondary duties, which every pilot in a squadron is assigned—such as the WEAPO (weapons officer), who maintains the weapons logs for the aircraft; the TIMESO (times officer), who ensures the hours flown do not exceed those allocated by Canberra; the NAVO (navigations officer), who maintains the navigation database; and, without a doubt the worst secondary duty that you could be allocated, the SOCO (social club officer), who was responsible for organising social functions without sending the squadron broke in the process. These secondary duties drive the fighter pilots insane because it stops them from flying or reading about flying or thinking about flying or even just thinking.

There was one morning brief that I've never forgotten, as it typified the frustration felt by most fighter pilots about these daily lobotomies. The morning brief is generally run by a senior officer and on this occasion it was our executive officer (XO), Rhino. Rhino was a highly intelligent (more so than normal), excitable (more so than normal) fighter pilot who had a tremendous sense of humour which had often gotten him into trouble with senior officers when he was a Bograt himself. Watching him take on a management role at the squadron was interesting to say the least, as he tried to corral a bunch of A-type personality junior fighter pilots into not killing themselves, either at work or at play.

On this particular day he didn't seem his usual funny self—indeed we could all detect a darkness about Rhino that we hadn't seen before. For something to rile Rhino like this, it must have been bad. I, like every other Bograt in the room, started to feel nervous. Hell, I hope it's not something I've done, I thought. Did I remember to safe the ejection seat yesterday? Did I leave the safe open? Did someone tell him I was out on the town last Friday in my flying suit (zoom bag)? Did he hear about the nudie run through the pub? Everything every guy had ever done at any time in our careers started to crowd into our minds. The suspense was asphyxiating all of us—for god's sake, Rhino, just get it out.

'OK, guys, I have something I wish to discuss with you all and, well, to be honest . . . I am a little embarrassed that I should have to bring this up. Supposedly you are responsible, intelligent officers of the RAAF. That is, some of you are; however, there is at least one of you—probably more—who is not.'

Oh, shit. This was bad. He was going to single one of us out.

Damn! But it wasn't just me that did the nudie run, there were at least ten of us . . .

Rhino gave us all a death stare and continued: 'It is to do with personal hygiene and responsibility. I am sick to death of going into the toilet, sitting down and taking a crap, only to find that someone has used the last square of toilet paper and not replaced it. I find it very hard to believe that the last sheet on every roll equates to the moment when your arse is clean. Either, A, you are not wiping your arse properly and being lazy, walking around the rest of the day with dags in your pants, or, B, you are over-wiping until you run out of paper—which is wasteful. Either way, someone is being lazy by not replacing the toilet roll. And in the worst case, someone sitting here has shit in their pants.'

If he had not been so visibly upset and angry, this would have been the funniest Morning Death ever—trouble was, he was totally serious. Rhino must have really got caught out on the can in a bad way to be so pissed off.

This was exactly the sort of thing that made the majority of fighter pilots, who wiped their arse properly and replaced the roll, so frustrated and patronised. Hell, the taxpayers trusted us to race around the skies with 50 million dollars worth of blowtorches strapped to our arses and drop thousands of kilograms of high-explosive bombs, and yet there we were, being treated like three-year-olds requiring tutoring in Potty Etiquette 101. It was completely bizarre.

Apart from toilet training, the portion of the morning brief that the executives (execs) favoured the most was new business. This was an opportunity for 'pearls of wisdom' to flow from the execs to the Bograts. Often, however, depending on exactly who the execs were, giant 'gherkins' could be launched that the squadron fighter combat instructor (FCI) would struggle to undo later. Things like, 'I don't even look at the altimeter in a dive bombing attack . . . I just use the force,' or 'You should not eject if you are conducting a high-speed abort . . . just jettison the stores to reduce your weight' (yeah, and have a couple of tonnes of high-explosive bombs bounce down the runway with you at 250 kilometres per hour). These sorts of gherkins could kill junior pilots if not extinguished by the real Jedi masters.

One such FCI was JC, a maestro who taught me the art of dog-fighting which I would use for the next ten years. I really thrived in the competitive environment of aerial combat and 76 Squadron was tremendous fun: who you could defeat in a dogfight, how quickly you could defeat them, who scored highest in the strafing and who could bomb the most accurately. For a young man with an unhealthy level of insecurity about his capabilities, the environment was perfect. I fed my insecurity with success which resulted from total dedication to my chosen career—a success that came at the expense of all other parts of my life, including relationships.

By the time I finished my Introductory Fighter Course I was 22 years old and living in Newcastle with my girlfriend, Kim, who I had met in the Northern Territory. She was a wonderfully free spirit who I loved, but I was emotionally immature. I could defeat most guys in the squadron in a dogfight but had absolutely no idea how to treat a girl. Even if I did, my career focus was so strong that I doubt I would have treated her the way she deserved. The fact that we lasted three years was a testament to her far more than it was to me.

With the introductory course out of the way I was assigned to the Operations Flight to await the F-18 course. For the next year I would turn the jet inside out, as much as you can in a Macchi, attacking navy ships and F-18s in mock combat. Strangely, the closer I came to the F-18 the more my sense of inadequacy and my obsession to win grew. The pressure cooker was now turned up to high.

5
Get off my bridge

SO WHAT IS a fighter pilot? The answer to this question depends very much on who you are asking. You will find knuckleheads have pretty bad reputations right across society—particularly within the RAAF's sister services, the army and navy. To the public a fighter pilot is a highly chiselled, glamorous flyboy, who plays volleyball and occasionally intercepts MiGs during negative-G pushovers. This misconception does not bode well for single Bograts who generally do not look like Tom Cruise, do not wear dogtags or have a mate called Goose. More than likely, you'll find a Bograt venting some steam in a bar using a loud voice and covering a wide range of topics centred mostly on himself. Not the best way to attract women. For junior fighter pilots the 'Take me to bed or lose me forever' line usually meets with the response of 'Yeah, right', 'Bullshit' or 'Yeah, and I'm a rocket scientist'.

Even within the RAAF, fighter pilots have a bad reputation and most of it is fully deserved. Let's imagine you are a transport pilot for a moment . . .

You went to the airshows your entire childhood and dreamt of flying those noisy fast jets (hmmm, sounds familiar . . .). You studied hard at school, achieved the grades in your Higher School Certificate, passed the RAAF's gruelling psych, physical and aptitude tests, and perhaps even completed a three- or four-year degree at the Australian Defence Force Academy (ADFA)—you are now on your way to the pilots' course. Look out, girls—here you come!

You then studied your butt off for two years on the pilots' course to be told you haven't got what it takes and you aren't good enough to fly jets—so you're posted to a transport squadron (hmmm, that sounds familiar too). After a couple of years of hauling trash around you become a captain, your morale lifts a bit and you convince yourself that hauling trash is really important. It's operational, it's crewed, you get fed onboard, you have a toilet, there are chicks in your squadron and you don't have to do too much to keep your position, rank and pay . . . life's pretty cruisy.

So there you are, standing in your squadron bar on a Friday afternoon when you sense a slight vibration in the floor, then the walls. It grows until the vibration starts to shake the windows. You don't know what it is. Other people stop their conversations in the bar. They look at you. You look back. Before anyone can say 'earth tremor' there is an almighty boom as a transonic formation of jets lifts the shingles off the roof—it's a Friday afternoon at the national RAAF Bar Hour of 1500.

The senior officer in the bar exclaims: 'Who was that? I want to know. Damn, I want his wings! Find out who that was.'

A few junior officers in the bar may have some knowledge. One of them squeaks: 'I think one of the Williamtown squadrons was coming down for the weekend. I'll find out, sir.'

Just as the bar conversation resumes (statistically researched by fighter pilots, for just this purpose, to take on average 55 seconds), another tremor starts and culminates in another formation beating up the bar.

You, the transport pilot, then have childhood recollections of an airshow you attended when you first saw the jets . . . but you push them out of your mind. You're a transport captain now, you have a crew, multi-engine rating, an operational task, frozen meals . . . but then . . .

Elvis enters the building—followed by another fifteen Elvises. A fighter squadron has arrived at your bar and the pilots are arrogant, loud and clearly intoxicated from the one beer they had in the crew van on their way from the flight line to the bar. They're dressed in real Elvis suits with comic velcro sideburns and hairspray. The apparent senior-ranking Elvis, although it is hard to determine any organisational structure to the melee, is immediately intercepted by your base commander.

'Was that you? Did you just conduct an unapproved fly-past of my base? There will be damage! I want your name! Who is in charge here?'

At this point the bar bell would ring, signifying money is across the bar and all drinks are free. It appears to be one of the Elvises who has put the money over the bar. The crowd cheers and is immediately drawn to this larger-than-life group of young men who are so generously shouting the whole bar. The base commander cannot be heard over the cheering, and soon realises his cries of displeasure are not being noticed by anyone . . . The Elvis he was talking to is now chatting to the new barmaid, who is giggling and blushing. Indeed a number of the Elvises appear to be chatting to girls, who all appear to be giggling and blushing.

It is about now that you shake yourself from your delusion and realise that boxed meals and in-flight toilets on your aircraft only go so far . . .

The navy's perception of fighter pilots is largely unknown to fighter pilots as we rarely get to meet our nautical brethren, what with aircraft requiring 2000 metres of bitumen and all. Generally our meetings are similar to one-night stands: quick, exciting and largely embarrassing to one party . . . the navy. They like to think that their small, aged, overpriced and strategically irrelevant fleet can use some sort of Klingon cloaking device to defend itself against multiple, off-axis, low level, supersonic, precision-guided attacks. I guess ignorance is bliss—especially when you're stuck in a pitching sardine can with a few hundred blokes and you have to share your bed with at least a couple of them. Hence our caution in not getting too close to them.

Fighter pilots, on the other hand, only fly Monday to Friday, knock off early Fridays, never share beds (with blokes anyway), stay in hotels and don't work when the weather is bad—it's no wonder the navy despises us so much. The poor impression the navy had of fighter pilots was made very clear to me on one particular exercise—Exercise Tasman Link 1991.

This was a very large joint exercise involving all military services from the Australian Defence Force (ADF), as well as US forces, in a scenario that required an opposed amphibious lodgement onto Townsend Island in the Shoalwater Bay Training Area, near Rockhampton. The joint activities included close air support of troops on the ground with live high-explosive weapons—an inherently dangerous exercise that required a lot of sound planning and execution management.

I had been seconded to the exercise to act as a fast jet air liaison officer in the tactical air control party (TACP) that would start aboard one of the amphibious ships, conduct the amphibious landing and then live in tents and foxholes for three weeks. What? No Hilton? This was not good!

I was flying Macchis at No. 76 Squadron at the time, preparing for the F-18 course, and had no interest in doing anything other than flying. I did everything I could to get out of the exercise. 'I have no kit', 'I haven't done my weapons training', 'I have an assignment due for my officer development course', etc. etc. Nothing worked, and to make it worse there was no precedent for this folly—fighter pilots do not get dirty, shot at or roll their own sleeping bag! More importantly, I joined the RAAF to fly, and all fighter pilots hate anything that stops them performing their passion.

Truth be told, though, I was going to enjoy this exercise. I have always been an outdoorsy sort of guy, having completed my first overnight trek when I was just five years old. I was visiting my grandparents' farm in Gippsland, Victoria, when I first got the urge to be alone in the wild. My mother helped me pack my backpack and I walked to the dam which was at the far end of the property, out of sight of the farmhouse. My uncle Brad came down at some stage to help me pitch my tent and I spent my first night fending for myself—a personal trait that would grow and serve me well into adulthood.

That was then, though, and this was now. Once the echoes of my bleating had faded, I headed down to the base warehouse at RAAF Williamtown to receive my field kit. As part of the exercise I was required to carry a weapon—now we were talking. The weapon had to match your duty-specified weapon, which for fighter pilots was the Glock 9-mm pistol. I struggled to see how I was going to instrumentally influence the ground war with this pea shooter and protested that I needed my own MAG 58 machine gun—despite the fact that the weapon weighed more than me. The armourer's response was that if I could fit it in the cockpit of the fighter I could take it—which made my MAG 58 dream of Rambo-ing my way into the enemy's command post disappear. Well, I thought, if they're only going to give me a pea shooter, I'd better get a few bags of peas then!

I convinced the armourer to fill all my webbing bags with blank 9-mm rounds, totally oblivious to the purpose of all these bags or the fact that I might have to actually carry the additional 20 kilograms of ammunition further than to the boot of my car. Three weeks and a thousand rounds—that's a lot of dead guys, I thought, a bit like bombing. Maybe I could make a difference against the enemy after all.

I received my deployment orders to turn up to Sydney airport for a Qantas flight to Townsville, together with a whole bunch of joining orders that I felt were not really for me but for the army. Hell, I was a fighter pilot! These army clowns weren't going to tell me how to win the war—they should've been grateful I was going to plan the bombing campaign so that the RAAF could win the war for them.

I arrived at the terminal in my camouflage fatigues so new that they were still creased from the packaging. In the interests of safety I didn't think it was a good idea to check in my gun and ammunition together—far smarter to break the weapon down, remove the breach and firing pin, and place the gun in my check-in luggage with the RAAF's entire supply of 9-mm blank ammunition.

When I got to security I placed my metal items in the tray and walked through the security screening point. On the other side of the metal detector I discovered security personnel starting to get a little concerned, calling for supervisors, lots of *ksshhh ksshh* on the radios, and looking at me weirdly.

'Is there a problem?' I asked.

'Sir, what is this?' one of the security guards asked me, holding out the barrel and breach of my pistol.

'It's the barrel and breach of a Glock 9-mm pistol—what does it look like?'

It was about this moment I started wondering what else was in the joining orders the army had sent me that I hadn't bothered to read—I'd taken a quick look, but they read like assembly instructions for IKEA furniture. The security guys explained to me that gun parts were illegal on aircraft. I attempted to explain the security risk of checking in operational weapons and ammunition and why I had done what I had done. Yeah, you know I was never going to win this—negotiating with security folk at airports is like trying to convince Paris Hilton she should join a convent. The gun parts were placed in an envelope marked 'gun parts' and put on the baggage belt—oh, that's a better idea, now the baggage handlers that drive around wearing camel heads and smuggle hash in Schapelle Corby's boogie board can have handguns as well.

Arriving in Townsville I hooked up with an F-111 navigator, Willie, who was going to be in the tactical air control party with me for the exercise. As he was the only other RAAF person around, and the only person who would talk to a 'Raafy crab' (always stepping sideways) in fatigues like me, it was apparent that we would be getting to know each other a lot better over the next few weeks.

We boarded the HMAS *Tobruk* which was the Royal Australian Navy's (RAN) training ship and apparently crewed by children—they had to be, as I was only 21 and they all looked a hell of a lot younger than me. The boat, as we called it (because they demanded we call it a ship), was designed to sleep 200 sailors and we had 500 person-nel onboard. That's OK, being a fighter pilot I was sure they'd have a private cabin somewhere on this gin barge reserved for me. Wrong! I was told I would be sleeping on the helipad with the other 300 soldiers. Weirdly, I was a bit relieved—at least I wasn't hot bunking with a navy guy.

We set sail on the first day and Willie and I managed to invite ourselves onto the bridge of the boat. The officer in charge was a female lieutenant who was extremely officious—extremely anally so, we thought. I mean, there we were travelling at 20 kilometres per hour and it wasn't like we were going to run into anything with less than an hour's notice. Willie and I were used to operating with more than 50 aircraft travelling at the speed of sound where midair colli-sions or hitting the ground can happen in seconds. And we were used to doing this in relative silence—but these guys were like a bunch of monkeys chatting incessantly about nothing:

'Ops officer, report.'

'Aye aye, skipper. Ops log zero five hundred zulu. Position south nineteen fifty-three point-eight. East one-forty-eight, fifty-eight point-nine. Speed 10 knots. Course one-five-zero degrees magnetic. Closest point of approach Hayman Island, bearing one-eight-zero for 15 nautical miles. Depth 330 feet, steady. Current three-six-zero at 3 knots. Wind one-five-zero degrees at 15 knots. Next turn point in 18 nautical miles, time zero six four five zulu. Steady as she goes.' Breathe, breathe, breathe.

'Aye aye. Steady as she goes.'

Willie and I couldn't believe it. In this modern age of satellite GPS, depth sounders, autohelms, digital mapping, etc., we felt like we had just walked onto the bridge of Captain Cook's *Endeavour*. I even turned to the back of the boat expecting to see a guy throw a bucket overboard and count out the knots in the rope. The thought occurred to me about now—no wonder boats were so easy to sink.

This cacophony was continuous for 30 minutes until all hell broke loose—a charter yacht appeared on the horizon. Funny that—we were in the bloody Whitsunday Islands.

'Ma'am, Ma'am. New contact. She bears one-five-zero magnetic. Range 12 nautical miles. Line of advance zero-nine-zero degrees magnetic. Speed 7 knots. Steady as she goes.'

'Steady as she goes. Request you monitor.'

'Ma'am, Ma'am, second contact. She bears one-eight-zero magnetic. Range 12 nautical miles. Line of advance zero-nine-zero degrees magnetic. Speed 6 knots. Steady as she goes.'

This second contact pretty much burst the calm of the ice maiden on watch.

'Quick—wake the captain,' she commanded.

Willie and I, both dumbfounded at the temporal distortion occurring on the bridge of this boat, started chatting about range/aspect/range rate—the three critical parameters used by fighter pilots to visually assess and engage a bandit. By our calculations there was at least one hour to impact and we figured the captain would probably prefer an additional 45 minutes in the rack.

'You two—do you have a problem?'

'Ahh, no, Ma'am,' I said. And that's where I should have stopped; however, I really felt the RAAF, particularly the fighter community, had a lot to offer the navy in this instance—and pretty much everyone else who we felt could do with some of our 'gouge'. Gouge is also known as 'good gen' and we would often say that 'an ounce of gouge is worth a pound of knowledge'. And I was quite happy to offer her a pound of gouge.

'I just thought your communications could be a lot briefer if you were to use the 81 Wing communication brevity code that we use when flying the jets. For example, in this situation we would say, "Two groups azimuth 5 miles, nearest tactical 150/12, Zac 020." You see what I did there was anchored the nearest threat and . . .'

'That is enough, thank you, midshipman,' she said coldly.

'That's flying officer, Ma'am.'

'Whatever. Just keep quiet or you'll be ordered off the bridge,' she snapped.

At this point the recently woken captain walked onto the bridge with sheet marks diagonally crossing his face and a morning hairdo—I half-expected fluffy bunny slippers.

'Captain on the bridge, captain on the bridge,' the gin bargers chorused.

'Aye aye, captain's on the bridge.'

'As you were, as you were. Steady as she goes, steady as she goes.'

My god—it was like a scene from *Master and Commander*. I'd hate to see how this drivel would work in a shooting match—the enemy could complete a broadside attack with cannons before we had all finished quacking about the fact that Russell Crowe was now at the helm. And thank god for that, because we still had another 55 minutes to turn the steering wheel and avoid a few blokes out for a Sunday sail. I could imagine them, beers in hand, rods out the back, trying to convince their mates that 'they knew boats'. And all with absolutely no idea that the operations room on Her Majesty's Royal Australian Navy ship, which they'd just spotted on the horizon, was in complete hysterics about their weekend sailing jaunt.

We left the bridge fearing that our presence might take up too many brain cells of the ice maiden, and we wanted to make sure she was entirely focused on the collision that was unlikely to occur in about one hour's time. We eventually found the ward room (officers mess to us), had our dinner and headed out to the helipad for some well-earned rack (sleep). Keeping Her Majesty's ship safe from dangerous bareboat pirates had been quite taxing.

Instructed to find a couple of stretchers on the helipad, Willie and I spotted them in the middle of a sea of olive-green oversized caterpillars where all the diggers were already tucked in nice and cosy. We unrolled our sleeping bags and allowed the cool breeze across the deck and the gentle swaying of the boat to rock us to sleep—maybe this navy life wasn't too bad after all.

During the night I woke with that pressing feeling in my bladder. The spotlights had been turned out on the helideck and it was now almost pitch black and the wind was quite strong. The ship was pitching a lot more and the occasional spray of seawater was coming across the helideck. I took back everything I said about navy life. Additionally, I didn't know if I had a torch or even where the toilets were. This was going to be interesting.

I decided the easiest option would be to take a leak over the side and proceeded to use my best tactile navigation techniques to make my way to the edge of the deck. This is a polite way for me to say that I pretty much kicked, felt and fell on every digger between my sleeping bag and the side of the ship. Sounds of 'uggh, aarrh, fuck off' could be heard as I made my way through the caterpillars.

After relieving myself over the side of the ship the best I could in the strong breeze and pitching conditions, I repeated the night assault on the diggers as I stumbled my way back to my stretcher. There was mainly just sounds of 'fuck off' this time, and I was starting to get concerned one of these guys would snot me. When I returned to my stretcher my heart immediately sank. Where my sleeping bag had been, now it was gone. I guessed the wind had blown it off my stretcher so I started to use my self-invented tactile navigation techniques again to search downwind of my stretcher—unfortunately for all the diggers downwind of my bed. I had searched pretty much all the way to the edge of the deck (lots more of 'fuck off') and was about to give up when I saw my sleeping bag about 5 metres away, clinging to the safety wire that surrounds the helideck. I'm sure there is a nautical term for this wire but to me it just looked a lot like a clothesline. I was able to rescue my sleeping bag before it blew overboard and then promptly tripped over all the diggers again ('fuck off') on the way back to my stretcher. Night one was going well.

The next day I awoke to a lot of bitching and moaning around me.

'Who was the fucker on night patrol last night steppin' on everyone? I'll fuckin' tear his balls off.'

So I joined in the general chorus. 'Yeah, who was that fucker?'

God, I really needed to get off this boat soon.

Willie and I invited ourselves onto the bridge again on the second day in the hope that maybe they liked the 'good gen' we gave them previously and there would be more opportunities to help them. We started at the steering wheel—helm, that is, to the gin bargers—where we struck up conversation with a young seaman.

'G'day, mate. So tell us about your training to drive this boat.'

'Well, Sir, I start off doing my basic seagoing course and then I . . .'

'Seaman Jones, eyes front, thank you very much, and you two, stop distracting my helmsman.'

There were some 'Yes, Ma'am's all round before we started up another conversation, this time with the poor bastard who had to keep a manual log of all the monkey chatter that was going on around the place. It just wasn't doing it for us. Then I saw the 50-calibre machine gun on the front (bow) of the boat.

'What about the gun? Who fires that?'

'Seaman Jones does, Sir.'

'What, the guy steering the boat? How does he do that without the ice maiden over there having a pink fit about him crashing?'

'It's his secondary duty.'

Willie and I locked eyes. Right, we had to have a chat to the gin boat pilot about anti-aircraft tactics so we could learn how better to attack ships.

'So, mate, we hear you're the gunner?'

'Yes, Sir.'

'Can you tell us how you aim the gun? I mean, if there was a jet moving from right to left across the front of the boat, how would you physically aim the gun?'

'It's pretty simple, really. I just put the cross hairs on the target and shoot.'

'Do you use lead?'

'What's that?'

Un-fucking-believable. The navy was so caught up in monkey chatter about collisions that took an hour to occur that they had no idea how to shoot the gun. I got out my field notebook (my 'brain') and started doing some lead calculations for him.

'So, what's your muzzle velocity? We'll assume 500 knots target with 90 degree heading crossing angle at 1 nautical mile . . .' Willie and I did the sums and then started teaching the gunner how to gun.

'OK, mate, here are some rough numbers for you. If you aim one aircraft length ahead of the target for every mile of range to the target . . .'

'You two, get off my bridge! I warned you not to distract Seaman Jones.'

'Sorry, Ma'am. We were just teaching Seaman Jones how to use the gun more effectively . . .'

'I said get off!'

I truly love organisations that strive to improve themselves.

By the end of the second day we were close to our anchor point off the northern top of Townsend Island where the amphibious assault was going to take place. We retrieved our kit from the helideck and prepared for our opposed beach assault. I loaded up three magazines of blanks and my water. I covered my face with so much camouflage cream it was peeling off like children's face paint, and headed down to the transfer dock where I boarded the landing craft. The landing craft is a flat-bottomed boat with a ramp exactly like the one Private Ryan used—though now it was 60 years later.

An opposed joint amphibious assault is about as complex as war-fighting operations get. You have the three services in close proximity, all contributing to sub-surface, surface, land and air warfare—with none of them really understanding what the fuck the other one is doing. Hence the need for liaison officers such as Willie and me. We, however, were determined to show these grunts a thing or two about land warfare.

With about 30 blokes packed into our little fishing dinghy, it was time to head for the beach. Jets were racing overhead and dropping bombs, choppers were lifting artillery pieces onto the beach and we were below them trying not to capsize. It seemed the swell was on the limit for this flat-bottomed boat and we were being pitched in all directions except the one in which we wanted to travel. We also started to take waves in over the side, which really pissed me off as now I was wet and it was causing my camo make-up to run. I kept my belt buckle undone on my pack in case we went over, and quietly wondered whether I could swim with the 1000 rounds of 9-mm ammo in my webbing.

I pushed my way to the front of the HMAS *Private Ryan*, determined to be the first man on the beach—the enemy would stand no chance. I heard the rustle of sand hit the bottom of the boat then the ramp started to lower—I wasn't waiting in the line of fire any longer and made a run up the ramp with a spectacular leap onto the sand while simultaneously firing my pistol on its side like some sort of mad gangsta rapper. The pistol fired only once and stopped before I hit the ground—literally. My heavy pack had overbalanced me and I went crashing, face first, into the sand. I scrambled to get up and out of way before the ramp squashed me.

Despite the adulatory comments from the grunts like 'Who the fuck brought him' and 'Fucking wanker', I continued on my solo assault of the island. It was only after clearing my gun for the third time in a row that I worked out that 9-mm blank rounds do not provide sufficient recoil to automatically chamber the next round and so I would have to manually slide my 'automatic' pistol 1000 times if I was going to use up my ammo. After approximately 50 rounds, and a few blisters, I quietly gave up on my Sly Stallone impersonation and made my way to the planned location of the tactical air control party tent.

On arrival I was greeted by a cranky warrant officer (WOFF) who I assumed must have been assaulted by a Raafy as a child because he had such a serious attitude towards Willie and I.

'Right, you two. Come with me.'

'We were told to rendezvous at this location . . .'

'Sir, when I need your input I will ask you for it, otherwise please shut the fuck up.'

'Roger, Mac going NOCOM,' I said, using the fighter brevity code for no communications.

He marched us to an apparently arbitrary piece of bush before shouting further commands at us. The way he was yelling at us, the thought occurred to me that the army maybe didn't have a similar rank structure to the RAAF—either that or they just didn't respect their officers. I was also thinking that the WOFF must have been an artillery gunner and was consequently half-deaf—he seemed unable to open his larynx without using the entire strength of his diaphragm. I also started to worry that one of the diggers on HMAS *Private Ryan* might have already reported me to him for my overly zealous beach landing.

'You will pitch your hooch there,' he shouted. 'And dig a foxhole there. You will then report to the command tent for further instruction.' The WOFF then quickly disappeared back in the direction we had come from.

Well, I guess an instruction is a little more respectful than an order.

This entire scene was going on beneath jets bombing targets, the navy shooting their guns at other targets and choppers continually moving back and forwards between the ships and the shore. Personally I thought there were far too many enemy remaining on the island to worry about digging foxholes and pitching tents, but I didn't want to get any further in the shit with this screaming dinosaur if I could help it.

Willie and I started to retrieve our hooches from our packs. A hooch is essentially a rectangular bit of olive-green plastic that, if you try really hard, you can convince yourself can be used for shelter. It was then I noticed there were old foxholes only a few metres from where the WOFF had told us to dig ours. As the exercise was a biannual event, it made sense that someone else had dug a hole somewhere else on this island—I just hoped it wasn't an old shitter. I cleared the leaves and loose dirt away and it looked fine—saving me about an hour's labour. Now we were getting somewhere. We'd be back in the fight in just a jiffy.

It was then that I had some sort of combat epiphany the likes of which Macarthur and Churchill could have probably related to. Why not pitch my hooch over the top of my recently seconded foxhole? That way, when WOFF Crankyarse started playing his little games in the night by running around screaming, 'Air raid, air raid, air raid,' which I knew he was dying to do, I could just stay snugged up in my sleeping bag. Well, it wasn't the RAAF's Hilton standard, but I was certainly moving in the right direction. So I threw my hooch over the hole, which ironically resembled a grave, and Willie and I headed back for 'further instruction'.

We met the rest of the command element of 3 Brigade who we would be working with over the next three weeks. We were allocated a corner of a tent in which we set up our radios and maps. We checked in with the joint fires element that had remained onboard the command ship and then took over the airspace coordination for the exercise.

Willie and I worked twelve-hour back-to-back shifts, making sure airspace was coordinated, ground forces were deconflicted from target areas, and the boats didn't shoot down the jets. After my first shift I knocked off at midnight then did the Stevie Wonder walk back to my hooch as I'd forgotten to take my torch to work with me. After some time I found my hooch, which was actually easy to identify as it was the only one with a grave underneath it. I unrolled my mattress, sleeping bag and mozzie net, and promptly fell asleep.

About an hour later I woke with a wet feeling near my arse. I initially thought I had pissed myself, but once I was fully conscious I realised I could hear torrential rain hitting my hooch and discovered that my foxhole was filling up with water. It didn't take me too long to work out why no-one else had had the same combat epiphany as me and slept in their foxhole. I quickly grabbed my stuff and dashed under Willie's hooch. My gear would remain wet for the next three weeks as a tropical depression set in over the north-east of Australia. I was really, really missing my RAAF hotel.

Outside of our twelve-hour duty period there was nothing we were allowed to do due to the live-fire nature of the exercise. This really pissed me off, and I snuck off early one morning to have a bath in the ocean, something they'd specifically told us not to do because of poisonous jellyfish. This part of my deployment felt more operational than the exercise proper, as I crept through 'enemy' lines before first light, made it to the beach, quickly undressed, scanned the beach one last time for sentries and then sprinted for the water's edge with my Palmolive soap in hand. I did a cursory scan for the famed box jellyfish before diving under and lathering myself up (which, by the way, never happens in salt water). It was then that I heard the beat of the drum.

Looking up I saw a Kiowa chopper coming down the beach towards me at about 50 feet. I sunk back underwater so just my nose was out, hoping against hope they hadn't seen me. *Bowwww bowwww!* No luck. The chopper slowed and hovered next to me with the pilot giving me angry hand signals to get out of the water. Fuck! This was not good. We had been specifically yelled at by WOFF Crankyarse not to go in the water because of the enemy jellyfish, and now I'd been caught red-handed and would have to do the walk of shame back up the beach in my birthday suit. I couldn't see the pilot's face because of the helmet and dark visor—could it possibly be a hot chick pilot?

With this highly dubious thought in my mind I did my best Daniel Craig swagger up the beach. The rotor wash from my friendly neighbourhood-watch chopper was driving sand into me that stung my legs all the way up to my groin. I quickly looked south to check if the tackle was handling the sandblaster and only then realised just how cold the water and the rotor wash were making me—*he* had gone. I broke into a sprint, no longer concerned whether the chopper pilot was a man, woman, hermaphrodite or whatever—in any case, it was embarrassing.

I got back to my hooch, changed into my still-wet clothes and headed down to the command tent in the hope they weren't all waiting there ready to bastardise me for not having a dick. Everything seemed normal when I arrived, so I went and spoke with the artillery officer I had been coordinating the joint fires with. He was of similar rank and a nice guy so I asked him if I could shoot some of his big guns. He said he would see what he could do, made a couple of radio calls and then sent me off in the general direction of the gun line.

'Do you have map or something, mate? I don't want to stray into the target area,' I said.

'Don't worry,' he replied. 'We have a fire serial about to start. Just follow your ears.'

So off I headed on an apparently arbitrary bearing that he had pointed out from the command tent. There were a few tracks that could have been wildlife tracks, and the target area was a few klicks away—it was unlikely I would end up at the wrong end of the gun line. But after I'd been walking for a few minutes the guns started to fire and I shit my wet pants.

I was only 100 metres or so from the guns but the thick scrub had prevented me seeing or hearing them until they fired—and fire they did. The percussion was amazing as it hit me in the chest through the vegetation. I hadn't brought any hearing protection so stuck my fingers in my ears and followed the pressure waves towards the gun line.

When I arrived there were twelve guns lined up next to each other with a team of three men on each gun and a few blokes at the rear preparing ammunition. I was in another scene from *Private Ryan*— I couldn't believe it. We had a navy that was still practising broadside cannon tactics and an army that was still using towed artillery. I resigned myself to the fact that there must be a good reason that I was not aware of for keeping these 50-year-old guns.

I had been told to ask for Bombardier Johns; he turned out to be a great bloke and we struck it off straightaway. He loved his Howitzer 105-mm and 155-mm and I wanted to learn all about them. I spent the next couple of hours helping the guys load the powder bags and set the fuses and finally they asked me if I would like to fire the big fuck-off guns. The guys gave me a set of earplugs so I could pull my fingers out of my ears, but I noticed they all wore earplugs and noise-cancelling headsets, as well as body armour to stop the percussive forces rupturing their internal organs. I was wearing my wet cams and a set of foam earplugs. I started to wonder if I would lose my hearing and my aircrew medical. How bad could it be?

I walked forwards to gun number eleven in the line of twelve and the trigger man briefed me up.

'OK, Sir, before you is a Howitzer 105-mm cannon.'

Thank you for pointing that out to me, Corporal, given that my head is ringing from the last hour of loading rounds.

'At the front of the gun is the barrel and recoil suppressor.'

He was joking, right?

'And at the rear of the gun you have the breach.'

I paid him the respect he deserved by listening intently—but I just wanted to let this bad boy rip.

'Unfortunately we just broke the firing mechanism on the last serial,' he said, pointing to a 30-centimetre long piece of cord on the ground. 'So you will be firing the gun with this,' he said, holding up a rubber mallet.

No, I thought, actually this was worse than *Private Ryan*—I'm pretty sure they weren't using rubber hammers to fire their guns.

The bombardier briefed me on the next fire serial. We would be firing a single spotter round initially. The forward observer would then apply corrections to this round, after which we would fire a second round. The forward observer would then apply a final correction after which we would 'fire for effect' for two minutes. However, I was not to use my Thor hammer of death until given the command, as to do so would kill the gunner loading the rounds into the back of the gun. OK, I was paying attention now.

Once we were all ready some radio calls were made and then Bombardier Johns started yelling down the line—hadn't these guys heard of Dick Smith and walkie-talkies yet?

'Gun line, ready, single round, on my command—fire!'

I checked the fall guy was out of the way and let the hammer fall.

'FUCK ME!' I yelled, stumbling backwards, slightly winded. My entire body was vibrating and my head was ringing. 'How the fuck do you guys do this all day? Aren't you fucking . . .'

Either the guys couldn't hear me, they were shell-shocked, or they were too focused on reloading.

'Gun line, ready, single round, on my command—fire!'

The gunners looked at me and I looked back with what I assumed was the expression of a stunned mullet. I didn't have to do it again, did I? I tentatively hit the firing pin.

'Aaaah . . . Faaark!' Knowing what was coming made it seem to hurt more the second time.

Were these guys really going to sit here and do this for three weeks? Was this going to be their career? Their heads would be permanently rattled. And the army commanders were worried about box fucking jellyfish?

I politely thanked the bombardier and excused myself, saying that I had run myself overtime and had to get back to the command tent.

With ringing ears I scurried back to the tent with some insight into why WOFF Crankyarse behaved the way he did. I enthusiastically reported to him about what I'd been doing and my newfound respect for artillery. Well, that did the trick—the WOFF and I got along fine for the rest of the deployment and he even gave me a polished 105-mm round at the end of the exercise. Despite the fact it was illegal to have one, required me to 'lose' my sleeping bag to make it fit in my pack, and my pack now weighed 75 per cent of my body-weight, I gratefully accepted his gesture and have kept the round polished in my study to this day. I needed to repay the favour.

On the last day of the exercise the simulated enemy capitulates after one final stand that requires one final comprehensive joint-fires serial from the ADF. We planned it to go late into the evening, with multiple ships shooting their guns, Bombardier Johns and his boys 'firing for effect', and F-18s and F-111s dropping a gut load of 230 kilogram and 900 kilogram bombs. Willie and I also planned a little surprise for WOFF Crankyarse and his mates.

On schedule the next day the gun lines opened up in a sustained rapid-fire serial. From the command tent all we could hear was the dull 'thud thud thud' as the rounds peppered the top of Hamburger Hill. The tropical depression was still over the island, which kept a low layer of cloud over the range, acting like a blanket that trapped a lot of the noise at ground level and amplified the explosive sounds.

'Excuse me, WOFF, what's that noise?' I asked.

'That, my air force friend, are the guns of 114 Field Battery preparing the target,' he replied.

'Sounds awesome,' I said innocently.

Shortly after, the sound of the thuds changed in tempo and tone to those of the naval gunfire. As the gin barges practised their broadside tactics, Willie's and my little surprise checked in on the radio.

'Colt check.'

'Colt 2.'

'Alpha 11, this is Colt formation, flight of two F-111s, four Mk 84 each, for single pass onto Townsend Island, presently 30 nautical miles (60 kilometres) north, below 500 feet (150 metres).'

'Roger, Colt, you're cleared on, maintain below 150-metres contact range control on range primary,' I replied.

A couple of minutes later Russell Crowe had finished his cannonball barrage and a strange quietness settled over the island. No helicopters, no guns, no naval gunfire. Then a vibration was felt through the ground, followed by a deafening shockwave that blew out the sides of our command tent, sending maps and paper flying through the air.

The brigade major, or God incarnate to the average digger, went ape shit.

'Tucker, what the fuck was that? Check fire! Your boys have missed the fucking target and dropped short!'

I listened to the range safety officer report good bombs to the F-111 pilots before turning to answer the major.

'That, Sir, are the bombs of the Royal Australian Air Force finishing the target that 114 prepared earlier,' I said, with a smile directed towards WOFF Crankyarse.

To be honest, Willie and I both thought the Pigs had dropped on our tent and were nervous until we heard the report from the safety officer. The atmospheric conditions and the shape of the terrain had focused the shockwave of the 7.5 tonne explosion directly onto the command tent, thereby comprehensively settling any rivalry about who had the bigger gun.

Since that exercise in 1991, I have often watched the services try and work together and regularly marvel at their inability to understand each other and work cooperatively. I wrote this chapter while working in Afghanistan across several different organisations, all of which act like hostile tribes towards one another. The RAAF are technology-driven, which enables them to adapt to change far better than the army, who are driven by manpower and understand how to manage men far better than the RAAF. I optimistically wait for the day when the different organisations can operate cooperatively rather than as adversaries. Once they do, the taxpayers might really start to get some value for their money.

6

Chemical warfare

MOST KNUCKLEHEADS WILL do anything to get out of any sort of course or activity that pulls them out of the cockpit. Annual medicals, pistol training, fire training, first-aid training, fitness tests, parades, safety courses—all are avoided like the plague because they have little to do with flying jets, and any day out of the cockpit is a bad day. There was one course, though, that a senior knucklehead advised me to do which I got selected for in 1991—the RAAF Weapons Course.

This course was an intense program in how to destroy anything you liked with any type of aerial weapon. I was the youngest on the course, as most of the other guys were already fighter or bomber pilots and navigators. I was still on Macchi jet trainers and my fighter career was not yet assured—I had a long way to go before I graduated from the F-18 Operational Conversion Course. But I figured it would be better to do the Weapons Course now and lose time flying the Macchi than lose time flying F-18s. The course was held at RAAF Base East Sale, Victoria, which was about the 'bluntest' base I had ever been to.

Someone, somewhere, early on in my career, sat me down and gave me their philosophy on 'blunts'. It went something like this: the RAAF is a pyramid with pilots at the top. For every pilot who flies there are a bunch of mechanics to service the jet. For every mechanic there are a bunch of cooks and bottle washers, etc., and so the pyramid expands towards the bottom. The pointy end is the top, the blunt end is the bottom. So RAAF Base East Sale was Bluntsville, and appropriately enough the home of the School of Navigation.

Now the School of Navigation was an enigma to most pilots and certainly fighter pilots. Navigation was no more than a couple of subjects in our basic training that taught us how to read a map and not get lost by day or night or in bad weather. I could understand it being complicated in the days of Wilbur and Orville Wright, but a handheld GPS is just not that hard to put batteries in and turn on. Here was an entire school dedicated to an iPhone application.

The No. 2 Central Flying School (CFS) was in East Sale also, which is where instructors go to learn how to instruct. It was getting up there in the RAAF pyramid but still lacked the dizzying heights of fighters. The RAAF's aerobatic team, the Roulettes—or Briquettes, as fighter pilots called them—were at East Sale too, as they were flown by CFS instructors. There was always a healthy rivalry between the Briquettes and the fighter community, as they required a lot of special training to do what we trained 21-year-old kids to do on the F-18 basic course. There was one advantage to being invited to conduct a fly-past at every special event around Australia—they always got invited to the gold chalet after parties for all the special events— which I guess evened things up a bit.

So there I was one night on Weapons Course in the back bar of the officers mess on the bluntest base in the RAAF. An old 75 Squadron mate of mine, Stu, was on course with me so I at least had someone to have a beer with and talk to about pointy subjects rather than the latest style of navigator wings, the correct way to trim the PC-9 (the bug-smasher flown by the Briquettes) or how awesome it was to pull up into the vertical at an airshow. Stu and I stuck to more important subjects like which chick in the bar was the hottest, whether it was time to move onto tequila sunrises, and how we were going to break into the CFS and put blotting ink on the inside of all their oxygen masks.

The course went slower for Stu and I than the rest of the students. While they were up all night studying the fuse sequence of a M904 bomb nose fuse, we were off in the wild town of Sale getting our groove on. Now, for those who may never have visited Sale in the early 90s, it was a pretty rough town, with Stu and I getting ourselves into more than one fight with the locals who did not appreciate our grooming (surely that's what pissed them off?). It was a miracle, but we managed to keep ourselves out of the lockup and the hospital while simultaneously passing our exams.

Around the middle of the course we headed off on a multi-day field trip to look at 'special facilities' and infrastructure which would assist us with our weaponeering. We inspected dam walls, power generation facilities, bridges, buildings and runways, looking at how we could optimise weapons to destroy them. Dropping bombs too fast into a runway will cause the bomb to explode on impact before it digs in far enough to cause a crater. Generator buildings require you to delay the fuse a considerable time period so that the bomb doesn't go off on the roof but penetrates the roof before detonating on impact with the generators themselves. Stu and I loved this part of the course because it was more practical than the classroom theory. There was one practical application that I, unfortunately, would be the only one to participate in—chemical warfare.

We covered the theory of chemical warfare in some depth from a defensive perspective, as the ADF does not use chemical weapons offensively. We learnt the broad types, active ingredients and biological responses, as well as protection and treatment for different chemical agents. Stu and I tuned out a fair bit during this part of the course as we never thought we would use the theory—wrong again.

On our field trip we visited a number of defence facilities in Canberra, such as the Defence Signals Directorate (DSD), Defence Intelligence Organisation (DIO), and Defence Imagery and Geospatial Organisation (DIGO). At the end of this taxing day we hit Australia's capital about as hard as you can . . . which means we had a couple of beers. Towards the end of the night I was kidnapped by a woman who must have drugged me, as I have no further recollection of the evening.

A week later, back at RAAF Base Bluntsville to complete our weaponeering course, Stu and I were again in the bar educating the blunts on the pointier aspects of life when he saw me scratching my balls.

'Mac, are you OK, mate? You've been at 'em all night like a Malaysian dog.'

'Mate, I'm not sure what's going on, but I've been as itchy as hell for a few days and I've rubbed my balls raw in my sleep.'

'You've probably got crabs, mate.'

'No. Do you reckon? How would I know?'

'Hang on, mate. There's a nursing officer over there—I'll just go get her.'

Despite me pleading for him not to involve the RAAF nurse, he walked off, looking back at me the entire time with a shit-eating grin on his face. Shortly thereafter the nurse came over with Stu smiling gleefully behind her.

'Hi, Mac, I'm Caroline,' she introduced herself. 'I'm the nursing officer here at RAAF Base Sale. Stu tells me you have a medical issue you need some advice about.'

I could feel myself going bright red in the face. 'Oh, it's nothing. I'm sure it'll pass. Thanks for asking.'

'Now look,' she said seriously. 'There is nothing you can't talk to me about. If you have a medical issue it's best to get onto it straightaway.'

'No, it's nothing . . .'

'He's got crabs!' Stu blurted out unable to constrain himself.

'I have not. He's being a dickhead. I'm fine.'

'Mac, pubic lice are nothing to be embarrassed about,' said the nurse.

Could she have said it any louder? 'I'm fine,' I insisted, my face flaming red. 'I told you, Dickhead here is just trying to embarrass me.' Which he was doing a fine job of, I might add.

Stu was like a dog with a bone. 'If Mac did have crabs, how would he know? What would be the symptoms?'

'Unexplained itchiness in the genitalia is the most common symptom. If you have a persistent itchiness in your pubic region without an associated rash, there's a good chance it's pubic lice.'

'Look, thanks, Caroline, but that's not what I've got. I appreciate your advice and if I need help I'll come and see you.'

The nurse walked away, smiling knowingly like she was thinking, 'Yeah, mate, I'll see you in a couple more days when your balls are bleeding.'

Stu was pissing himself laughing and the entire bar was now looking at me trying to work out what he found so amusing and why the nurse was involved. I had to do something. There had to be some way I could sort this thing out without having to do the walk of shame through medical. Then I remembered a lecture we had the previous week on nerve agents.

I went up to the bar. 'Excuse me, do you have any flyspray, please?' I asked the barmaid.

'Mate, that won't work,' Stu said. 'Just go and see the nurse.'

'Why not? Flyspray acts like VX nerve gas on insects. Remember how they breathe through their bodies? It's got to work.'

'Here you go, Sir,' the barmaid said handing me the can.

I headed into the men's room despite Stu's protests. I opened my flying suit, dropped my jocks, held the old fella out of the danger zone and started spraying for all I was worth. I'd been going crazy day and night with the itching and if it was crabs then my chemical warfare assault on their main base would fix them.

'Mate, that's gotta be enough. That shit will kill you,' Stu pleaded.

I kept spraying, left, right, under, my arse crack—everywhere. By this stage the flyspray was dripping down my groin and legs. And it was about then that one of the navigator cadets walked in and found two of Australia's war gods from the heavens doing something that looked very suspicious. He took in the picture of Stu watching me strangle my chicken neck with one hand while appearing to club the chook with a can of flyspray in the other and white liquid running down my crotch—he spun on his heels and left abruptly, with his bladder no doubt overflowing.

'It's not how it looks, mate,' Stu yelled out, in the hope of stopping any rumours spreading throughout the bar.

With most of a full can of flyspray applied, I felt certain I had drowned every living organism in my crotch. I pulled my jocks back up, zipped up my suit and headed back to the bar. I handed the can back to the barmaid and said, 'Bit of bug problem in the men's—all sorted out now. Thanks.'

The next morning I saw Stu at breakfast and greeted him with a big smile.

'You're shitting me?' he said.

'Nope. All sorted. Good night's sleep and my old fella hasn't started peeling.'

For the final week of the Weapons Course my experiment in chemical warfare was the chief topic of conversation. I was quite proud of my ingenuity, but then, after I'd been home in Newcastle for about a week, the itching started again. I couldn't believe it. How could they have survived my napalm assault?

I reluctantly booked into medical to see my doctor, Trev, who was luckily also a mate. I recounted to him the timeline of being kidnapped in Canberra, tearing my balls off in Sale, my chemical warfare attack (at which he almost pissed himself laughing) and how the itching started again. He listened intently while ripping out a handful of pubes to put under the microscope—I will forever appreciate what women go through at the beautician.

'The flyspray probably did a great job killing the lice but not the eggs. They lie dormant in your hair follicles for two weeks before hatching,' the doc explained. 'I'm giving you something that will work on both the eggs and the lice. It's pretty strong stuff so follow the directions.'

Those little fuckers were smarter than me, so I gave in to the wonders of modern medicine and took the bottle of milky fluid home for my second chemical attack. The directions said to apply liberally so I did, by pouring the bottle contents onto a washcloth and coating my nether regions. Instantly pain shot through me like acid—this stuff was burning the fuckers out. I went down on all fours trying to endure the agony. My flatmates, Honko and Mirty, thought it the funniest thing ever.

'Pass me the hairdryer—quickly!' I yelled.

I then started trying to dry off the acid-like chemical with the hairdryer—much to my flatmates' further amusement. The pain slowly subsided over a ten-minute period, after which my balls were bright pink. The next day they began to peel.

The bugs never returned but the stories flourished. The fighter pilot community is a very small one, comprising only 60 to 100 guys in total—and it is a very close community. My wingmen were my family for the best part of thirteen years—and many remain so today. I just wish they didn't know all my personal details.

7
Fly-by-wire

WITH THE ADVENT of computers, aerodynamic engineers started to get a little more creative with their aircraft designs and break away from long-held traditions such as aircraft generally having to point forwards and being controllable by pilots of average strength, reflexes and aptitude. The F-18 is a good example of the first point and commercial airliners are a testament to the last point. Microchips now fly airliners—pilots just act as high-speed cheerleaders and psychological reassurance for naive passengers who truly believe that the old guy with the four gold bars and dorky hat is some sort of demigod who is not bound by the same physical laws as us mere mortals.

Vertical surfaces on aircraft, such as vertical stabilisers and rudders, act like fins on a surfboard—they keep the surfboard pointing forwards. If you have ever tried to surf backwards you will know it is a bit of a struggle and the board usually wins by spinning itself around to point in the correct direction. The trouble with fighter aircraft is they require high levels of agility to evade enemy missiles and win dogfights. In order to have this high agility, fighters are designed with more vertical surfaces forward rather than aft (i.e the surfboard fins are on the front of the board). The canopy and fuselage both act as giant fins when flown at high nose-up attitudes.

In order that these supersonic surfboards remain pointing forwards and do not enter a spin, computers are required to fly the aircraft in ways that normal pilots cannot. This is the conventional definition of 'fly-by-wire'. There is, however, another definition . . .

Hang-gliding is my favourite form of flight (maybe as a result of my early childhood experience—thanks, Dad) because it's as close to free flight as humans can possibly get—except maybe that crazy Frenchman who strapped four jets to his back. There is no G suit, no oxygen mask nor a sardine tin to squeeze into. It is just you, hung from a strap to a kite that is made from carbon fibre, aluminium tube, dacron and stainless steel wires—these are the wires I prefer to fly by.

Keeping young fighter pilots entertained on their days off is difficult. If they're not sleeping off the night before, they can usually be found surfing, hang-gliding, kiteboarding, wakeboarding, snowboarding, parachuting, gliding, mountain climbing, racing motorcycles or ocean-racing maxi yachts. Anything to try and induce another dose of their preferred drug of addiction—adrenaline.

For me it was hang-gliding, and still is. There is nothing like it that makes me feel so alive.

Life is a condition of existence we take for granted. By facing death, and surviving, we teeter on the razor's edge of existence. Staring into the abyss we see the abyss staring back and start to understand what lies within it—and therefore appreciate all the more the life we enjoy every day. The psychological trait that encourages one to contemplate or even risk death on a regular basis is something that the armed forces screen for in their psychological tests. It is not a suicidal condition, but a belief in oneself to the point where you will risk your life if it becomes necessary, that is, if it's warranted by what's called the 'subjective need'.

My subjective need was self-discovery. How high could I go? How fast could I go? How far could I go? How low could I go? How short could I land? Could I stand on top of a power pole? Could I tiptoe on some fat-cat's outdoor dining table that was perched on a cliff-top mansion? Could I fly at night? Could I fly formation with a wedge-tailed eagle?

I answered all of these questions and more without ever breaking a bone. All these risks were calculated and managed to a very fine degree, and, unlike the RAAF, I did not have to employ a risk consultant nor write up a risk management plan to find the answers. Every day I fly my hang-glider I continue to learn—even now after competing and flying in the sport for twenty years. One lesson learnt sticks out in my mind more than any of the others.

While flying Macchi jets at RAAF Williamtown, I rented a top-floor apartment on one of the hang-gliding hills in Newcastle. This vantage point allowed me to be fully in tune with the weather conditions. I could see the wind lanes on the water and determine the wind strength and direction. I could even tell the direction and strength of the wind by the sound it made on the different windows in the apartment. Combined with the long-range forecasts I received as part of my day job, and my fellow hang-glider pilot 'Wingover Wayne' who worked in the lighthouse on an adjacent hill, I could anticipate when and where I needed to be with my hang-glider to ensure I got one of my 'three F's for the day'—a good fly. (Another of the F's could be satisfied at a restaurant—a good feed. You can guess the third.)

My glider was kept permanently set-up in my garage, which resulted in my BMW being evicted and consequently suffering terribly from the salt spray that perpetually coated everything on the hill. The benefit, however, was that within five minutes of heading out the door I could be flying—it was the perfect hang-gliding pad.

I woke one morning to the familiar whine of my balcony window caused by the south-easterly wind. It was on! Trouble was, I had to go to work and fly jets. Sometimes the decisions we have to make in life can be so difficult . . .

It is extremely rare for a fighter pilot to pull a sickie. It is usually the other way around. Generally an executive officer will see a half-dead corpse in a damp flying suit sitting in the main briefing room in a full-body sweat trying valiantly to look like he has just got back from a jog. A brief discussion ensues before the pilot is forced to medical to find out that he's suffering from glandular fever and he's running a temperature of 42 degrees. On this occasion, however, the wind looked just too good. I rang TVH, who was going to be driving me to work.

'Mate, I'm pulling a sickie and I need you to cover for me. Tell them that I have a cold or something, will you?'

'You're going flying, aren't you?' asked TVH straightaway. TVH was also a hang-glider pilot and loved the sport about as much as me.

'Yeah, I am. It looks awesome. It's going to be on all day. Listen, I was leading a maritime strike at ten hundred—can you lead it for me?'

'Yeah, alright. You're a prick, mate. Have a good one.'

Shortly after hanging up I was jumping off the hill with a good supply of water and muesli bars—it was going to be a long day.

Hang-gliding is definitely an art more than a science. There are no instruments to read—it is all sensory input. Height is judged with eyesight, speed judged with noise and feel, and thermals are found with skin temperature and smell. The honing of these senses, and the judgement of these senses, is what makes a good hang-glider pilot. On this particular day the south-easterly was bringing rain squalls onshore with associated low cloud. At the base of the low cloud there was a slight temperature increase due to the latent heat of condensation. Condensation is released when the warm, moist, rising air cools and forms clouds. This warmer air then starts to rise more aggressively, leading to a phenomenon that glider pilots call 'cloud suck'. At 700 metres, over the top of one of Australia's most populous cities, I was experiencing cloud suck in a big way—able to fly out to sea, back to land, over the city and back out to sea. It was like having a motor—I could go anywhere.

My mind occasionally turned to TVH and the maritime strike mission he was leading. The mission called for a four-aircraft formation (four-ship) to conduct multiple low-level attacks against a navy ship so that the ship's crew could train in anti-aircraft defence. They were fun missions but I really felt that I was having more fun discovering how to exploit this meteorological phenomenon. Eventually I went back to soaring above the largest cliff in Newcastle, and was perched comfortably at about 200 metres above sea level when I saw TVH and his three wingmen.

Knowing that I would be having a great day hang-gliding, and pissed off that he had to cover for me, TVH thought he would teach me a lesson. With his four jets in arrow formation, he was racing back from the exercise airspace off the coast of Nowra at 700 kilometres per hour and 75 metres above sea level. I had detected him quite late due to the effective camouflage scheme of the Macchi, but when I did, I was terrified.

Although I was a good 150 metres above the jets and at no risk of being hit, I was at risk of being flipped over or having my hang-glider structurally fail due to their jet wash. TVH had brought the jets in close enough that the turbulent air left behind them was going to blow into the cliff and then up the cliff face to where I was perched. As the wind was climbing at about 500 metres per minute I had about twenty seconds.

I started a mental clock and attempted to dive and fly out and over the jets to put their wake behind me. But the wind was too strong and I couldn't make sufficient headway to clear their wake. After the longest twenty seconds of my life the wake hit me.

It was like being thrown around in a washing machine with one major exception—this washing machine was 150 metres above sea level. I felt the strap that attached me to the glider become extremely taut and I could envisage it breaking under the strain. Then my thoughts turned to the glider flipping end over end, or perhaps it would just break up in midair and spiral to the ocean, crashing against the rocks below. I always carried a parachute for special occasions just like this, but I was too low to deploy it. I hurled an expletive at TVH who was by now out of sight—and then I became weightless. Shit.

Weightlessness in a hang-glider is like losing your rudder in a boat or having your steering wheel fall off in a car. Pilots steer hang-gliders by pushing their weight left and right, forwards and back. Without any weight, however, the glider cannot be controlled. I held onto the control bar with cold hands and waited. This was uncharted territory for me and I had no idea how my little sick day would end. I guessed if I ended up in the hospital I would at least pass the scrutiny of my Commanding Officer wondering why I wasn't at work. I might just have to avoid telling him exactly when it occurred and how my 'car' ended up crashing into the rocks on Newcastle beach.

The glider pitched nose-down, past 90 degrees, so all I could see were the rocks, and then the underside of my wing—as I started to fall onto it. This is about as bad as it gets for hang-glider pilots. I continued to fire my expletives in TVH's last known direction and prayed that the glider didn't tumble.

After what seemed like an eternity the glider regained airspeed and started to climb out of the dive. Thankfully the climb gave me back my weight and my control—but I was now pointed directly at the cliff, approaching it from the ocean side and beyond the maximum speed my wing was designed for. Smoothly pushing the bar out, I climbed and rolled past the 90-degree point until I was parallel to the beach and upside-down before returning to normal. For those watching below it looked like an intentional aerobatic display. Fortunately for me they couldn't see inside my boardshorts.

I landed on very shaky legs and did an inspection of the structural parts of my glider, looking for any signs of overstress. It all looked OK so I continued flying for the rest of the day.

After work, TVH turned up at the take-off site with his glider, bragging about the mission. 'Mate, you missed a good day. Sunk those fuckin' navy pussers in their gin barge. They never stood a chance. Did you see us on return to base?'

'See you?' I yelled. 'You nearly fuckin' killed me! I went totally weightless and almost tumbled straight into the cliff, you fuckwit.'

'Yeah, yeah, Serge, whatever you say,' he said, laughing. 'Come on, let's practise some night formations. I brought some glow sticks so we can tape them to our gliders. Everyone will think they're seeing UFOs.'

And with that we were off, using our fighter NOCOM signals to change position and put on a hang-gliding night airshow of military precision.

A couple of years later, TVH and I headed up to the Carlo Sandblow on Rainbow Beach in Queensland to teach some fellow knuckleheads how to hang-glide. The sand blow is the coastal mecca of hang-gliding in Australia, where perfect conditions present themselves every day during summer. Ironically, two of my hang-gliding students would end up being instructors on my F-18 course a year later. As expected, all the F-18 guys picked it up within a few days and were soaring well. It was time for the 'Cherry Venture Express'.

Just north of Noosa Heads, not far from Rainbow Beach, is a ramp launch site called 'Teewah' which has been constructed by hang-glider pilots to prevent sand dune erosion. The sand dune is over 55 kilometres long and finishes at the wreck of an old ship that ran aground years ago—the *Cherry Venture*. The weather was perfect so we packed up our four-wheel drives and drove the 70 kilometres along the beach to the ramp.

Ramp launches can be difficult in strong winds as the ramp juts out well forward of the dune, resulting in vertical air passing up the face of the dune and into the ramp. This means that the airflow is at a 90-degree angle to the wing, which places the wing in a deep stall. If the wind is strong enough it can lift a glider vertically in this stalled state and flip it. TVH and I therefore decided we would help launch all the other gliders before launching ourselves.

We used three 'wiremen' to hold the nose and two wing wires. This allowed the pilot to concentrate on getting into his harness and observing the conditions. Once the pilot called 'clear', the guy on the nose would let go and lay down, and the two on the wing wires would hang onto the glider to stop it from lifting vertically while running forwards to the front edge of the ramp, where they literally threw the glider off with forward airspeed such that the stall was broken and the pilot could control the glider.

Our plan worked well and we successfully launched the other six gliders. Then it was down to the two of us. I volunteered to go last and acted as a lone nose man for TVH. We struggled to hold the glider down, with the strong wind occasionally lifting both of us off the ramp. I started to get nervous about how the hell I was going to do this without any assistance when TVH called clear and I leant back to use my weight, which wasn't much, to assist his launch. TVH's launch was fine and all seven gliders circled overhead, waiting for me as the 'Tail End Charlie'.

We were all on radio, and the encouragement started to come through my helmet as I strapped in.

'Be careful, Mac.'

'Don't fuck it up, mate.'

At the start of the ramp the wind began to buffet just the nose of my glider. With less than a metre of my nose in the vertical airstream, it already felt like I was holding on to a bucking bull. I leant forwards aggressively to pin the nose to the deck and started walking out hesitantly. At the halfway point enough of the gilder was in the airflow to lift both me and the glider. It was here I probably should have stopped, but there was no other option I could think of if I was going to join the gaggle circling above.

Eventually I had the entire glider onto the ramp and had stepped through the control frame to hold its nose down. I couldn't do my harness safety checks in this position so I did a visual inspection, stepped back through the control frame to the flying position, took a deep breath and then . . .

'Faaaaaaaark!'

I was upside-down, sitting on the underside of my wing, 20 metres in the air and moving over the back of the sand dunes at about 20 kilometres per hour—this was going to hurt. Fortunately, the glider settled gently upside-down on some bitou bush like a magic carpet, with no bending of metal or snapping of limbs and I quickly climbed out of my harness.

'Mac, you OK?'

'Mac, come in. You right, mate?'

'Yeah, I'm good. I'll just be a minute,' I replied. I rolled the glider over and walked it forwards to the start of the ramp, then got into the nose wireman position. In this position you can hold the nose down while the tail of the kite buffets like a crazed shark thrashing around. This time I used a tie-down strap with a quick-release knot to secure the nose of the glider to the front end of the ramp. With the glider secured I could walk around to the pilot position, strap in and complete my safety checks. I then braced myself in the take-off position, grabbed the long tail of the quick-release knot and gave it a huge tug.

'Faaaaaaaark!'

It happened again. This time the glider remained the right way up and flew backwards at 20 metres before falling where I experienced my first bitou bush enema.

'Mac, you there, mate? Give it away. You're going to kill yourself,' TVH wisely transmitted.

The glider was fine and I only suffered some minor bruising and cuts. I had one last play left in me and probably less in the glider itself.

'I'll give it one more go, guys. If I don't get off then, I'll see you at the other end.' I was now full of adrenaline and a bit of emotion. It wasn't the embarrassment that was worrying me, it was my frustration at not being able to sort out the take-off—even if it wasn't normally done solo.

I got the glider out of the bushes, walked it back to the start of the ramp, clipped into my harness, did my safety checks and gave my final harebrained scheme a crack. I pushed the nose of the glider onto the ramp then, like a bulldozer, started running with the nose grinding along the full length of the 10-metre ramp. The mylar nose cover ripped off immediately and then I could hear the aluminium scraping away as I sacrificed the nose plate for flying speed. At the front of the ramp I was still running flat-out with the nose in a 30-degree dive as it left the end of the ramp. At exactly that moment I jumped forwards and took up the tension on my harness so I'd have control of the glider. It worked—I was off.

The boys cheered as I joined them and we headed north on our 55-kilometre run. It was a great experience teaching these guys then enjoying two hours with them along one of the world's most beautiful beaches. We saw sea turtles, rays, dolphins and got to fly with sea eagles. Strangely, though, I was unable to reach the height of the other gliders and I couldn't keep up with them. I only just made it to the destination, taking a lot longer than the others.

After I landed TVH took one look at my glider and raised his eyebrows. 'Good job getting off, Serge. But you might want to get out of your harness and have a look at your leading edges.'

I got out and immediately realised why I'd had such a difficult time keeping up. At some stage during my two take-off aerobatic shows, I'd put a lateral tear in both leading edges, causing them to open in flight like giant airbrakes. I pulled out some thousand-mile-an-hour tape and fixed the tears, which thankfully held together for the rest of our sky-surfing safari.

A year later TVH and I had both been posted to 75 Squadron at RAAF Base Tindal to fly F-18s. There were no beaches within a three-hour drive and the wind in Darwin was never strong enough to fly the low cliffs unless there was a cyclone off the coast (TVH actually tried this once). But we weren't about to let a small matter of geography stop us from doing the thing we both loved the most. So we set about designing and building a system using a car to tow each other up in our hang-gliders like conventional gliders use. How hard could it be?

The first task was to learn how to tow our gliders. For this TVH, FE and I used the opportunity of an air-to-air gunnery camp in Perth to enrol in a hang-glider towing course. We shipped our gliders in the C-130 Hercules, booked our 'rent-a-bomb', sorted our accommodation and deployed with the squadron to Perth.

Air-to-air gunnery in a Hornet is really quite easy; you simply lock up the target with your radar, select your gun, put your pipper on the target and when the 'green shit' in the heads-up display (HUD) starts flashing 'in range' you pull the trigger. To score well during training is, however, incredibly difficult, largely due to the safety constraints that have to be observed. The target is an oversized tennis net towed behind a business jet at 500 kilometres per hour. The tow aircraft flies a continuous orbit so the target is never directly behind it. This ensures a degree of safety for the crew of the tow aircraft as the firing aircraft approaches the 'banner' (or 'rag') from behind and the rounds travel past the banner and away from the tow aircraft. The tow aircraft are flown by contractors who are all ex-fast jet aircrew, as they are also required to conduct intercepts and maritime strikes for training purposes; this further increases the safety levels.

There is a safety management theory that suggests all accidents are manmade and therefore preventable. While this is true, if you're going to reduce the risk to all personnel involved in the design, manufacture and operations of an aircraft, you will be required to manage the system to the lowest common denominator. This has the effect of constraining the operation for the majority in order to accommodate the minority—a bit like modern-day politics. One such example where RAAF management was required to use this 'best practice' approach to safety was when a US navy F-18 almost shot down the tow aircraft.

We had been conducting exercises off the coast of Newcastle with a US aircraft carrier when the F-18 squadron onboard requested the use of our tow aircraft for gunnery training. Now I know I started by saying that air-to-air gunnery in the Hornet is really simple; however, I did also say that you have to select the gun.

On this occasion the F-18 pilot wrongly selected AIM-7 Sparrow, which is a 225-kilogram semi-active radar-guided missile. There is a dot in the HUD when this missile is selected which tells you where to fly to maximise the range of the missile. Somehow, for reasons unbeknown to any Australian F-18 pilot, this US naval aviator was able to put the missile steering dot on the rag, generate a shoot cue and fire his AIM-7.

The copilot in the tow aircraft saw the giant smoking telephone pole coming straight for them and could not even warn the pilot.

'M-m-m-m-missile,' was all he could get out before the it flew over the top of the tow aircraft. Through pure luck the radar lock was inside the minimum range of the AIM-7 and it didn't have sufficient time to arm its proximity fuse before the missile flew over the business jet. Needless to say, the RAAF no longer conducts air-to-air gunnery with missiles onboard.

The greatest risk in air-to-air gunnery is not shooting down the tow aircraft, but running into your mates. Four F-18s conduct gunnery at the same time, each flying his own 800 kilometre per hour circular pattern relative to the banner, which is itself moving in a circular pattern at 500 kilometres per hour. The pattern is a bit like leapfrog where the guy immediately ahead of you shooting the banner ends up behind you and then you end up behind him. It is almost impossible to describe in words and best left to the bar where you can use hands and beer coasters to explain the procession.

Each member of the four-ship has his bullets dipped in different-coloured paint so that when the bullets pass through the rag they leave a slight discoloration. Post-mission the tow aircraft conducts a low pass adjacent to the runway and releases the banner, where it is recovered and returned to the pilots for 'adjudication'. Now I have mentioned a number of times how close squadron buddies are; however, this is not always the case during the marking of the banner. Air-to-air gunnery is one of the most competitive activities, and often sees major disputes between the best of mates—particularly if someone is shooting blue. All the 20-millimetre ball ammunition is painted blue at the factory and then dipped in various colours by our 'gunnies' at the squadron. With the friction of the air on the bullets as they leave the muzzle, you're lucky if any of your squadron paint makes it to the rag—the factory blue, on the other hand, always seems to be present. The confusion that this causes often leads to serious altercations during the mark-up. Amazing how many fighter pilots come down with a bad dose of colour blindness during an air-to-air gunnery camp.

After two weeks of gunnery it was time to head to the wheatbelt of Western Australia for some inland flying. Inland hang-gliding is inherently more difficult and dangerous than coastal flying due to the turbulent air that you must fly in—including take-offs and landings. By this stage we all had the minimum experience required to have a crack at this more challenging form of hang-gliding and the weather was primed for an excellent weekend. There was just one little thing we had to do before we headed off—a quick wafer-thin brewski at the bar . . .

It was around 2 a.m. when FE, who was our designated driver, cracked the shits and said we had to be leaving. Now! By this stage we had pretty much completed our pub crawl of all the good bars in Perth, which is a fair few, and were on the dance floor of the Cottes-loe Hotel. And, oh yeah, we were still in our flying suits. Even our intelligence officer, Diggsy, was getting into it, wearing his 'service dress tropical'—also known as the RAAF summer safari suit. With the khaki shorts and long socks, which were now around his ankles, he was a hit on the dance floor. TVH was a write-off and I was some-where in between.

FE had already picked up the bongo van, which was a 1970s *A-team*-style Bedford van with a two-tone rust and white paint scheme. It had roof racks though, and that was all we cared about. By the time FE drove the one hour back to base, TVH and I were snoring our heads off. FE woke us up and we started the task of packing and sorting all our flight gear for the weekend as we hadn't had the forethought to do it prior to 3 a.m.—plan early, plan twice!

TVH's approach to packing was simple. He got out of the van, walked to his upstairs room in the officers mess, picked up his mattress complete with all the linen, walked back down the stairs, threw his mattress in the back of Mr T's van and promptly went back to sleep. TVH was never a morning person.

After FE and I packed some clothes for TVH and all of our gliding equipment, we started heading inland. It was well past sun-up when we reached the hotel where we were to meet our hang-gliding instructor. FE had not slept a wink and pretty much had done everything to get us there. TVH was still asleep, or unconscious, when the instructor arrived.

'Hi, guys, I'm Dave. Was there meant to be three of you today?'

'Aaah, yeah. TVH is still asleep in the van. He's been working some long hours . . .'

'So, FE tells me you guys are pilots in the RAAF and have been hang-gliding for a couple of years,' Dave said. 'I have to warn you that normally this is a full-week course so I can't make any promises that I'll have you rated by tomorrow, but I'll do my best.'

An hour later we arrived at the paddock. It was about 2 kilometres square and the wheat had been recently harvested, leaving a short stubble. As we pulled up, the van door opened and TVH stumbled out with sheet creases up his face and an asymmetric hairdo.

'You must be TVH,' Dave said. 'Good to meet you. I was saying to the boys that normally this course is . . .'

'I'll be right, Dave,' said TVH. 'You just go hook up the car, I'll get my glider ready and we'll get going. I want to have this thing knocked over today if we can.'

I'm not sure if it was the smell of the brewery when the van door opened or TVH's bloodshot eyes, but Dave started to look concerned. TVH didn't notice, though. He was on a post-bender high, singing and whistling as he set up his glider. FE and I started to worry that Dave would find out TVH was still pissed and cancel the course on us, so we made sure we stayed between them and let Dave start giving us some instruction on how to safely perform a car tow launch. Despite TVH wanting to tell Dave how it could be done better, we managed to get through the instruction without Dave losing his cool.

'Alright then, who wants to . . .' Dave started, but TVH interrupted.

'I told you, Dave, I was ready when I got here. Let's get going.'

'Well, it's too early for the thermals to be working, so be prepared for a sled ride back down from 400 metres. Just land back here and we'll launch you again.'

Dave got in the car and TVH got into his harness. He locked on his microphone so that he could tell Dave when to go, stop, speed up or slow down. Dave acknowledged by tapping the brakelights of his car.

'OK, Dave, I can see your brakelights. Let it rip, mate,' said TVH.

The car revved up and kicked up some dust as it accelerated. The 500-metre tow rope is semi-elastic so the car can get up to speed before the drag of the glider is felt. After about five seconds the rope went taut and TVH started to run. He did a perfect foot launch before climbing effortlessly to 300 metres. He released the tow line and we watched him immediately enter a thermal and start spiralling up. So much for it being 'too early for thermals'. After fifteen minutes we realised he wasn't coming back any time soon, so FE got into his harness and set up for his first take-off.

Some time later, both FE and I had completed our first couple of tow launches and were discussing with Dave where TVH might have had got to.

'That doesn't normally happen on my student's first tow,' said Dave, looking a bit baffled. 'I mean, it's not even warm yet. I told him to come back here for another take-off. Where do you think he's gone?'

Our instructor was very worried about TVH but FE and I weren't—we knew what he did for a day job.

Dave then noticed a stray sheep that had walked through a fence and was now trapped in our paddock. 'Mac, could you go grab that sheep and put it back into the next paddock? There's no water in this paddock for it.'

I jumped into our rent-a-bomb and started herding the sheep along the fenceline—well, at least, trying to herd it. After fifteen minutes of it doubling back on me I was worried I would kill it through exhaustion, or blow up the gearbox in Mr T's van. I got out of the van, did my best steer-roping impersonation and got dragged along on my knees holding onto its woolly arse. Eventually it gave up and I half-carried the poor animal back to the van. I was almost as buggered as the sheep by the time I got it to the van and threw it in the back before driving it to the next paddock and releasing it.

An hour or so later, FE got a glimpse of TVH's glider and we watched him circling back around for a perfect landing on our designated landing spot. We gave him a clap and Dave looked suitably impressed. TVH professionally parked his glider, stepped out of his harness and then performed the largest projectile vomit I had ever seen.

'Had a pizza last night, did you?' asked Dave.

'Yeah, I think the prawns were off,' replied TVH.

FE and I pissed ourselves laughing, knowing the real reason had something to do with the 30-odd tequila sunrises he'd consumed during the pub crawl.

'OK, I'll leave you guys to it. I need to go lie down for a while,' TVH said as he headed over to our bongo van. He climbed into the back of the van and closed the door behind him before throwing it open again in a fit of expletives.

'OK, who was the smart-arse who put sultanas in my bed? Pretty fucking funny, guys.'

FE and I exchanged looks of 'What the fuck is he talking about?' And then it hit me. The little jolly jumback I had saved from certain dehydration had got so excited by TVH's comfortable bed it had left him a little present . . . or a few dozen little presents. I started snickering and shared the truth with FE.

'Yeah, sorry 'bout that mate,' I said to TVH with a straight face. 'I spilt my raisins.'

TVH was none the wiser. He brushed off his mattress and got straight back to the task of recovering from his hangover. The boy was a machine.

FE and I continued our instruction which included headwind, nil-wind, crosswind and—my least favourite—tailwind launches. One of the more widely accepted rules in aviation circles is that you should always take off in a headwind. This ensures the ground speed is minimised—particularly important in hang-gliding where your 'wheels' are your own legs and you have to carry a 30-kilo glider while sprinting for the take-off.

To take-off in a tailwind we had to coil 1 metre of rope on the ground in front of us for every 2 kilometres per hour of tailwind. On this particular day there was a 20 kilometre per hour tailwind so we coiled 10 metres of rope on the ground in front of us. We told the driver to 'GO GO GO' and watched as the rope rapidly uncoiled and the elastic in the rope stretched, with the car approaching 60 kilometres per hour by the time the force was sufficient to start to pull us. With a 10-metre running start, plus 500 metres of elastic in the rope, we were basically human slingshots. Even if we said 'stop' at the moment of launch, there was so much elastic potential built up in the rope that we were going into orbit regardless. The idea was to minimise the period between maximum running speed of the pilot and minimum airspeed in the tailwind. We would literally fall forwards at maximum sprint speed with the glider still in a stall for about one second before the tension pulled the glider fast enough to fly away from the ground.

I hated tailwind launches because they were dangerous—the pilot wasn't in control, the horizontal bungee was. The trouble is that the best time to launch is in a tailwind when the thermal is in front of you and sucking the air in from behind you. So upon returning to Tindal I set about designing a trolley that would act as a set of wheels for tailwind launches so that we wouldn't be required to do a Carl Lewis impersonation every time we launched.

I started by setting up my hang-glider in my backyard and taking some measurements. Transferring these to some graph paper over a few beers and then having some highly technical aerodynamic discussions over many tequila sunrises, I came up with a design.

The next day I took my patent-pending design to the metal bashers who normally make and repair parts for F-18s. I told them what I wanted to do and asked them if they could possibly make the glider trolley for us.

'You must be fuckin' nuts, Sir. Firstly for designing it, and secondly for asking us to make it for you!' was their response.

With my confidence bolstered, I left them with the plans and set about building a tow meter. Through some hang-gliding contacts I was able to source a car brake cylinder attached to a hose and a pressure gauge. The idea was that we would attach one end of the master cylinder to the back of the car and the tow rope to the other. The gauge would rest on the dash and tell the driver how many pounds of force he was pulling the glider with. Too easy.

A week later I went back to the metal bashers to pick up my invention. There, in the middle of the hangar, shining under the spotlights, was a polished aluminium frame that resembled the base of an oversized shopping trolley. The one difference was a large fork that stood vertically at the rear of the trolley for supporting the hang-glider keel tube. It looked even better than my design as the metal bashers had built it out of aircraft-grade aluminium and modified the trolley to be stronger, lighter and have a more professional appearance. I slipped them a slab of VB cans and hitched the trolley to the back of our squadron crew van. Then I towed the trolley down to an old WWII hangar that I had secured for our weekend antics. It was a perfect and appropriately nostalgic location for the auspicious occasion that lay before us.

'Mac, I don't think we can just start driving down the runway without authorisation from the Civil Aviation Safety Authority,' FE pointed out.

I looked up the regulations and, sure enough, hang-gliders were not allowed to fly at Tindal due to airline operations at the airfield. I put together a risk management plan for the authority and applied for dispensation to this regulation. After a phone call it became apparent that the clearance would not be granted by the following weekend when we were planning on testing our human shopping trolley. We decided to move the test program to Manbulloo Airstrip, an old WWII airstrip which was next to Tindal but away from prying eyes.

We spoke to the station manager and used another green-can mind-control device to convince him to let us use his airstrip. We set up our gliders and laid out all our equipment. Hawks, kites and eagles were circling overhead in thermals 1-kilometre wide—it was going to be a great day.

TVH, FE and I started to discuss who was going to be the first crash-test dummy, but I never finished my sentence—TVH was going first and there was nothing we could do to stop him. I was worried that I had designed the trolley and if it didn't work it would be my responsibility. TVH wasn't worried, though, and had complete faith in me . . .

So I got into TVH's Bombadoor, he clipped onto the tow line and we did our radio and brakelight checks.

'OK, Mac, I'm in the trolley. Ready. GO GO GO.'

I floored the Bombadoor, which was actually a V8 but performed like a straight six. I could hear TVH's breathing over the radio and it was increasing in both volume and rate.

'Faster, faster, faster, fucking faster, Mac . . . Faaaaark!'

I had my foot to the floor and the Bombadoor was howling in protest. I was doing 80 kilometres per hour when I checked my rear-vision mirror to see what was going on. TVH was still lying horizontal on the trolley with his face and body no more than 3 inches off the bitumen. Then in an instant I saw his glider pull up vertically.

'Stop, stop, stop, fucking stop, Mac . . . Faaaaaaaark!' was the next thing I heard on the radio.

I locked up the Bombadoor and put my head out of the window to look back. I saw TVH point straight up, tail-slide backwards, then drop nose-down before flaring and landing on his feet, followed by his knees and finally his stomach—it was the world's lowest hammer-head aerobatic manoeuvre.

I drove straight back to TVH and found that, thankfully, he had no more than a few grazes on his knees and a slight bump on his head.

'How did you set up the angle of attack on the trolley, Mac?' he asked when he could speak again.

'I just took a pluck. Why?'

'I had a negative angle of attack and had to use all my strength to get out of the trolley.'

In designing the trolley I had incorrectly set the keel support too high, which meant the faster I drove, the greater the air pressure was on top of the glider and the harder it was for TVH to push the nose up. By the time he had used all his strength to push the nose up, I'd been doing over 80 kilometres per hour, which approximated the maximum speed the glider could fly before structural failure.

'No worries, mate,' I replied. 'I've got my hacksaw in the boot of the car.' I didn't feel too bad as TVH was by far the best pilot among us and he had done a great job of recovering a bad situation. I adjusted the keel support with my hacksaw and five minutes later we were ready for test-flight number-two.

'Do you want me to go this time?' I asked TVH.

'No fuckin' way, mate—we've got it sorted. Now get in the car.'

I had to hand it to him—he had balls of steel.

The next launch was perfect. At around 20 kilometres per hour, TVH let go of the trolley and gently lifted into the air.

The trolley worked perfectly and with the castering front wheels we could launch in crosswinds or tailwinds without running our legs off or feeling like we were being slingshotted into orbit. Eventually we received our approval from the Civil Aviation Safety Authority for hang-gliding operations from the main runway at Tindal, and some big flights were had by all.

One of my most memorable flights occurred after releasing from a car tow at 300 metres above the Tindal airfield. I wasn't planning on a particularly long flight and was wearing only shorts and a singlet, with no water or food. Shortly after releasing I entered a strong thermal and climbed to over 3000 metres above mean sea level. Now 3000 metres is an important number in aviation. It is the maximum authorised altitude without oxygen—above this the air becomes too thin for pilots to perform their duties reliably. Parachutists are authorised to 4000 metres because they don't hang around up there for long—they freefall back below 3000 metres in just a few seconds. The other thing about 3000 metres is that the temperature is 20 degrees Celsius below the temperature at sea level. On this particular day it was around 30 degrees on the ground, resulting in a temperature of 10 degrees where I was flying. When combined with a 20–30 kilometre per hour wind, it meant my 'five seasons, extreme weather technical clothing' (boardshorts, singlet and thongs) wasn't up to task—I was literally freezing.

I let the guys know that I was going to start heading north following the Stuart Highway and see where I got to. While we had all completed good endurance flights, the lack of suitably cleared areas outside of the base meant that we had never really gone far cross-country. I figured that despite the Stuart Highway being Australia's National Highway No. 1, and the main supply route of quadruple-semitrailer roadtrains, I should be able to find some bitumen or a shoulder to land my hang-glider on—well, that was the theory anyway.

I flew over Katherine and headed for a good clearing north of the town, which turned out to be the agricultural research station. I traded most of my altitude for distance and now found myself down at 6000 metres. I wasn't nervous about landing on the highway at this stage, as there was a decent clearing at the research station, but I did have to find some lift if I was going to continue my flight much further. I tried finding some lift from the buildings of the station, with no luck. I tried the black bitumen highway with the same result. I started to think that I wasn't going to get any further when a friend found me.

On the opposite side of my orbit, seemingly from nowhere, appeared a huge wedge-tailed eagle. It looked at me as if it was wondering, 'WTF is that thing?' I was definitely the first hang-glider this magnificent creature had ever seen. We stared at each other—both mesmerised. I watched its tail roll left and right for angle of bank. I could see its tip feathers curled up like the wingtips of a modern airliner, trying to squeeze as much efficiency out of its form as possible. I didn't want it to end but I was low and had not found any significant lift. I started to unzip my harness to lower my skinny undercarriage when my newfound friend rolled out of the turn and started to fly away.

Without really thinking about it I instinctively mimicked its track and followed approximately 50 metres behind the raptor. Then I saw the wedgie rise and I felt the positive G on my hang loop, followed by the warm air on my face and the smell of dust. My feathered friend had led me to a 'boomer'—a massive thermal. The bird turned left—I followed. Right—I followed. Together we set ourselves up on opposite sides of the same circle and perfectly cored the centre of the thermal. My instruments showed my rate of climb was over 500 metres per minute and stayed that way almost all the way to 5000 metres. I wondered what an eagle was doing up here. I mean, I know they have good eyesight, but unless he was circling for cows I doubted very much whether this altitude was about hunting. Personally, I was higher than I had ever been before.

Then I heard the Air North airliner call up on the radio: 'All stations in the Tindal area, this is November Oscar Papa, 30 nautical miles north of the field passing 10 000 feet on descent, estimating the field at zero five.'

As much as I wanted to brag, I didn't want to transmit the fact that I was well above the maximum authorised altitude for hanggliders. I looked down and saw the airliner a good 2000 metres below me. I tried not to let my teeth chatter as I transmitted back to the airliner: 'November Oscar Papa, this is Wind Beater 001, a hangglider, I am presently 30 nautical miles north of the field, well clear of you.'

The airliner pilot then went mental on the radio, worrying about hitting me—it was me that should have been worried, as I'm pretty sure I would have come off second best.

With our thermal squeezed of all the lift, the wedgie headed west and away from the highway—my only possible landing area. Additionally I was starting to get concerned about my brain oxygen levels and how long I was going to hold off the hypothermia. The temperature was now below zero and the wind chill was freezing my tears and nose snot. I started to head north and entered a glide aimed at maximising the distance I would cover.

I picked up another couple of small thermals below 3500 metres; however, I was still very cold from my little jaunt to the stratosphere in boardshorts and singlet. I wasn't so concerned about getting another thermal—I just really needed to warm up a bit. But at 2000 metres I hit strong 'sink'.

Some smart bloke a long time ago said that what goes up must come down—and the same is true for hot air. Thermals eventually cool down, as I was discovering firsthand, and the cold air sinks as rapidly as it rises, which means the cows start getting bigger really quickly. I changed track left and right, trying to get out of the sink, but to no avail. I hit my landing threshold of 600 metres and searched the highway for a clearing—none. Bugger. I then started looking for a break in the traffic—none. There was traffic heading in both directions with no maximum speed limit and I also sighted a number of roadtrains in the throng—they took a lot longer distance to stop than I needed to land. With my shorts gripped between my arse cheeks, I contemplated putting the glider into the trees—at least the trees weren't travelling at over 120 kilometres per hour. And then I heard an angel calling to me.

'*Kssshhhh*, Mac, *ksssshhhh*, see you, *ksssshhhh* traffic.'

One of the boys must have been relatively close to me, as they could see me and I could hear them on the radio.

'Whoever is calling me, I need you to stop the traffic,' I half-screamed into the microphone.

'Roger, Mac. Standby.'

The signal was now much stronger and I recognised the voice—it was Trev, our flight surgeon, and hang-glider pilot extraordinaire and the guy who had given me the poor man's Brazilian the year prior when my flyspray didn't work. Trev was arguably more insane than I was, having previously jumped off the Sydney Harbour Bridge in his hang-glider, even managing to successfully evade the fun police at the same time. I just hoped he was capable of stopping these high-speed freight trucks or I was going to be in a world of hurt.

I scanned the highway back towards Tindal, looking for Trev's vehicle, when I saw him half-run a roadtrain off the northbound lane. He swerved across the front of it, waving madly out the window, before slowing down and preventing the roadtrain from overtaking. The roadtrain complied, as did the one behind that, and the one behind that. Having a truck driver for an uncle, I knew Trev was going to be in some serious shit.

Trev was a legend—but I wasn't out of trouble yet. Only one lane was closed and my wingspan was wider than the single lane. Additionally, I was landing in the peak heat of the day with thermals popping off everywhere, resulting in severe turbulence the lower I descended. It was highly likely I wouldn't be landing in a headwind even if I could fight the turbulence enough to keep the glider pointed in the same direction as the highway.

I dropped my legs out in preparation for a controlled crash and was relieved to feel the warm air on my semi-frozen chicken thighs. Just like cold hydraulic fluid in aircraft undercarriage, my wheels came down slowly and felt half-cramped. They were about to get one hell of a work-out if I wanted to avoid faceplanting directly into the bitumen of Highway No. 1. I circled around behind the truck to set up my landing towards the north and could see the driver leaning out his window to give my guardian angel the bird. I felt awful for Trev, and thought I would do my best to take some pressure off him.

I pulled the bar in as hard as I could to enter a steep dive and lined up the truck's cab. Passing over the truck at 100 kilometres per hour, I had to raise my legs to prevent them slamming into his cab. I imagined the wind noise was going to be enough to stop the guy raving, let alone the sight of some moron in a hang-glider landing on the north lane of Australia's National Highway No. 1 no less than 50 metres in front of him.

After a near-perfect inland spot landing I put the glider down and turned to wave to the truck driver, while Trev just wore his semi-permanent shit-eating grin. The look on the driver's face was priceless. I carried my glider off the highway and into the scrub beside it. By this time there were a number of trucks and dozens of vehicles backed up. As they drove off slowly past us, Trev and I gave them a wave and thanked them all very much for their patience.

Trev was also a big microlight fan and a few months later convinced me that our 'club' needed a microlight and that I should buy one—which I did. A microlight, or trike, is simply a hang-glider with an engine on the back and a two-seat motorbike underneath. We intended on using the trike as an aerotow so that we could get higher when towing up into thermals. Sometimes, though, the best of intentions go astray. Somehow our aerotow plan morphed into the development of a weapon platform.

Hunting was another pastime of most knuckleheads in Tindal, and Trev was a big gun lover. We started scheming about how we could conduct 'micro-Spooky' missions with the trike and simulate an AC-130 'Spooky' gunship. The AC-130 are specially modified C-130 Hercules that have sideward firing guns and provide precision support to special forces. The theory is simple: you fly a circle and the centre of your circle never moves—that is the target. The theory came from the original US air mail service, where they would lower a rope to the ground while the aircraft flew orbits. The rope at the centre of the circle would be stationary on the ground and permitted the mailman to untie the incoming mail bag and replace it with the outgoing bag. Shit, if the postie could do it in the early 1900s, surely we could hit a pig from 30 metres with a 30/30 rifle out the side of our modern trike.

Trev and I headed off one early morning to trial our latest theory of flight. I flew in front seat and Trev was the gunner.

'Now listen, mate, whatever you do, make sure you don't hit the "Jesus" wires,' I instructed him, pointing at the stainless steel wires that hold the wing on.

'No worries, Mac, you just get me in the slot and we'll be eating ham for a month.'

I had no idea where he thought we were going to land to pick up our 100-kilogram prized boar, nor where he thought he might stow the pig given we were at our maximum flying weight with the both of us onboard, a tank of gas and Trev's small arsenal in the back.

We headed south to a couple of known pig-watering holes looking for our prey. Unlike the low frequency drone of a Spooky, we sounded more like a brushcutter on steroids. I doubted we would be sneaking up on anything that had at least half a brain. Though that did leave the feral donkeys.

Thirty minutes south of Tindal, at 20 metres, paralleling a power-line cutting in the trees, Trev caught sight of one of these intellectually challenged creatures.

'Tally, donkey, left ten o'clock low, 30 metres. I'm going to shoot out the left side.'

'Roger, positioning,' I replied, offsetting the donkey to place it at the middle of our orbit. The donkey didn't seem too interested in us . . . for a little while, anyway.

Craaaaack, chhhhk, chhhhhk, ting. Craaaaaack, chhhhhk, chhhhk, ting.

With every shot the recoil would wobble the trike base and cause the trike to slightly turn. Concentrating on countering the recoil-induced roll, I couldn't pay much attention to the sounds Trev was making in the back. It was a lever-action 30/30 and I could hear the *craaaacks* and the *chhhk chhhk* as he reloaded but couldn't make any sense of the *ting* that followed each reload.

The donkey wised up to this lead-spitting bird of prey and started to bolt.

'We've got a runner, Mac, keep coming left,' called Trev.

'Roger, I'm on him,' I replied as I tightened the turn to try and keep the centre of our orbit on the bolting beast.

Trev kept unloading his magazine and I kept trying to anticipate the recoil effects on our trike and decipher the noises I was hearing. As he emptied his last round, it hit me like a cattle prod to the back of the head.

'Check fire, check fire,' I yelled.

'Yep, I'm out, Mac. What's up?'

'Mate, where's your brass going?' I asked.

'Out the back . . . and . . . ahhhh . . . through the propeller,' came Trev's sheepish reply.

The *ting* noises were the sounds of his spent 30/30 cartridges going through the thin fibreglass propeller. We both sat there quietly listening to the prop and looking at the engine instruments before limping home at minimum power for fear the prop was about to depart the engine. We made it back to Tindal safely with minimal damage to the prop; however, this would be our first and last 'micro-Spooky mission'.

8
Lost and found

I COMPLETED MY Hornet course in 1993 at 23 years of age and was posted back to RAAF Base Tindal, the home of the 'Murderous Marauding Magpies'. Having spent eighteen months at 75 Squadron previously, I knew what tools I would need for the job so I headed out and bought a Toyota FJ40 'bull catcher' and a 44-Magnum handgun. The bull catcher was essentially a short-wheel-base four-wheel drive without any doors or roof, used by cowboys in the Northern Territory for catching bulls. I loaded up all my belongings, which had by now grown to the size of an entire box trailer, and headed north. I left Newcastle and made it to Rockhampton in one day and then Mt Isa the second day.

It was summer, and midway through the second day I was really starting to feel the heat: from the sun above, the road below and the overheating engine in front of me. I drove to Mt Isa wearing my straw sombrero and boardshorts for protection, and I was going through water quicker than I could stop and find it; for both the radiator and for me. I ended up falling into the pool at the first motor lodge I came to at Mt Isa with severe heat stress. I didn't last long in the pool before I had to quickly exit and look for a toilet, whereupon I promptly lost control of my bowels. I have never had heat stroke so bad!

The memories of Foxy came back as soon as I arrived in Tindal. I was gutted that he never got to see me achieve my goal of flying jets. I'd only been away from Tindal for a couple of years and things hadn't really changed much, except now I was a fully qualified fighter pilot. My first night flight at Tindal, however, would call on everything I had learnt about flying over the last five years.

With twenty seconds gone on the clock in my heads-up display (HUD) I released the brakes, lit the afterburners and started a radar-trail departure behind Scrowt, my lead. Scanning the engine instruments during the take-off roll, I gently nudged the rudder pedals to keep the jet running down the middle of the blurring runway-edge lights. Once airborne, with the wheels and flaps retracted, my radar automatically locked onto my lead, who was now 3 kilometres in front and commencing a right turn at 800 kilometres per hour. With the jet cleaned up the acceleration rate increased, helped along by the extra thrust generated in the cool night air: 400 kilometres per hour, 500, 600—airspeed digits rolled quicker and quicker in the HUD. And then the jet started to pitch up with a purpose all of its own.

The pitch-up continued until I felt like I was pointing vertical, and then continued over onto my back. I was suffering from a sensory illusion known as 'head-up illusion' that I had only ever read about. I had never experienced the sensation because the conditions required to generate the illusion are generally only experienced in high-performance aircraft being shot off aircraft carriers on moonless nights—or RAAF Base Tindal on moonless nights, so it seemed. The area is so remote that there are no streetlights to discern on the horizon so the brain starts to interpret the acceleration without the sight inputs and convinces you that you're looping over onto your back. I don't think I have ever glued my eyeballs to the flight instruments any harder at any other time in my life. It took all my discipline and training to fly the instruments and discount what my brain was telling me—that I was upside-down and heading in the opposite direction from my lead.

With the acceleration complete, Scrowt and I climbed to 10 000 metres feet at Mach 0.85 and carried out our weapon system checks while tuning our radars and targeting pods for our night-strike mission. The mission would take us 300 kilometres south of Katherine and then north again to fight our way through simulated enemy MiGs, before finding our target and dropping some 33-pound (15 kilogram) practice bombs, or 'blue death' as we called them.

Night flying in a modern fighter is exhilarating to the point of terror—a bit like your worst roller-coaster ride. Night, low altitude, large numbers of aircraft, high-explosive weapons, high-power lasers and tropical thunderstorms all mixed together to raise my adrenaline to the point that my legs shook on the rudder pedals and my hand on the joystick. Tonight's mission, being my first in the unit, was planned to be simple—well, that's the way it was intended.

At the first turn point Scrowt turned on time, with me following twenty seconds behind. I watched his aircraft symbol drift to the right side of my radar screen as I leant down and selected the next navigation waypoint that I would steer to once I had turned the corner. Surprisingly, instead of seeing the number 2 appear on the horizontal situation indicator, I saw an AIM-7 Sparrow missile symbol appear. I had never seen this before, but since I'd only been flying these jets for six months I figured this must be some special mode that 75SQN had in their war-ready jets that I was not briefed on. I pressed the waypoint selector button again but a bomb symbol reappeared, and nowhere could I find my number 2 waypoint that I needed to track to. Never mind, I thought, I'll just follow Scrowt all the way to the target and bomb it visually. It was then that I noticed he'd disappeared off the screen.

My radar screen had gone blank and a test pattern appeared. Again, this was something I had never seen. Again, I assumed that these 75SQN jets were totally wired for the business and I was now in some time-warping, laser-beam generation mode. With no way to know where my next navigation point was, I found the bearing on my map and turned right onto the planned heading for waypoint 2. In the turn I started to turn the radar on and off and looked at my air-to-air TACAN (tactical air navigation system) range that would tell me how far I was from my lead—blank. It was about now that I started to question my 75SQN deathstar modification theory and started to think the jet had some gremlins loose in her. I looked up at my compass rose in the HUD and found I was still going south—my original direction out of Tindal. I kept turning and discovered the compass rose had frozen at my last heading of 180 and I now had no idea where I was going. Time to 'fess up and tell lead, I figured.

'Magpie 1 from 2.' No answer. I continued trying to call Magpie 1 on both radios and all frequencies, including the emergency distress frequency 243.0 which we all monitored—nothing. I tried air traffic control, approach control, tower, squadron operations—nothing. So there I was in a $50-million blowtorch with more computers than the space shuttle and I was seriously lost—at a minimum, I was geographically embarrassed, but at the speed of sound it could quickly get much, much worse.

I looked across to my NATO-standard E2B compass—a small oil and ball compass the size of a golf ball that was invented in WWI. It was working. Great—now I knew which way I was going. The problem was I had been flying in a turn for somewhere between 180 and 360 degrees for the last couple of minutes at 1000 kilometres per hour—I was probably somewhere within 40 kilometres of my first turn point. OK, I thought, so all I have to do now is head back to base by the reciprocal of 180—which was north—and find the base. It was a clear night and I felt confident I would see the lights of the base and Katherine at about 80 kilometres—ten minutes flight time—no problems.

Those ten minutes were among the longest ten minutes of my life. I was using the navigation techniques of Wilbur and Orville at the speed of Chuck Yeager—how the hell did I end up here? And where was I going to end up? Darwin and East Timor weren't that far away at 1000 kilometres per hour—the world can seem very small in an F-18. I started scanning the horizon for the lights of Tindal and with huge relief I soon saw them about 20 degrees right of my nose.

The lights seemed to be getting closer than they should have been if they were the lights of Katherine—but what else was out there? What else could the lights be? I found out soon enough. It was a standard Northern Territory dry-season grass fire that was approximately 20 kilometres across—shit. Now I was off my planned track because I had been suckered into following a fucking bushfire. I started to panic and search the horizon for lights—they were everywhere. It seemed there were bushfires from horizon to horizon but I couldn't see the lights of Katherine anywhere. Things were not going well for my first night flight at RAAF Tindal.

It was then I saw some other lights below me. First one, then another, and then another. They were vehicle headlights on the Stuart Highway—fortunately for me the only main road in the Northern Territory—and I knew where they were going.

I paralleled the imaginary line I had drawn in the night sky to join the dots of vehicle headlights and leapfrogged from one set to the next until I found the lights of Katherine and the RAAF base. I flew a visual approach to the airfield and the tower shone a steady green light to me indicating that I was cleared to land. I landed safely and taxied the deaf mute of an aircraft back to its ordnance loading area.

The subsequent investigation revealed the jet had suffered a 'CNI computer failure', which means its communications navigation interface computer went belly-up. I couldn't believe that in this modern day and age I would be using World War I navigation techniques to find home. Scrowt got in more trouble than me for breaking that *Top Gun* maxim of 'Never leaving your wingman'. I was comfortable with him heading to the target alone and unafraid, especially given he shot both bandits, found his target and got a direct hit with his bombs. He would have done the same thing in war—and that's how we should train.

My sense of inadequacy was stronger than ever as I arrived back to my old squadron—now filled with a new group of pilots. I think most fighter pilots would agree that the friendships they form on their first fighter posting are some of the most enduring friendships of their lives.

The 75 Squadron also has a United States Marine Corp (USMC) pilot permanently assigned to it on a foreign exchange program. For my first fighter tour Captain Barry 'Spook' Moore was our resident USMC jarhead and I, reluctantly, owe my tactical callsign 'Serge' to him.

Tactical callsigns are not just used in Hollywood for Maverick, Goose and Iceman, but are utilised by fighter pilots as an informal way to communicate on the radio when airtime is short—such as when 35 other aircraft are talking on the one frequency. Official callsigns can become difficult to use as they change mission by mission, such that one day you are Ford 21, the next day House-fire 33, then Doghair 14 and Drynurse 32 and so on. When you're closing at faster than three times the speed of sound, you don't have time to look at your kneepad to work out who is who to ask a time-critical question. In such a situation a quick 'Tool, confirm hi lo' (or whatever) will ensure a more immediate, accurate response.

Despite my poor wardrobe decision the first Friday night of officer training school that led me to wear my Topgun badge–clad leather jacket, I didn't have a tactical callsign that had stuck—primarily because I had been moving every year. This all changed when I arrived back at Tindal and Spook saw my 'gourmet rolling pin' in my room.

'Dude, what are you doing with that?' Spook asked.

'Oh, it's just something my dad gave me when I left home. I'm sort of keeping it for when I eventually get my own place.'

'What are you going to do with a rolling pin?' he persisted. 'What are you, some kind of gay boy? Like Serggggggeeeeyyyy with a twist of lemon, you know, the gay hairdresser from *Beverley Hills Cop*.'

And that was that. Even my wife and kids call me 'Serge'. I often allow people to presume that my callsign has something to do with an engine surge, or a surge of energy, or anything other than the truth.

The backgrounds to callsigns are often the most protected information within the fighter community—classified SECRET NO CUNT! While some guys are lucky and end up with bogan aberrations of their surname, like Robbo, Simmo, Honko and Tobes, others end up with highly derogatory callsigns. Over the years I have heard, and allocated, some very imaginative callsigns. It seems the more guys try to fight them, the harder they stick. Here are a few to give you the gist:

Helmet	The guy's surname is Polish
COAB	Cunt Of A Bloke (just add alcohol)
Carloss	The guy had his car stolen

Spanka	This guy grunted in his sleep one too many times on deployment (his wife particularly hated being called Mrs Spanka)
Ballbag	No, he was not named after the corner pocket of a snooker table
Spook	He was born on Halloween
Flange	According to dictionary.com—a projecting flange, collar or ring on a shaft, pipe, machine housing, etc., cast or formed to give additional strength, stiffness, or supporting area, or to provide a place for the attachment of other objects.

It is not the derogatory nature of the callsigns that's a problem (unless you're a 'Spook' who's required to monitor fighter tactical communications and therefore has to put up with the obscenity), but the fact that in order for them to work in combat every pilot must practise using your callsign so they have it embedded in their melons. This means that these names will be used at formal dinners, media interviews, social gatherings and in front of your family. I'd be a rich man if I had a dollar for every lie a fighter pilot has told about his callsign.

Journo: 'So, Flange, why do they call you Flange?'

Flange: 'It's a tactical callsign, used on the radio in time-critical moments when a wingman needs my attention.'

Journo: 'Right, got it. And where does that name come from, Flange?'

Flange: 'Well, umm, when I was training I, ahh, walked into one?'

Journo: 'Yeah, right.'

End of interview.

The executive officer (XO) is the deputy commander of a fighter squadron and probably has the most influence on the morale and performance of the squadron. I was extremely fortunate to have JP as my first XO—he had the perfect balance of professionalism and larrikinism. He was a great leader who inspired guys to follow him, be it at work or play, and he was incredibly selfless. He was also never afraid to prioritise the reputation of his squadron or his junior pilots over his own career progression. JP soon became my mentor and for the next three years he would guide me towards both professional and personal success.

The day JP arrived at Tindal the commanding officer (CO) asked me to organise an informal dinner to welcome him. I met up with JP at the officers mess and arranged to meet him for dinner at Kirby's back bar in Katherine later that evening. Unbeknown to JP, Kirby's back bar is one of the roughest pubs in Australia, and pretty much only safe for black guys. I had talked up the place to JP on the premise of the squadron wanting to take him out for an upmarket welcome dinner. A couple of other junior pilots and I waited in an abandoned lot behind Kirby's, peeking through a crack in the fence. Sure enough, exactly on time, JP walked into the back bar wearing his perfectly ironed chinos, polo shirt and boat shoes.

The bar momentarily went silent—which is pretty hard to do when 50 drunk guys all want to kill each other, not to mention the white man that has been oppressing them for so long. JP briefly looked around then headed to the bar. He didn't make it halfway before he was aggressively intercepted by a number of the Indigenous patrons who wanted to know his name, where he was from, if he had a smoke, did he have any money and did he want a 'puck'. The other guys and I pissed ourselves laughing at our juvenile joke, delaying the moment when we'd go in and 'save' him.

Much to our surprise, though, JP remained totally calm; not only did he never lose his composure, he started befriending each and every one of the locals. Before we could extract him he had pretty much won them all over, such that when we arrived to drag him away we were the ones set upon by the newly formed JP fan club.

'Sorry, JP. The restaurant is around the corner, mate,' I said.

'What's wrong with this place?' he replied. 'The locals are very friendly.'

And that moment pretty much sums up why I respected JP so much.

During this first tour the commander of the US Pacific Air Force (PACAF) visited RAAF Tindal in order to hold some high-level discussions on defence cooperation. JP announced the importance of the visit to us and put together an itinerary for the visiting grand poobah that included taking him flying to drop some live ordnance on the Delemere weapons range, which the US air force was interested in utilising. JP had us all drag out our service dress uniforms, which few of us even owned at Tindal. We had knuckleheads greeting cars, opening doors, driving crew vans, and simulating dumb MiGs that died easily—all to JP's precise schedule. The visit culminated in a VIP dinner that only the Kool-Aid drinkers in the squadron would be invited to. Somehow I ended up on the list.

'Hey, boss,' I said to JP. 'I think there's been a mistake—I got an invite to the poodle-faking event tonight.'

'Nope, Serge, there's been no mistake. You will be there at 1800, smiling and acting professional. If you want to be a true leader you need to learn when to spit and when to swallow. And I wouldn't recommend getting on the tequila sunrises before the general has left if you want to deploy to Singapore next month.'

Tequila sunrises were the 75SQN drink as the colour matched our squadron patch, which depicted a northern Australian sunset.

JP was one of the few bosses I ever had who could balance the poodle-faking with the fighting and the partying. The difference with JP was that most bosses would rather give me a leave pass off the base than invite me to an official function. But JP knew how to manage and how to lead and he did it all while setting a perfect example. Well, almost . . .

JP's dinner, like everything the guy did, was planned for precise strategic effect; who sits next to who, who says what to who, who is tasked to find out what information we're lacking, etc. The guy should have been a diplomat. JP was the senior hosting officer and was seated next to the PACAF commander, who was a tall, well-built African–American. It was a mixed delegation of about ten Yanks and ten Aussies, small enough that the conversations could be heard by all. Things were going well for JP with the general declaring the visit a huge success, and how appreciative he was of our hospitality, etc.

'So where is your CO tonight, JP?' the general asked.

'He sends his apologies, Sir, but he had a family commitment he couldn't get out of,' replied JP smoothly.

'So what is he like to work for? Do you guys get along OK?' asked the general.

'He's a real white man, Sir.'

Silence. Long silence. Suddenly the cold peas on the side of my plate seemed like the most interesting thing in the room. All the other guys seemed really interested in their dinner as well. This was the one and only screw-up I ever saw from JP and it looked like it was going to cause a massive diplomatic issue.

'Ahh, sorry about that, Sir. That's just a saying we have down here in Australia. It means the CO is a really good guy . . . Not that black guys like yourself are not really good guys . . . it's just . . . umm . . .' He needed to stop now.

'That's fine, JP,' the general said. 'I would probably use similar language to describe your lack of skills on the dance floor.'

The table erupted in laughter . . . except JP.

The remainder of the visit was incident-free and in fact so success-ful that it wasn't long before B-52s from Guam started to conduct regular training with 75 Squadron.

JP, meanwhile, continued to unintentionally clear dance floors with his Peter Garrett dance style.

I worked extremely hard on my first Hornet tour but it never felt like work—I still had to remind myself they were paying me to have this much fun. My first love, the F-18, left little room for a serious relationship . . . until Lil.

We met at an airline party in Rockhampton when I was there for an exercise flying Macchis and she was a flight attendant. She was the happiest person I'd ever known and her personality was infectious. Her father was a retired senior RAAF officer and she had grown up as a RAAF brat living on all the fighter bases in South-East Asia. I figured she was a perfect match for me and my job, and after a year keeping a long-distance relationship together we got married.

Lil left the airlines and we moved into a house on the 'baggers' patch'—a term used to describe married guys who turn up to work with their lunch in a brown paper bag rather than microwaving a $1 meat pie the social club officer had left in the freezer. It was a massive change for Lil, leaving her circle of friends and the job she had loved so much to come and live in the middle of the desert with a husband who was very much in love with his job.

Weekends at Tindal were generally spent four-wheel driving, camping, fishing, sailing, waterskiing, hunting or hang-gliding—none of which Lil was really into. I eventually convinced her that a romantic camping weekend together was going to be the ticket for our first-year anniversary.

So I hired a Canadian canoe, we drove out to the Katherine Gorge, filled up the QE2 with everything we could possibly need for an overnight camping trip and started heading upstream. It was a gorgeous dry-season day and we were chatting away, enjoying each other's company. The Katherine Gorge is actually a series of gorges separated by short banks of rock and sand that you have to porter your gear across. We arrived at the first of three portages where we unloaded our canoe, walked it across, reloaded and continued on our way. Lil started to lose her sense of adventure on the first portage, causing me to lose mine by the third.

Eventually we found a nice sandbank on which to make camp and promptly pitched our tent for an afternoon siesta. We were in a truly beautiful place with no-one around and nothing but the sound of flowing water to lull us to sleep. Sometime later I woke to what sounded like a yell. I lay there listening, wondering what it was, and had just about fallen back to sleep when I heard it again—this time louder. The Katherine Gorge is like a giant amphitheatre and the sound of whoever was coming up the river was resonating all around us. I could just start to make out voices when Lil elbowed me in the back.

'You set this up, didn't you?' she said through gritted teeth.

'Set what up?' I honestly didn't know what was tripping her over the edge.

And then I heard the voices, or more importantly, what they were saying: 'How far up do you think Serge and Lil went?' and 'I hope it's not too much further, I want to crack these beers.'

I felt sick knowing what Lil's response was going to be, yet I was amused and keen to see the guys. Squadron life is very 'inclusive', which was one of the reasons why Lil and I had tried to get away for some time alone. On top of that I enjoyed socialising as much as anyone, which meant the guys weren't used to not having me around on a weekend—they were missing me. I was really touched, but Lil was furious.

Before long a tandem surf ski and a single surf ski cruised around the corner with Flange, Honko and TVH on the paddles. Their mock surprise was comical.

'Serge? Lil? What are you guys doing here?' asked Flange, trying his best not to smile.

We could all see that Lil was about to hit critical mass.

'Come on, Lil,' said Honko. 'We just thought we'd drop in for a little fun. We brought you some beer,' he said, pulling in a towline with a six-pack of beer tied to it. Flange and TVH opened the access hatches on their ski and produced beer, wine and cheese. They really had gone to a lot of effort—at least I was appreciative.

Later that night a guided camping tour set up on the opposite shore to us (so much for romantic solitude). We had consumed most of the supplies by this stage and so naturally I started painting my naked body with the green fluid from a couple of glow sticks— I looked like a neon skeleton. Against Lil's protests of carcinogens and crocodiles, I paddled my canoe to the middle of the natural amphitheatre where I performed my own Indigenous dance for the tourists including drums, sticks and didgeridoo before paddling off again. I was proud of my physical achievement to stand on one leg in a Canadian canoe, performing my best Bangarra Dance solo, all while half-cut. I also wondered how the tourist guide on the opposite bank would explain the spirit dreaming spectacle the campers had witnessed. I am sometimes so thankful that YouTube was not around when I was younger.

Things were tough with Lil, and we lasted only another couple of months. I know it had nothing to do with Flange, TVH and Honko's anniversary present—but I didn't let them know that. Professionally, I was going great guns, and was awarded the fighter pilot of the year in 1994 and selected for the fighter combat instructors' course in 1996. Personally, however, I couldn't keep a relationship together and was soon one of the youngest divorcees in the RAAF at 27 years of age. It was hard, but I was too immature to make the connection between my career and my personal life.

During this time JP provided me with another great example of leadership when he heard about Lil and I. On top of my marriage failing, my mum was in hospital with cancer, Dad had a tumour and my brother was struggling with depression, drugs and self-harm. JP called me into his office to 'have a chat' and I was pretty sure he was going to ground me for flight-safety reasons.

'You know, if it was anyone else in the squadron I'd ground them, Serge, but I think that might be the worst thing for you—you'd probably fall apart if I took you out of the jet. So I'll be watching you closely and I want you to watch yourself even closer. If you need to talk about anything, my door is always open. Don't prove me wrong and turn yourself into a smoking hole.'

JP knew that if I creamed myself through distraction he would likely lose his job, but he also knew that my sense of self was so closely tied to the jet that if he had grounded me I would have sat at home contemplating my navel lint and become overwhelmed with depression. His leadership and insight were impressive, although in some ways the strategy only fed the monkey on my back even more, driving me further away from solving my personal issues.

Sadly, JP died in 1997 while hang-gliding in north-western Australia. He had survived A-4 Skyhawks off aircraft carriers, ejected from a Mirage, flown F-18s in the RAAF and the USMC, only to be killed by a small gust of wind he had not anticipated.

His death struck me hard in a number of ways. I lost a close friend and career mentor, and I lost my nerve for hang-gliding for a number of years. The hang-gliding was relatively easy to get over— replacing my mentor, however, was not. It was always going to be a tall order for any senior officer to fill his mentoring role, but it seemed the higher I moved up in rank, the less operationally focused the 'managers' became and the more worried they were about their careers and their retirement benefits.

JP was a true warrior and leader—qualities that are increasingly hard to find in today's politically correct defence force.

9

Dining-in

WHILE RAAF TINDAL is arguably one of the best places in the world to fly a fighter, it is also very remote, which can be hard on young men and their families. As such, the Fighter Wing Headquarters will usually organise formal training of one sort or another to justify an annual trip to RAAF Williamtown: the epicentre of Australian fighters.

Newcastle, a former coalmining and steel-works industrial city, is the cultural foundation of the majority of Australia's fighter pilots by virtue of the fact that most of us spend our formative years training at Williamtown. During this impressionable time of our lives we are only 30 minutes from the Delany Hotel (often referred to as the Williamtown Back Bar), the Brewery and Fannie's Night Club (pronounced 'Fanwahs' in a vain attempt to make the place sound more sophisticated). This trifecta makes up the majority of Friday nights for young fighter pilots, and is usually followed by the greasiest hamburgers ever manufactured in history at Hamburger Haven. The fighter pilots had affectionately dubbed this cholesterol depot 'Hamburger Asian' as all the hamburger cooks were Asian and spoke poor English. I'm unsure whether they had actual chef qualifications, or immigration visas for that matter, but at 4 a.m. when Fanwahs shut there was only one place open—and what was cholesterol anyway? MiGs couldn't touch us, so a few greasy burgers hadn't a hope in hell.

Just like humpback whales, the timing of 75 Squadron's migration south was always in summer, when the thermal shock was less likely to stress our delicate bodies. During the wet season we could leave Tindal at 35 degrees Celsius and arrive in Williamtown three hours later where it was 30 degrees Celsius. This was far better than scheduling training courses in Williamtown during the dry season, where we would leave Tindal at 30 degrees Celsius and arrive in Williamtown at 10 degrees Celsius. The summer months in 'Willy' were also far more congenial to surfing, which was expensive or dangerous in Tindal. To surf in Tindal we had to either attempt to surf a cyclone swell in Darwin or fly to our nearest surf break in Bali. We often joked about Uluwatu being our local break—times were tough.

Timing of the Williamtown migration also usually coincided with an 81 Wing dining-in, which is the military equivalent of a black-tie dinner and a rare occasion when all Australian F-18 pilots would be in the same room.[2] Don't be fooled by the black tie—once the Queen is toasted there is little decorum at these events.

Every year 75SQN would devise a different 'theme' for these dining-ins, such as 'The Flying Elvises'. Being the consummate safety-conscious professionals we were, we had our own Elvis suits made that could be worn underneath our flying suits or 'zoom bags'. The Elvis suits were made at little expense while on an overseas deployment to Singapore and had nothing to do with one of the pilots dating a local seamstress at the time. By ensuring their compliance with RAAF safety regulations (not!), we could wear our suits on cross-country transits, land, undress in the cockpit, and taxi the jets in wearing the correct dress of the day—Elvis Presley sequined suits.

On one occasion an air traffic controller, aware of the impending arrival of sixteen supersonic Elvises, got right in on the act:

Magpie 1 (in a very good Elvis voice): 'Oh mama in the tower, this is Magpie formation, I gotta flight of four and we're all hungry, mama, requesting a low flyby.'

Tower Controller: 'Roger, Magpie, you're clear low initial, report on base. All aircraft in the pattern, be advised: Elvis is entering the pattern.'

I'm not quite sure who invented dining-in, or why, but it included some of the most ludicrous traditions, both official and unofficial, that I've encountered in my life. (And after 25 years with the RAAF I've seen some corkers.)

The evening begins with '7 for 7.30' or 'international dining-in time'. This would be the pre-dinner drinks and horses hooves (hors d'oeuvres) at the officers mess[3]—dressed in our finest 'summer mess kit'. The mess kit is similar to a tuxedo and includes a squadron-crested cummerbund, cufflinks and, hidden somewhere on the pilot, his Hornet pin. The Hornet pin is presented to every F-18 pilot when he completes both his day and night solo. About the size of a small key, these three-dimensional brass Hornet models are to be kept from sight until the magic word is called. Now that I think of it, the whole tradition doesn't fit with a quote I once read on the wall above a fighter pilot's desk:

Do not ask a pilot what type of aircraft he flies.

If he is a trashhauler, you will embarrass him.

If he is a fighter pilot, he will tell you.

Anyway, back to the magic word . . . When someone calls out 'flash', all pilots are required to to produce their Hornet pin. Failure to produce your pin results in a fine, which is placed in a beer jug along with all the other fines from forgetful knuckleheads. This jug, in turn, goes over the bar at closing time to bribe the waitress to risk her job by keeping the bar open past its licensed hours—oh, the wonders of a capitalist society! If all pilots are able to produce their Hornet pin (a thing rarely witnessed), then the pilot making the challenge of 'flash' is responsible for placing his own, significantly greater, amount of money over the bar. (Over the years though, I have often wondered when this fun tradition would be deemed 'unbecoming of an officer', by virtue of nothing more than the call 'flash' and some overzealous, intoxicated knucklehead taking the word too literally.)

Then there's 'Mr Vice'[4], the privileged position of the most junior fighter pilot who is responsible for maintaining order over the evening's proceedings. This designation is ironically appropriate as the younger fighter pilots usually do have a drinking problem—like most nineteen-year-olds they don't know when they've had enough. To appreciate the hilarity of this tradition you need to understand that Mr Vice sits at the counter–head table to the President of the Mess Committee (PMC). Where the fun starts is when Mr Vice has his drinks spiked so that the more experienced pilots can undermine his authority and introduce whatever unsavoury activity they have concocted. Most important, however, is the timing of these antics. Until the meal is complete, and the Queen has been toasted, all members present are on their strictest behaviour.

This behaviour is outlined in a little blue book given to officer recruits and includes forbidden dinner conversation topics such as politics, religion and women. Most knuckleheads don't have much trouble avoiding the first two topics but the third . . . tough rule. Other draconian rules included hushed conversation only to your immediate company, all members to remain seated and no toilet breaks. Having a Chinese bladder I found the latter impossible.

Drinking usually started in our personal quarters at around 5 p.m., then moved to the pre-dinner drinks at 7 p.m., a last toilet break at 7.29 p.m., and then drinks with dinner until the Queen was toasted around 10 p.m. I could never hold it! So I had to devise ways of discreetly relieving myself without being caught.

At my first dining-in, I foolishly believed that my immediate dinner company would cover for me while I commando-crawled underneath the long table to the kitchen door and used the cooks' toilets—wrong. I stealthily crawled back to my place only to find my chair had been removed. I was forced to squat for the remaining hour.

The next dining-in I tried the good old empty wine bottle. It seemed by far the easiest and the most covert. It worked a treat until Monday morning when the PMC rang my commanding officer to lodge a workplace harassment case against me. Apparently the waiter, who was not an ADF member but a civilian contractor, was embarrassed by being asked to place my bottle of rare vintage in the bin.

It took me ten years to work it out but I finally resorted to a tried-and-true method which I utilised almost daily while flying my toilet-less single-seat fighter—I used my 'pisser pack'. These packs are full of highly compressed foam that expands to ten times its size when wet. Utilising the pisser pack, which surely must have been designed for such an occasion as the military dining-in, I was able to simultaneously continue my tightly controlled dinner conversation, utilising a hushed tone and limited to my immediate company, while not losing my seat, nor embarrassing delicate civilians, and even quaffing a good glass of wine. Mission accomplished!

After we made it through the dinner, and stayed awake during the guest speaker, the port would be passed in silence—and I mean silence. No snickering, no whispering, no scraping of chairs on polished floors—nothing except the *nook nook nook nook* as amateurs attempted to decanter the port in too much of a hurry. This would often be echoed by the more experienced knucks who had learnt to mimic the sound of decanting port throughout their careers. There were also other weird protocols that needed to be followed, such as not spilling the port, not allowing the decanters to touch the table, and circling the decanter three times counterclockwise around the glass before pouring it. Not allowing the port to be spilt was due to its historical connotations with the blood of fallen fighter pilots in past conflicts. Not allowing the decanters to touch the table was just another form of bastardisation of the weaker pilots and I was sure that the execs ordered the heaviest decanters for this purpose—it is called lead crystal for a reason. The circling of the glass prior to pouring was to do with the warding off of evil spirits. This mumbo-jumbo never worked, however, as we all suffered shocking hangovers the next day from the cheap evil spirit used to fill the decanters.

When all port glasses were full, the PMC would bang his gavel and ask Mr Vice to carry out his second most important duty—toasting the Queen. I cannot describe the excitement most knuckle-heads had to restrain at this moment in the night. I would like to say it was due to the loyal monarchists among us having an opportunity to pay homage to our esteemed ruler; however, it was more like the excitement a sprint car driver feels as the lights drop from red to amber. We were almost at the point of unleashing the hounds and all their frivolity.

After banging his gavel, Mr Vice would prompt everyone by nervously saying, 'Ladies and gentlemen, please be upstanding.'

Shuffle, shuffle, shuffle . . . silence . . . pause . . . Mr Vice then raised his glass in the direction of the spotlit portrait of Her Majesty and, in case there was any confusion, boldly pronounce, 'The Queen'.

All: 'The Queen.'

This was followed by everyone immediately sculling their port in silence with the ambience morphing within seconds. Glug, glug, glug . . . pause . . . Who's going to sit down first? . . . He has . . . OK, I can sit now too . . . Is it OK to start the banter? . . . Murmur . . . Look at other squadron pilots ... Murmurs getting louder ... Are you going to start it, mate? ... Conversation moves outside of immediate company ... Do you think the CO meant what he said at morning brief about not getting him in the shit? ... More murmurs ...

Anonymous shout: 'Mr Vice!'

Upon this icebreaker, all eyes would turn to the person responsible who would by now be the only one standing. Our attention would then focus on Mr Vice to see how he would respond. Generally most Mr Vices would be under strict instructions from the PMC to control the banter, including its tone and level, suitability, legality and tempo. It was a lot to ask of the most junior pilot present, and often an acid test for the burdened individual. By the time I left the force I had learnt to pick the future leaders by their performance in this daunting position.

Mr Vice: 'Identify yourself.'

Once the individual identified himself, he now had the floor for a time period that was based on his ability to entertain a highly intelligent audience ... not long. He could cast aspersions about another squadron. He could tell a joke (although it was hard to find one that didn't involve the three taboo topics of women, politics and religion). Or he could distract the audience while the main event occurred elsewhere in stealth. Some examples have included transonic low-level fly-overs at night, the firing of cannons and even beastiality. I can assure you they all sound far worse than they actually were (however, in the latter case, this was literally how the police report was completed). The banter was predominately inter-squadron: The milk drinkers (3SQN) would defame the poor sisters (77SQN) while the cowboys (75SQN), being the non-resident squadron, were often ganged up on by the two local squadrons.

One year I was involved in some inter-squadron banter that nearly lost me my aircrew medical. A pilot from 3 Squadron, Gumpy, had had an engine fire in flight. He hadn't shut the engine down in accordance with the checklist; rather, he'd kept flying around using his nose as his primary fire detector. The aircraft was in fact on fire and significant damage was done to the internals of the jet while he flew around taking in the scenic sites of Newcastle. This buffoonery was unbelievable and became the theme of one of our skits.

Now I must say that from day one in the air force we were taught the importance of wearing fire-resistant flying suits . . . particularly when the opposite sex was around. This WWII carryover had little to do with fighters as we had a bang seat that would do much more for us than a protective suit; however, from basic pilot course onwards, the lifesaving qualities of this wardrobe accessory were drummed home. So Honko and I planned our piss-take of Gumpy and the entire No. 3 Squadron based on the almost mystical powers of my flying suit. Ladies, these suits have mystical powers against you and resistance is futile, but please, let me finish the story.

I think Honko and I spent an entire 30 seconds planning our stand-up comedy routine on the way to the dining-in with enough pre-dinner drinks in us that at least we thought it would be funny. Once the banter started, and Mr Vice authorised the first pisser break, Honko and I loitered in the toilets until everyone had resumed their seats. I then quickly put on my Nomex 100 per cent fire-resistant flying suit and Honko helped me stuff all seven pockets with paper towel.

'You sure you want to do this, Serge?' he asked cautiously, pausing with the lighter just out of range of the paper towel.

'Go for it, mate, it'll be fine. These suits are fireproof,' I replied confidently.

Honko started lighting me up, one pocket at a time. By the third pocket the first was well and truly aflame. By the sixth my legs were seriously burning and I couldn't wait for Honko to light the last one. I headed out of the toilets towards the dining hall but the pain became unbearable. In the hope of fanning out the flames I ran straight into the dining hall, yelling: 'Mayday, mayday, mayday, Gumpy 1, I am not on fire, I say again . . . I . . . ahhhh, am . . . ahhhhh, not . . . ahhhhh, shit, I am on fire, fuck, it's burning . . . Help!'

It was no longer the paper towel that was on fire, it was my supposedly fireproof flying suit.

Honko had seen the look on my face change from, 'Fuck, we're the funniest guys in the place,' to 'Fuck, I'm the dumbest prick in the world' in a matter of seconds and ran to help. He grabbed a fire extinguisher off the wall, pulled the plug and started spraying white powder all over me, the carpet and nearby dinner suits.

Once the fire was out I ran back to the toilets to get some water onto my burns. The audience exploded in laughter and applause, believing Honko and I had scripted and executed this fine piece of fighter force humour. No-one had any idea about how much pain I was in, how bad the burns were and the fact that I was never acting from the time Honko had lit the last flame.

10
Fight or flight

A HIGHLIGHT OF squadron life is the annual deployment to South-East Asia. The location of these deployments seemed to be random and based on the proverbial dartboard in the Minister of Defence's office in Canberra. Iswahutti Air Base in Indonesia, Korat Air Base in Thailand, Butterworth or Kuantan Air Force Bases in Malaysia, Payar Lebar Air Base in Singapore or Clark Air Base in the Philippines were all possible destinations that the minister could send us to in order to maintain defence relations with our regional neighbours. For young twenty-something-year-old knuckleheads, our deployments had little to do with international relations and a lot to do with beer, Asian food, Elvis suits and testing out our diplomatic immunity.

In 1994, No. 75 Squadron (SQN) deployed to Payar Lebar in Singapore as part of Australia's contribution to the annual exercising of the Five Power Defence Agreement which included the UK, Singapore, Malaysia, New Zealand and Indonesia. For one month we would be staying at a five-star hotel in downtown Singapore and flying in mock defence of the island state. This was the way wars were meant to be fought, with cold beer, chilli crab and rotis. It was times like these when I knew why I had opted for the air force—no foxholes, slit trenches and 'meals ready to eat' (MRE) for this little flyboy.

The flying was fun on these exercises and generally not too taxing for Australian fighter pilots, due to the technological advantage we enjoyed over the other nations. It became embarrassing at times and so we would create scenarios that would even up the odds for our regional brethren. 'Heaters and guns' was one way of levelling the playing field for them, where we would simulate that all our radar-guided missiles had been expended, leaving only short-range heat-seeking missiles and guns to fight with. As this was equivalent to the weapons used by the A-4s, F-16s and F-5s of the Royal Singapore Air Force we would find ourselves in a more even fight, requiring our pilots to use their flying skills more than relying on their superior weapons.

After a couple of weeks of rehearsals, the exercise proper would kick off, with strike raids ingressing down the Malaysian Peninsula to carry out mock attacks on Singapore. For these large-force employment exercises we would not restrict our weapon types but would fight with our full complement of missiles, as we were generally seriously outnumbered. We would sit at the end of the Payar Lebar runway on 'strip alert' with one engine shutdown to save fuel while the running engine would keep all our avionics online, cool and ready to be airborne within three minutes of being scrambled—we called this readiness state 'Alert 3'.

The Singaporean air traffic control (ATC) was superior to Australia's because their government was not afraid to interrupt commercial operations once a year to train their defence force. Upon receiving a scramble order the Singaporean ATC would hold commercial flights clear of the fighters to enable us to efficiently engage with the hostile aircraft, which would often be close to Singapore by the time we were scrambled. Additionally, they would allow the civilian airliners to fly through the middle of our military airspace by using restricted 'tubes' that we were required to remain clear of. There were many times while exercising over the

Malaysian Peninsula that I would be 'pencilling' down vertically to engage low strikers and pass an airliner. I can only imagine what this might have looked like to a passenger in a Malaysian Airlines flight as they gazed out their window and saw a pair of supersonic Hornets diving past.

In the words of JP, 'Air defence is a mug's game.' It flies in the face of most of the tried-and-true principles of war, including maximising surprise and concentrating your effort. Here, the enemy had all the surprise and we rarely managed to get more than four aircraft up, while our opponents could strike with twelve or more aircraft at any time. It was on a previous exercise in Singapore when I first joined 75 Squadron that JP had shown me how to deal with being 'numerically challenged' by the adversary.

Sitting at Alert 3 at the end of the Paya Lebar runway, I was flying as JP's wingman or 'Dash 2'. He had us both listening in to the 'big picture' frequency, which broadcasts an overall disposition of enemy and friendly forces as the fight progressed.

'Hermes, big picture, single group, bullseye 360, 60, heading south,' said the Singaporean big-picture controller.

The bombers were 120 kilometres north of Singapore and heading straight towards us. JP and I knew if we could launch now we would intercept them at 60 kilometres, but we still had the second engines to start. JP started talking to our tactical controller to get us airborne as soon as possible, as the strike package was only seven minutes away and we didn't want to be straffed in our jets while sitting on the end of the runway.

'Hermes, Magpie 11, request scramble,' JP transmitted.

'Magpie 11, hold Alert 3,' the controller replied bluntly.

'Roger, Magpie 11 hold, suggest you scramble us, Hermes, so that we can engage the strike group before they strike the base.'

'Negative, Magpie. I say to you, hold position,' the controller ordered in a frustrated tone.

'Roger, Magpie holding,' JP professionally replied as he gave me the wind-up signal to start my second engine.

I figured I must have missed something as I was so junior and JP knew everything about air combat that there was to know. I quickly performed a cross-bleed start, drawing high-pressure air from my running engine to start the dead engine, and ran through my pre-take-off checklist. Halfway through my checklist, JP pushed us back over to the squadron operations frequency.

'Ops, Magpie 11, can you get onto Hermes and get us scrambled before the strikers hit the base? Break. Magpie, Channel 2 go.' Then JP ordered me across to the tower frequency. 'Magpie, check.'

'Magpie 12,' I responded, still stuffing around with my checklist.

'Paya Lebar tower, Magpie, ready immediate scramble, 350 departure, flight level 210,' JP announced.

'Aaah . . . aaah . . . standby,' the tower controller stumbled, trying to work out exactly whose authority Magpie were intending to get airborne on. 'Roger, clear . . .'—JP powered up and started turning onto the runway before the controller had finished speaking—'. . . for take-off, make left turn, vector 350 climb to flight level 210.'

My heart was now racing as I tried to get my jet ready for take-off while watching JP's burners light up and his jet accelerating down the runway. I started my clock. I had twenty seconds to finish my checklist, power up, turn onto the runway, check my canopy, flaps, seat and stabs, look at the clock . . . eighteen, nineteen, twenty. Time to go.

I pushed both throttles through the afterburner gate as I watched JP lifting gently into the air about 2 kilometres ahead of me. I scanned the engine panel to check the engine parameters, 100 kilometres per hour in the HUD, quickly scanned to JP so I wouldn't lose him, 160 kilometres per hour, corrected slightly for centreline, back into the HUD, 240 kilometres per hour, rotate. The jet leapt into the air with a motivation all of its own, though my mind was still back at the end of the runway, wondering why we were asking for take-off clearance when we didn't yet have approval to start our second engines. I locked up JP with my radar and started to check my sensors on his aircraft, including my air combat radar modes and heat-seeking missile track. As I powered up to overtake JP in order to reciprocate the weapon system check for him, our tactical control had a baby over the radio.

'Magpie, Magpie, scramble now, vector 350, climb to flight level 210, you have strikers north 25 miles (50 kilometres).'

JP spoke ever so calmly over the radio, the same way Obi Wan Kenobi does when Luke Skywalker starts freaking out about the stormtroopers and the force not being strong enough: 'Magpie, make switches, roll 260, 20 miles, 5000.' JP was directing me to arm my weapons now and point my radar ahead 40 kilometres at 1500 metres for the enemy strikers.

Most intercepts start at a minimum 80 kilometres and happened far too fast for junior pilots like myself. This one was at 40 kilometres and happening now. I rolled my radar down to look at 1500 metres, where I found a strike train of over twelve aircraft. Up until this mission I had never seen more than four blips on my radar. While trying to make sense of what was what, where I was, who I should shoot, and staying visual with JP around the cloud, I quickly armed my weapons and forced my heart to calm down below 250 beats per minute.

'Fox 1, lead group, western, engaged,' JP transmitted.

I watched in awe as the Jedi master then rolled inverted and pulled to 45 degrees nose-low. I was now behind my timeline—way behind. The contract JP had briefed me on was to have a missile in the air no later than when the bandits hit 30 kilometres. We were now at 20 kilometres.

'Magpie 2, locked far group, Fox 1, press,' I replied. I had a rocket on the way to the far group, though I wasn't sure exactly who in that group, and I was maintaining visual contact with JP. Flying in a slightly swept position 2 kilometres off his left wing, I mimicked his WWII Pappy Boington peel-off and pulled aggressively nose-down. I was now pointing at my group and able to look through the radar-lock box in the HUD to gain tally of one, two, three, four . . . I stopped counting at eight.

'Magpie, freezer freezer, take face shots and blow through. Magpie 11, Fox 1 kill, Fox 2 near group.' JP was telling me to reduce my power to idle and dispense flares to reduce the likelihood of being shot by a heat-seeking missile. JP had killed one of the leaders and had now sent a heat-seeking missile on its way into the wingman of the guy he had shot.

I took this cue to look at the time to go on my missile as it counted down towards its target: three, two, one, zero. 'Magpie 12, Fox 1 kill far group, second Fox 1.' I boresight-locked another bandit and took a minimum range Fox 1 while locking a heat-seeking missile onto another.

By this stage JP had merged with the near group from high to low at over 2000 kilometres per hour. I pulled back up to remain clear of all the aluminium as I was unsure where everyone was. JP kept firing down the train until he ran out of missiles. We eventually blew through the train until we were 20 kilometres behind them and climbed into a cover position on the remaining bandits—we had killed six on the first pass. After transmitting our claimed kills to the opposing force, six aircraft removed themselves from the strike package, leaving six remaining. JP again committed low for a follow-on attack.

'Magpie, gate go.' JP ordered me to light my afterburners as we started a descent to catch the strikers. Descending through 5000 metres we were close to breaking the sound barrier, which would have caused serious damage to half the windows along the Malaysian Peninsula. At 1200 kilometres per hour we had 360 kilometres per hour of overtake and soon got back into weapons range. I was out of Fox 1 missiles but JP still had one and I had one Fox 2. Trouble was, there were six bandits ahead—three more than we had missiles for. What was JP thinking? This was suicide.

'Fox 1 western bandit, near group,' JP transmitted.

Then we both continued our aggressive descent down to the strikers' altitude and soon had tally of the six bandits. The rear pair started a break turn to the left to defend against our attack, which provided me with a second missile opportunity.

'Magpie 12, Fox 2 eastern bandit in the break turn,' I transmitted.

The time of flight on both our missiles was only short and we claimed two good kills on the rear pair. The remaining four strikers were approximately 10 kilometres ahead in a box formation—but I now had no missiles left and only my gun pack, and JP was the same. They, on the other hand, probably had sixteen missiles between them. Time to retire to the bar gracefully, you would think. Not JP.

'Magpie, fuel check,' JP asked.

I replied, '6.5 on 7.0,' indicating I had 2300 litres (6500 pounds) internal and 2450 litres (7000 pounds) total fuel remaining.

JP transmitted back, '7.0 on 7.3, Magpie, buster,' letting me know his fuel state and that he wanted me to come out of afterburner to conserve fuel. He then contacted the controller. 'Hermes, Magpie, we have four strikers approaching Singapore at low level, request hot pursuit.'

'Roger, Magpie, you are clear, hot pursuit into Singapore control below 5000 feet (1500 metres).'

I couldn't believe it. JP hadn't yet had enough and felt he stood a chance at 2 vs. 4 with guns only and a useless D cat like me on his wing. He was a legend. And to top it off he'd just got clearance to chase the four-ship of bandits over downtown Singapore. It seemed insane but he was the boss and I trusted him—I just needed to stay visual and not hit the skyscrapers.

The bandits, who we could now see were F-5s, flew directly over the middle of the island before starting a hard turn to head back north. JP started a lead turn which placed us directly over Orchard Road—one of the busiest shopping districts on the planet. I was flying in a 2-kilometre combat wing on JP as he flashed in and out of skyscrapers. I remained slightly higher than JP so I could look down on him in the concrete canyons. The picture was surreal; however, my contemplation was soon shattered by JP on the radio.

'Magpie 11, engaged eastern trailer.'

You've got to be shitting me! I thought. Oh well, I guess it's one way for the Singaporean taxpayers to see where their money goes.

The four-ship were still in their hard turn to go north as JP merged with the leaders and saddled up in a turning engagement on the trailing aircraft right over the top of the Singaporean CBD at 150 metres above ground level (AGL).

'Fox 3 kill, come out south,' JP unemotionally transmitted. He had achieved a guns kill on an F-5 and wanted me to head out south with him.

'Magpie 11, visual, your right, three o'clock, 3 miles (6 kilometres),' I replied.

We had been airborne for less than ten minutes and claimed a total of seven kills between us, as well as recreating the Battle of Britain for the good people of Singapore. Our tactical controller was very quiet throughout the entire engagement—probably wondering how we had time-warped ourselves off the runway without his authority to even start our engines.

One weekend in Singapore my squadron mates decided they would head to Thailand to let their hair down a bit more than you can in Singapore. I was married to Lil at the time, who had made it clear to me in no uncertain terms that there would be no ping-pong displays or special massages. This was going to be one of the first tests of my marriage . . . and one I would fail miserably.

All week the guys maintained their psychological stress on me. I was under the thumb, not a real fighter pilot, gay, unlikely to pass my upgrade and never to be a fighter combat instructor (FCI). The pressure was seriously killing me—until now I had been the one instigating squadron social functions and now I was the one defending my absence.

On the Friday night we all retired to the Paya Lebar officers club for a quick beer before the guys had to head to Changi Airport to catch their flight—as usual they had left their run to the airport until the last moment.

'Come on, Serge. You know you want to.'

'Nope. I've told you I can't go—I made a promise to Lil.' The peer pressure was excruciating. These guys weren't just work colleagues—they were squadon buddies, wingmen, brothers in arms. We trusted each other with our lives.

'You can still make it, Serge.'

'No, I can't. I left my passport at the hotel, I have no clothes and I haven't even got a ticket.'

'We'll hold the flight for you, mate.'

And that's all it took. 'I'm in. Buy me a ticket,' I said and quickly called a cab.

Paya Lebar is halfway between downtown and Changi—the trouble was I had to go back into town to get my passport. When the cab arrived I asked him the fare. I offered him double if he could get me there in half the time (the maths seemed simple enough to me). Speeding in Singapore can lose a taxi driver his licence—he needed serious incentive. At the hotel I quickly raced inside, grabbed my passport and overnight bag, and raced back down to the waiting cab . . . still wearing my flying suit.

I continued throwing $20 notes over the front seat of the cab, spurring on my driver to make it to Changi in record time—which he did. I arrived at the airport at the scheduled departure time and the airline staff met me, handed over my ticket and escorted me through security. I was still in a jog, with sweat staining my flight suit dark green, as the staff then informed me that I had missed the flight. I was deflated and disappointed, having agreed to sacrifice my marriage, spent a week's wages on taxi fares and broken the land speed record to Changi airport—the guys had left without me.

At that moment the airline staff radios erupted in rapid-fire Thai and the security staff started going mental. I looked up and saw the cause of the commotion. Two fighter pilots were claiming diplomatic immunity and threatening the Singaporean staff with an appearance at the Hague Criminal Court if they even looked at them the wrong way. The bluff worked—it stalled the security staff long enough for me to board the flight.

Thailand was shocking for me. I could not believe that middle-aged white men would openly walk around with teenage Thai girls. Despite whatever laws were or were not involved, it was wrong on so many fronts. I just couldn't stand by and watch it happen for the two nights I was there. So I bought every Thai teenage girl we found who was being exploited. Like some sort of Pied Piper I ended up with a dozen girls following us around. We even bought them dinner and let some of them crash in one of our rooms while we slept on the couches and floors.

The guys made fun of me, pointing out that as soon as we headed back to Singapore the fat middle-aged men would be back onto the girls—it was sad but true. Even so, I still felt good about giving them a night of wholesome fighter pilot shenanigans, a decent meal and a bed.

When I got home I attempted to explain what happened to Lil.

'I'm sorry. I was weak and succumbed to peer-group pressure from the guys.'

'What did you spend all the money on?'

'Well, I bought a dozen teenage hookers . . .'

There was no way I was going to stay out of the doghouse on that one . . . no matter what I said.

With some great flying by day, Singapore also offered some wonders by night for its aerial saviours. The Elvis Bar was a favourite for the 75 Squadron pilots. It was probably one of the few places on the planet where we could go out as a twelve-ship formation wearing our Elvis suits and be treated with the appropriate amount of respect that 'the King' deserves. Unfortunately, our flying suits were not permitted to be worn outside the base, for fear the pilots would give the uniform a bad name. Having said that, this was a constant area of friction with the squadron executives, as the junior pilots tried to stretch this rule further and further. We had even devised a cunning plan to protect ourselves from incrimination if seen in public in our flying suits—we all wore 'Mick' name tags, the name of our CO. One night in particular the no-flying-suit rule would be stretched well beyond its limit and the executives' worst fears would come to be realised.

The night in question started at the officers club at the Singapore Air Base. We had enjoyed an 'international night' with the other pilots where we exposed Singaporean pilots to the joys of boat racing with beer jugs and combat rules crud (a semi-violent competitive ball game played on a billiard table), and they did their best to reciprocate with karaoke and some local cuisine. With our regional brethren now educated in Australian fighter culture, we headed to the best hotel in town—the Hyatt.

The Hyatt Hotel in Singapore was a pretty posh place that attracted the right sort of clientele that we were sure would appreciate our Friday night antics. Branigan's nightclub was in the basement of the Hyatt and was generally packed to overflowing, selling five-dollar jugs of beer and frozen margaritas. This strange arrangement of pricing spirits and beer equally always led to one outcome—the blenders got a good workout.

The guys were on fire with a crewload of flight attendants in town, good music and an overdeveloped desire to vent some stress from a hectic week. It was around 11 p.m. when I left the dance floor, having just done my best dance medley of the sprinkler, lawn-mower, chainsaw and walking frame, to find the men's room. On my way there I was abruptly stopped by something that resembled a half-man, half-gorilla, with facial hair and muscles that would have rivalled King Kong's.

'Where do you think you're going?' the *Homo erectus* grunted.

'To have a dance—want to come?' I replied with my best smart-arse face.

He then reached down from his towering height and promptly ripped off the Australian flag that was velcroed to my flight suit. Having watched *Gorillas in the Mist* I remembered I should not run or make eye contact, but back away slowly.

'Keep it, mate. Courtesy of the Australian Government,' I said, and went immediately to let our senior ranking officer know trouble might be brewing near the toilets, and perhaps guys should take a wingman with them for mutual support. The trouble was that the FCI I approached, JC, was one of the hotter heads in the squadron who just happened to be a black belt in taekwondo and by this stage of the evening had a gut full of Mexican courage.

'Which fuckin' guy?' JC asked.

'Mate, it's not important, just tell the guys to travel in pairs,' I said, trying to calm him down.

'Fuck that, I'll sort this cunt out,' JC barked and promptly stormed off in the direction of the gorilla's lair, where there now appeared to be an entire tribe of silverbacks looking our way.

'Which one of you pricks took my mate's patch?' JC demanded.

On cue the original silverback stepped forwards. 'I did. What you going to do about it?'

'You and me, outside,' JC replied.

How clichéd, I thought. Where was I? Back at school?

The worrying thing, though, was that JC was only about 170 centimetres tall and of slight frame, while the near-Neanderthal had to be at least 190 centimetres tall and almost as wide. The gorilla tribe followed their leader outside and the 75 Squadron pilots followed our FCI.

It soon became apparent that, despite my pleas, JC was determined to set this bloke straight, and the gathered throng soon set up a perimeter around JC and Kong. An argument ensued about who was more of a tosser when, out of nowhere, JC planted a very fast uppercut into Kong's jaw. His head snapped back, paused and then slowly came forwards, looking JC in the eye. And then it was on.

Kong threw a single punch to knock JC flat on his arse before Vag stepped forwards to replace JC. Vag was also a black belt in something—well at least he looked like it as he rose into a leaping grasshopper pose before also being dispatched by Kong into the beautifully manicured Hyatt gardens, where he remained with a pop-up sprinkler jammed up his arse. Hecka then moved in with some sort of Vulcan deathgrip on Kong, which also resulted in some sort of arse impact for Hecka. It was about now that I decided to use my greatest fighting asset—my legs.

I jumped the garden into oncoming traffic and beat feet-up Orchard Road. I know it was cowardly. I know it's not what you're meant to do when confronted by a tribe of silverbacks, but I figured that 150-kilogram-body wasn't going to be able to keep up with me, which it didn't. It didn't have to. Its territory regained, Kong's tribe could now return to their spoils of war: the British Airways crew who were still on the dance floor, wondering why their steely-eyed killers in flying suits were taking so long in the toilet. Must be applying more musk . . .

The next day we all woke with sore heads and went into work for a no-fly safety day—as if those days weren't painful enough. JC's left eye was completely closed and the other guys had some minor scratches and bruises from their tour of the Hyatt gardens. I had nothing but a couple of blisters from my sprint down Orchard Road in my flying boots. We waited patiently for the CO to arrive for morning brief. Being late was very much out of character for him. Fifteen minutes later he walked in . . . and we knew immediately something was up.

'As you were,' he said, staring down each of us. 'I have just had the defence attaché on the phone from the embassy claiming that you guys were in town last night in flying suits and were involved in some sort of pub brawl with a Special Air Services (SAS) patrol. Who wants to tell me what the fuck he is talking about and why he wants to see me? And you might want to start with why the only name he has been given is Mick!'

Special Air Services—that explained the genetically modified, performance-enhanced, overdeveloped half-men that were able to defeat all martial-art tactics known to humankind—well, at least the three pissed ones who were stupid enough to try.

JC started explaining what had happened but didn't get very far. We were all assigned to cleaning duties awaiting further disciplinary action while the CO visited the embassy.

At the embassy the boss stood at attention next to the SAS warrant officer who was in charge of the patrol that had been enjoying some leave after an exercise. Both the officers were drilled new arseholes by the defence attaché. The CO returned to the base and promptly grounded us from the exercise for two days while we cleaned, did paperwork and generally bored ourselves into doing even more stupid things after hours. JC's eye got better and he kept his aircrew medical. Vag stopped watching Bruce Lee films, while Hecka no longer believes Dr Spock's Vulcan deathgrip is fair dinkum.

Ten years later while consulting in Canberra I was invited to a dinner with friends where I met a former SAS operator who we were getting into business with. I recounted the Sasquatch story over dinner to much laughter from all the guests except 'Steve', who sat in the corner with his standard 'grey man' facial expression until I got to the punchline:

'. . . and so I do my best Bruce Willis impersonation by jumping over the garden, over car bonnets and sprinting down Orchard Road, one-eighty flat-out with all the traffic—the whole time wearing my flying suit.'

At this Steve cracked a small smile and I congratulated myself, once again, on my ability to win over even the toughest audience with my tales of fighter heroics.

Then he drawled, 'So you were the rabbit.'

It turned out Steve had been the warrant officer in charge of the SAS patrol that had beaten the shit out of 75 Squadron ten years prior.

'Umm, yeah, could you, ahh, pass the salt, please, Steve?'

11
Chuck's dead

WITH ADRENALINE SPIKING through my veins, I felt my heart stop as I looked into my rear-vision mirror to see the lifeless silhouette of my mate strewn across the road behind me. I stared, waiting for the guillotine of reality to slice through the fog of my dream. A little longer, I thought. He will move soon. I will wake up soon. I should slam the handbrake on now and return to his aid. I imagined him squashed flat by my rear wheels. Had I really had that much to drink? Move, dammit! As awful as it was for me to accept, it had happened—I had run over my best mate.

For you to understand how a seemingly intelligent fighter pilot might have got himself into such a mess, I will have to rewind a couple of weeks to Exercise Kangaroo 1994. This was the pipe-dream of some deranged senior RAAF officer in Canberra who had convinced the government that despite their best-intended plans to downsize the RAAF, in fact the boys in blue needed extra troops to defend their valuable aircraft from ground attack as well as air attack, as clearly the army was not competent enough to fulfil this highly technical task. I mean, how hard is it to stay awake with a rifle? While I am sure the government's decision to entertain the moron made many senior RAAF bureaucrats (aka blunts) in Canberra very happy at the increasing size of their phallus, the rest of the air force felt otherwise, as now we would be regularly required to exercise in ground defence—something fighter pilots are born extremely allergic to.

The first test of the RAAF's new lethal air-base defence capability would be during Exercise Kangaroo '94. This exercise was without doubt one of the most ridiculous waste of taxpayers' money that I have ever witnessed while in uniform. The scenario was that there was an imaginary island state of Kamaria just north of Australia that was starting to get a little froggy. This island state had been created by blunts in Canberra who worried more about their PC careers than actually training the ADF to defend against a discrete threat such as, say . . . umm, ahhh, I don't know, ahh . . . say, Indonesia for instance. These blunts seriously worried that if we trained against a real-world threat and that country found out about it, they would attack us. Ironically, 'intelligence' also told us that the Indonesians weren't as worried about our sensitivities when it came to training for war as they regularly trained against Australian capabilities. No worries, then, we'll just tie our hands behind our backs. As such, this fairy-dust country of Kamaria had an entirely fictitious order of battle that had us flying against pretend aircraft that fired magic mushroom missiles.

The 75 Squadron's commitment to the exercise was two jets on Alert 15 (fifteen minutes to take-off) and two on Alert 60 (60 minutes to take-off) for 24 hours per day for a month. The scenario had Kamaria's magic jets conducting probing raids across northern Australia at all times of day and night—although there were actually no other aircraft flying. It was a giant multi-billion-dollar game that was being played out so the senior blunt in Canberra, having delusions of commanding his 'special air forces', could fulfil his fantasy. This meant that 24/7 we had two aircraft running in their ordnance loading areas (OLA), each with one engine shut down, while another two pilots were kitted up in the crew room ready to step to their aircraft once a scramble call came in from the sector operations centre. Now I need to stop and explain right now why JP had taught us that 'air defence is a mug's game'.

The aircrew have duty limitations imposed on them for fear they may get a little tired during war and hurt themselves. The limit is twelve hours per day for five consecutive days, after which they must have a couple of days off to rest their bodies that have grown so weary sitting around waiting for something to happen. Another wrinkle-preventative limitation is not allowing the pilots to sit on alert in the aircraft for more than three hours—the monotony of sitting alone for this long without telling a war story to your mates was also deemed by the blunts to cause steely-eyed fighter pilots to suddenly fly into the ground. These limitations therefore meant that sixteen pilots are needed for the four aircraft to be on alert for a 24-hour period. In order for pilots to have their two days of R&R per week, the squadron had to borrow pilots from another squadron just to meet the four-aircraft commitment and, oh yeah, the pilots have not yet done their stint in the gun pit. Thanks to Air Commodore Blunt, the RAAF not only had to fly, fix, fuel, arm and maintain their aircraft, they now had to defend them as well. Promote that man!

Additional to their Easter bunny air force, Kamaria also had some special forces which were being simulated by members of the Australian Special Air Service (SAS) regiment—or 'chicken stranglers' as we more affectionately call them—acting as the red team. And in the blue corner defending the base we had highly trained RAAF Base Tindal killers, including clerks, cooks, dental nurses and sixteen fighter pilots with their blank-firing Glocks who could only sit watch for an hour or two for fear their handsome features might permanently be damaged by having less than twelve hours sleep per night. The chicken stranglers stood no chance.

Frustrated by the lack of flying and the ridiculousness of the situation, I decided to convince the red team that they needed a pilot on their side who could assist them in finding strategically valuable targets around the base, like the liquid oxygen facility, flight-safety shed or officers bar—all vital infrastructure for the continuation of the war. While I wasn't able to convince the SAS operators of my highly valuable skills, I was able to get myself onto the B team for the red side. These guys were air base defence guards from another RAAF base who seemed to be getting a lot of enjoyment out of testing their Tindal brethren. So, after I knocked off work, exhausted from all the sitting around, I snuck back to my room at the officers mess and filled a bag with some dark clothes for my 2300 report at the base armoury. Well, I was legal as I had left the squadron after the mandatory twelve hours and what the CO doesn't know about won't hurt him—though it just might hurt me.

I arrived to a room full of Dad's Army members wearing jeans, AC/DC T-shirts and bandanas. There was even one guy who looked like he was taking it all too seriously, wearing a Neo-Nazi jacket and Doc Martin boots, though I was pretty sure he hadn't gone wardrobe shopping just for the occasion. We were issued blank-firing Steyr rifles which I had never seen before. I pretended I had some idea and stood next to one of the Free Australia militia members who looked like he knew what he was doing and started loading up some magazines. We then painted our faces and hands black. I purposely left my lips white so that I looked like a mime and performed a couple of moonwalks along an imaginary glass window. With my band of miming brothers I was ready to take on 1500 base personnel.

The white force acts as a neutral party during exercises and ensures the safety of personnel, as well as stage-managing the whole show to achieve training objectives. I wasn't exactly sure what our objectives were, but felt my Neo-Nazi comrade was pretty sorted so long as there was at least one non-Aryan person on the base. White force drove us outside the base and dropped us off a short distance from 'the wire'—an elusive geographical enigma that demarcated good and evil, red and blue, danger pay from normal pay, and

Starbucks from ration packs. Well we were now on the 'other side of the wire'. I grinned at myself about the entire lunacy of the situation, including the fact that I was meant to be sleeping in order to regain my strength for another three hours of sitting in my flightless chariot tomorrow. This was way more fun.

Our seemingly self-nominated leader, who probably had a rank and a real day job, cut 'through the wire' to put us back in from whence we had just come. We moved with stealth the likes of which I hadn't experienced since tripping over my shorts while trying to take a covert crap in a bush campsite as a kid. There was little ambient light—at least that was my defence when they started waving their hands around in secret code that I had no fucking idea about. I tried to squat when they squatted. I walked when they walked—though I worked out that was possibly what they didn't want by the way they increased the tempo and size of their sign language towards me and how the white portion of their eyeballs stood out extra-well against their black face paint.

Soon we could make out the headquarters building of 75 Squadron, which was both good and bad for me. Good, because I might get a chance to scare the shit out of some of my pilot mates who I knew would be guarding this building, and bad, because if they caught me I would be in deep kimchi with the CO. I figured it was death or glory—there would be no way I would allow them to capture me alive. The rest of my posse had no idea what I did for a day job and I guess they had chosen the HQ as the most vulnerable building for inflicting damage on the blue team. Either that or they knew the knuckleheads would be asleep in their foxholes, totally exhausted from reading their *Ralph* magazines while on alert for an entire three hours during the day.

Once we were within a couple of hundred metres of the HQ, we dropped down onto our stomachs and started a long slow crawl towards the razor wire. Our lead militiaman cut the razor wire and we snaked through in single file. I started to get seriously nervous at this point—not so much about the bullshit toy soldier game I was playing, but the fact that I would seriously get in the shit if caught. My senses went into overdrive as I listened, stopped, listened. I could make out some idle chatter in a gun pit not more than 30 metres away. Can't we just lob in some hand grenades and be done with it?, I thought. Nope. Red 1 was intent on slaying the enemy where they slept, which meant that with every piece of razor grass I slithered my stomach across I was another step closer to getting grounded. And then my good associate of Hitler set off a trip-wire.

Night instantly turned into day as a flare ignited 10 metres off to my side. The knuckleheads in their gun pits thought heaven had come and started unloading everything they had, which included Glocks, Steyrs, a machine gun—where did they get this stuff from?— smoke grenades, illumination rockets, pen gun flares and a truck load of fireworks. It was definitely getting dangerous, so much so that the red freedom fighters were forced to make a run for it. It was like someone had dropped their cigarette butt into a pile of fireworks on the fourth of July. With our team now running for their lives I saw the razor wire ahead and, having the additional incentive of not being able to fly my jet the next day if caught, I attempted to Steve McQueen my way over the top and got my leg caught on the razor wire—finding out immediately how it got its name.

By this stage our environmentally challenged aerial warriors felt they no longer needed concrete and sandbags to protect them and had the enemy in retreat. Leaving their posts to try and capture what they assumed to be members of the SAS, they started wailing like screaming banshees as I negotiated the razor wire. Fuck. They were nearly on top of me. As luck would have it there was no chivalry among the Free Australia militia, as they had left me impaled on the wire like a roasting spatchcock. Leaving half my trouser leg behind and gaining a good gash down my thigh, I freed myself and bolted with one naked leg through the razor grass—which I also soon learnt really deserved its name. Unsure whether the razor wire or the razor grass was more painful, I ran for all my career was worth with my best mates behind me, unknowingly chasing me down like a witch in the fifteenth century. I could hear them yelling and recognised their voices:

'This fucker got caught in the wire,' said Scrowt.

'Die, you mutha-fuckin' pussies,' screamed TVH.

'Who's your daddy now?' yelled Flange.

To them this was a once-in-a-lifetime shot at instilling fear into their strategic counterparts. I'm not sure if the SAS guys would have been scared by the barrage of gangsta movie quotes, but I was shitting my one-legged pants. They were closing in on me as I did my best pirate run on one leg, with sweat running into my wounds, increasing the pain significantly. I couldn't hear my panting over the sound of my heart in my eardrums and resigned myself to one of them recognising me. I started to anticipate the inevitable 'Serge, what the FUCK are you doing?'

I eventually made it into some tall timber and, despite being reduced to a monopod, was still able to outrun my fat mates. I think I ran/limped for 5 kilometres before I had the guts to slow down and started to circle around to the front gate of the base where white force checked me back 'inside the wire'.

'Holy shit, what happened to you?' asked the officer in charge of white force, who also had no idea what I did for a day job . . . which, by the way, I was not about to give up after this evening's entertainment.

'Oh, I just snagged my leg on a tree, Sir,' I replied sheepishly, praying he wouldn't start asking me for my personnel details and send me off to medical . . . which of course he did.

'Right, lad, you had better go with the sergeant down to medical right now,' he said, in that 'aren't you fucking thankful that I'm here as you'd probably die without me and where's my next medal' tone.

'Yes, Sir,' I replied, wanting to make as little impression as I could on the throng that was now gathered at the front gate. Thank god I was in civvies and still had my Marcel Marceau disguise on. It occurred to me at this point that I had no ID on me and could have been anyone turning up at the front gate. In fact, I could have been anyone turning up at the armoury earlier that night and been handed a Steyr and taken along on the 'Raid of the Gashing Leg'. Wish I had known about that at high school—could have been seriously fun.

The sergeant who accompanied me to medical wanted to know where I worked. I told him some big ones about being a mechanic on Hornets at 75 Squadron and how much the pilots really pissed me off. We arrived at medical and I insisted I could walk myself in; then, when he'd driven off, I cut a beeline straight back to my block at the officers mess. By the time I limped back in it was almost sun-up and I was exhausted. I dropped into bed for an hour before the alarm went off—I was shattered.

I woke to a dried puddle of blood in my sheets and took the first real look at my leg. The razor wire had made a nice gash but the half-marathon in the early hours of the morning through the razor grass had done more damage and was certainly more painful. I cleaned up in the shower before trying not to limp to breakfast and back to work for Morning Death. We sat through our morning lobotomy of unchanged weather and NOTAMs (notices to airmen) before the intelligence officer (there's that proverbial oxymoron again) got up to do his update.

'Thank you, Sir. Good morning, gents. Most of you would now be aware that in the early hours of this morning, 75 Squadron head-quarters came under attack from a company-size force of Kamarian special forces.'

YGTBSM! I thought. Special—yes. But not in the generally

accepted military meaning of the word—my thigh was a testament to that.

'The night shift, led by TVH, were successful in defending against the attack which included both direct and indirect fire against the headquarters building, simulator building and flight line diner.'

What bullshit—we hadn't got a round off. We had popped up like rabbits in the headlights and hightailed it, and I had then attempted to give myself a vasectomy before hopping 10 kilometres home. I started to see how the intelligence cycle really worked. Military intelligence is simply the process of transforming the fantasies of desire into reality.

The intelligence officer kept going on with his citation for the award of Victoria Cross: 'TVH then led a quick-reaction force that was able to isolate elements of the force and came very close to capturing one of the special forces soldiers.'

The fighter pilots went mental. *Whoo! Rahhh!* They really believed this shit. I was laughing too, hysterically, just not at the superhuman efforts of the gangsta rappers who had tried to subdue me by yelling smack at me. My thigh started throbbing as I went red in the face from laughter, though I sobered up slightly when I realised I hadn't checked if I'd washed the black cam paint from behind my ears.

That day I was on Alert 15, which was going to be hard given how little sleep I'd had during 'the night of a thousand cuts'. Additionally, JP had chastised us all after Seagull (you had to throw stones at the guy to make him want to fly) had fallen asleep at the controls during one of the recent night shifts. When the shift change came, they couldn't wake Seagull over the radio and they couldn't safely approach the aircraft until he had cleared them. If they approached the aircraft without a clearance, the ground personnel could be sucked into a jet engine or hit by a moving flight control. So they called him and called him on the radio for half an hour before the replacement crew rocked the jet by hanging from the wingtip missiles. Seagull's helmet started bouncing off the inside of the canopy and he eventually woke. No surprises there, I thought. If you want your guys to practise bleeding by sitting in running jets all night so some blunt in Canberra can get his rocks off, you're going to have guys fall asleep— especially given the fear induced by the mushroom-shooting fairy jets that they may be scrambled to intercept.

I got to my jet and the pilot signalled me to approach. I lowered the ladder, pulled myself up like a one-legged rock climber, changed over the memory unit that had all his mission data on it for my memory unit with my data, and changed the videos. The pilot then gave me a quick update on the status of the jet, including fuel and avionics, and then we swapped positions. I checked the ejection seat was safe before I (gingerly) lowered myself in, so that if I inadvertently pulled the handle while strapping in (which has been done), I would not violently launch myself into the hangar roof above. Once seated, I immediately plugged in my helmet lead and checked in with my mechanic who was plugged in below. I then went through the task of 'strapping a jet on', which is exactly how it feels.

First the survival raft is clipped on, then the G suit hose is attached. Next come the gaiters, which attach to the bottom of your legs and stop your legs getting caught in the airstream during high-speed ejections. Then come the lap straps, shoulder straps, negative-G strap—all adjusted as tightly as you can get them. The helmet liner goes on next to absorb sweat, followed by the helmet, the oxygen mask, adjusted left and right, visor down to look cool and stop the wind blowing your eyeballs out in a high-speed ejection, gloves on and finally your kneeboard, with all your mission data in hard copy, wraps around your right thigh.

After strapping in, I quickly ran through my 'left to rights' to check every switch—and there are a few in the Hornet—was in its right place. Then the navigation data was checked, correct airspace, correct frequencies loaded, identification friend or foe (IFF) codes. My radar was next—scan widths, heights, pulse repetition radio frequency (PRF), tracking modes, special modes—followed by weapons, including air-to-air and air-to-ground, chaff and flare programs set to defeat the magic mushroom missiles . . .

'Blackbird, scramble, scramble, scramble,' came booming into my helmet.

YGTBSM! Not today—I've only got one leg. I'll have to turn left at the first merge, I thought, because my right leg wasn't going to be able to push the rudder pedal. This was unbelievable. We'd been sitting alert for two weeks with not one of us going flying and now we were going? Against what? Oh yeah, that's right—the fairy jets. This exercise was not about air-to-air, it was about bleeding for the dickhead blunt in Canberra. This was a test to see if the chicken stranglers could take us out while taxiing off. Prior to the exercise the special forces guys had posted us a very nice black and white 10-by-8-inch glossy picture of one of our pilots with a set of cross hairs on his head. It was meant as a warning. Well, I was going to take it as it was meant.

I was parked next to TVH, who gave me the wind-up signal to start the left engine. After start we did a final run-through of our mission systems to make sure that the second generator had not thrown a stray zero into the mission computer, and then we taxied. Determined not to be shot by our friendly neighbourhood chicken stranglers, I lowered my seat all the way to the floor and hunched forwards so that my head was below the side of the cockpit. I used my forward-looking infrared (FLIR) pod display as a heads-down display to track my nose wheel on the centreline and occasionally scanned up to make sure I wouldn't run into the back of my lead. I managed to keep my head down all the way until lining up on the runway, when my lead looked across and saw my jet was missing its pilot. I imagined the sniper commentary:

'Two aircraft entering the taxiway left to right.'

'Contact.'

'Target is second aircraft. Wind, left to right, 5 knots, range 800 metres.'

'Eight hundred metres set.'

'Call ready.'

'Hey, mate, there's no fucking pilot in that second jet . . .'

TVH and I were lined up ready to take on the marauding hordes of Kamarian fairy jets when the knobber from Canberra got involved again: 'Blackbird, this is the tower, scramble cancelled, return to Alert 15 status.'

Noooooooo! I swore I would track that dickhead down one day, and kill him.

At the end of the disaster otherwise known as Exercise Kangaroo '94, the CO hosted a large party in the hangar for all participants, which the pilots really weren't because we had essentially sat on our arses for a month and burnt fuel without achieving a single training objective—other than my personal lesson in how not to leap razor wire.

Stories came out at the party, including how a female switchboard operator had been sitting outside the base communications centre when she thought she heard a noise and so flicked the switch for the outdoor security spotlights. She caught four genuine special-operations guys cutting their way through the perimeter fence. The teenage girl opened fire with her blanks, rang the alarm and the entire ground defence force descended on these four guys. In true 'who dares wins' style, the SAS boys jumped in their tricked-up Landrover and floored it—straight through every security checkpoint the base had—and threw in a few flashbangs for fun.

Without the traditional war stories that come at the end of an exercise, most of the fighter pilots just got pissed—depressed that switchboard operators were now the 'defenders of the realm'. After a couple of beers to drown our sorrows, Chuck and I jumped into my 'bull catcher', which was parked out the front of the hangar next to an F-18.

When I started the engine Chuck began egging me on: 'Smoke it up, mate. Come on, Serge, smoke it up.'

'No, mate. The CO's just there with all the honchos and the NCOs. I can't or . . .'

'Mate, I'll tell the CO that I ordered you to do it,' Chuck said.

So, as if all the frustration of the last month entered my right foot, I let it rip.

'Hold on, mate,' I said, as I locked the steering wheel and let the back wheels break into an almighty howl right next to the F-18, across the flight line and down the street. The only sound louder than the tyres was whoops and yells from the troops as two of their fearless leaders set an upstanding example for them. The adrenaline was pumping again as we took off around the corner, and I was laughing so hard I could hardly breathe.

'Haa haa, mate, haa haa, that was so fucking funny. The CO, haa haa is going to fucking kill us, haaa haaaa.' I looked at Chuck in the hope he would reiterate his offer of defending me from the CO only to find he was gone. With adrenaline now spiking coldly through my veins, I felt my heart stop as I looked into my rear-vision mirror, only to see the lifeless silhouette of Chuck strewn across the road behind me. There was no movement. Move, dammit! As awful as it was for me to accept it, it had happened. I had thrown my best mate out of the bull catcher and probably run over him with the back wheels.

I swung the car around as quickly as I could and raced back to him. When I arrived, he didn't move or speak. There was blood all over his forehead and he just kept making a noise that was somewhere between moaning, whimpering and drooling. Now, the latter noise was something Chuck did on most Friday nights; however, the amount of blood and the lack of movement had me seriously worried. I got down next to him and held his shoulder.

'Mate, can you move?' I asked.

'Urrrgggghhhhh,' was Chuck's reply.

'Mate, move your feet.'

'Urrrgggghhhhh.'

Shit, I had turned my best mate into a window licker. 'Chuck, talk to me. Say something!'

'Urrrgggghhhhh.'

I was swept with emotion—guilt, fear, sadness, loss. Fuck! 'Chuck, can you sit up, mate?' I pleaded.

'Urrrgggghhhhh. My hand.'

Relief! He could talk—though he might still like the taste of glass. I eventually coached him into sitting up and then helped him to his feet. He kept making the noise which I started to think was more about him being too pissed to speak than being brain dead. His head and arm did look bad, so I loaded him into the car to drive him to the base hospital. On the way he broke through the alcohol-induced mantra, insisting that I take him back to the officers mess. Not wanting to cause an aneurysm I agreed, providing he let me tend to his wounds when we got back.

On arrival at the mess I broke out my first-aid kit and washed his forehead. It looked like he had rolled out the door, braced his fall with his hand and then rolled onto his head. Not being fully qualified in the treatment of head trauma, I told Chuck I had some painkillers from a surgery I had recently undergone and supplied him the maximum dose. He took them, lay on his bed and immediately passed out. I was so worried I sat with him for ages, cleaning his wounds, applying antiseptic and making sure he kept breathing. Eventually I felt more confident that he would survive and went to bed myself in the adjacent room—leaving the door open in the hope of hearing him if he needed anything.

In the morning I woke with the jagged memory of my last conscious moments and rushed to Chuck's room. The door was shut so I knocked . . . and knocked . . . and knocked. No answer. I then remembered I had played doctors and nurses with Chuck and ran back into my room to read the label of whatever I had given him. And there it was: 'not to be taken with alcohol.'

Shit! Once wasn't enough—I had killed him twice. I half-broke the door down to find his bed empty, the sheets strewn all over the place and blood all over the sheets. Fuck! He did have an aneurism. He died in his sleep from the Friday night cocktail of Jack Daniels and prescription-strength painkillers and someone else had found him. I raced out of his room and was on my way to medical when Chuck walked in the front door.

'Hey, Serge. What the fuck happened last night?' He was talking, and walking, and not tasting the windows. Praise the Lord.

'You're OK? Where have you been?' I asked, breathless with relief.

'I just went up to grab some fat for breakfast. Great night last night, wasn't it?'

'Shit, mate, you scared me. I thought you were brain dead last night when you fell out of the truck . . .'

'Is that what happened to me? I was wondering where I'd lost that bark off my melon.'

We laughed for an hour as I rebuilt the events of the previous night for him.

Monday morning the CO stood up at morning brief. 'I'd like to see Evel Knievil and his driver straight after this in my office.'

Chuck and I waited outside his office until he called us in.

'You two, get in here.'

We walked in and stood at attention.

'Chuck, are you OK?'

'Never better, boss.'

'Right, well get out of here.'

We both turned to go.

'Not you, Serge, you can stay right where you are!'

Chuck left and with him my only defence—weak as it was—about being ordered to lay my rubber by a senior officer.

'If I ever hear of you hurting another one of my pilots with a harebrained antic like you pulled on Friday night, I'll fucking shoot you. Are we clear?'

The scary thing was that this CO owned and regularly used a very large arsenal of guns—somehow his threat seemed quite real.

12

The octagon of death

RAAF BASE TINDAL is home to No. 75SQN, Australia's most combat-ready squadron, which deployed to the Middle East at the start of the Iraq War. The high level of readiness is not so much due to good planning from the blunts in Canberra as to the environment Tindal provides the young pilots—unlimited airspace and no chicks. So what did we do with our spare time? We trained hard.

Fighting hard in the Hornet involves continual study to understand the academic side of aerial combat prior to practising the tactics. Aerial combat is a true art and a science—a science to understand and an art to execute. Like Sun Tzu calls it, 'the art of war'. During the 90s scientists performed some studies on UK fighter pilots to map their brain activity during aerial combat. The study found that fighter pilots predominately used the left side of their brains while starting, taxiing, taking off and flying to the airspace. Once established in the airspace, much to the scientists' amazement, the fighter pilots' brains appeared to switch over to the right, or creative side, of the brain when they were engaged in dogfights. It would appear that scorching around at the speed of sound with eight times your body weight strapped to a couple of 7200-kilogram blowtorches is quite artistic.

The other part of fighting hard in the Hornet is the practice. We would generally fly once a day for one hour and talk about that one hour for another twelve: two hours to plan, one hour to brief, one hour of pre-flight administration, one hour to fly, one hour to review video tapes, three hours to debrief and then another three hours in the bar to really work out what the fuck we had done. That was how we squeezed the most out of the $75 000 for each hour that we flew. With all of the academic preparation and debriefing that goes into each hour, a RAAF Hornet pilot is lucky if he cracks 200 hours of flying per year, which his airline pilot mates laugh at when they regularly log 900 hours per year in a little over 50 days of work.

And after practising, there is only one philosophy we live by: Never give up. Ever. In fact it is part of the 'Wingman's Creed', which we were taught during initial formation training:

Mustard, mud, shit or blood,
Grit your teeth and stay there.

The saying came from the trenches of WWI and I often wondered if my great-grandfather John, who fought in the Somme and was shot through the head yet continued to fight, had lived by it also.

Never giving up means never getting shot. Getting shot during training is easily assessed with an electric jet like the Hornet. The radar tracks an aircraft and the mission computer uses navigational models to determine if a missile hits or misses the target. The way to survive is to never be in a position to be shot at. If you are, never let the bandit get a radar lock. If he does, you've got to break the lock. If you can't, degrade the radar lock with chaff which is an expendable store made up of millions of aluminium-coated glass fibres designed to confuse the enemy radar. If you're out of chaff, descend into terrain. If you don't have spare altitude below you, manoeuvre hard.

If you have no airspeed, trade your altitude for a tight manoeuvre. If you have no altitude, chaff, airspeed or fuel, then you're an idiot and deserve to be shot.

When I was on my second tour at 75SQN I was pissed off that a couple of weak pilots (lemons) were getting shot on the majority of missions but hiding it in the noise of the busy squadron routine. This really got under my skin, because your wingman is your best defence in combat. In other words, you're more likely to be killed in combat if you've got a lemon on your wing. I often joked that if I was ever unfortunate enough to find myself airborne in a combat zone with one of those wallies, the first call I would make would be 'Magpie, break right' to my wingman, then promptly select a heat-seeker and accelerate the outcomes of the ensuing fight for them. Better to fight alone than to be hampered by incompetence.

I decided to develop a weapons board and annual competition for the squadron's Top Bomb, Top Shot and overall Best Weapons prize. I did this in the hope that it would start driving some self-respect into these lemons—and because of the fact that I had a particularly overdeveloped competitive streak, just like most of the other non-lemons in the squadron. As part of the competition, for one year every pilot had to complete mission report cards which logged the number of kills taken against the number of times they were killed and the results of their bombs.

After a couple of weeks into the program the XO (executive officer), JP, called me into his office to ask me stop the competition because he was worried it was getting too serious and might lead to an accident. I begged him not to and told him that I would make sure the guys flew within the rules and did not compromise safety. I knew he was telling the truth about the risk, as my normally overdeveloped competitive 'streak' had grown into a complete competitive 'paint job'—particularly against two of the other senior pilots, TVH and Simmo.

Between TVH, Simmo and myself, the weapons competition started ballooning out our days as we insisted on reviewing each other's weapon videotapes to make sure no one was cheating. Watches were cued, TV contrasts adjusted, volumes maximised in the hope we would find a fault in each other's shots. TVH and Simmo were absolute guns and the weapons prize was going to be very hard for me to win. Despite being of equivalent experience and great mates, relationships started to get strained. We kept our disagreements between us, to hide from the XO the fact that we had totally ignored his request. It was time to get serious. It was time for the 'octagon of death'.

The octagon of death was a particular fight set-up between three pairs of fighters. Each pair starts outside non-adjacent edges of the octagon and collects points by killing other bandits and/or flying out through the opposite gate where they would be in a safe sanctuary. Each pair could lose points by being shot, whereby they would have to exit the octagon to regenerate. What made the fight incredibly difficult was the octagon was only 30 kilometres across and you were only allowed to shoot heat-seeking missiles. This meant you could be shooting your opponent (or be being shot at) very soon after entering the octagon, merging with your opponent within 30 seconds. Worse than that, you could only engage one pair at a time, which meant the other pair were free to engage you. This air-combat quandary led to many crew room tactics discussions.

TVH: 'I'm going to come in at 50 000 feet (15 000 metres) and Mach 1.5 and shoot you guys before I enter the octagon.'

Simmo: 'That's crap, TVH. You can't squeeze the trigger until you're through your gate.'

Me: 'Let him try it, Simmo. I'm going to come in at 250 feet (75 metres)—he won't even see me but I bet he'll be conning[5] like a big dog.'

Simmo: 'Fine, we'll just skirt around the octagon until you guys start shooting each other and then we'll shoot you all.'

This is where 75SQN had its advantage. The airspace allowed us to fly as high, low or fast as we could go while dispensing chaff, flares and jamming electronics. And in the middle of this you could employ any high-explosive weapon or laser. Tindal was a fighter pilot's heaven and would evoke comments from visiting US pilots such as 'Is this really legal?' and 'What about the folk who live out there?' Once they arrived and looked out of their canopies, they found the answer themselves. This was the GAFA—great Australian fuck all (just another quick FLA).

So with our trusty titanium steeds, the world's best fighting airspace, and squadron mates overly keen to shoot each other, we entered the octagon of death. My brief to my wingman, Slime, had been simple: 'Keep your eyes on me so you don't get caught up in the green shit. Don't hit me or shoot me. Shoot anything your radar locks or your eyeballs see, and if I'm not talking about what you're shooting then tell me about it.'

I entered the gate and immediately turned away from the opposite gates and commenced an aggressive descent at high G. This would slow down the intercept and give me time to visually acquire the other jets while reducing their ability to shoot us.

Looking sideways over my shoulder I strained to see the other jets, did a quick scan to check Slime had matched my turn and was abeam me, checked my altitude, speed and radar warning receiver (RWR) on the HUD to determine if the bandit's radar was locked on us, dispensed some chaff to degrade their radar locks, then looked back to the bandits' last known position . . . tally.

I transmitted to Slime 'Magpie 1, tally 2, left nine o'clock high, 8 miles.'

The opposing aircraft had also performed a turning manoeuvre away from us but by doing so provided a large platform for us to visually acquire. Anticipating their radar losing lock once their turn away was complete, I initiated a 6G turn back towards them, pointed the radar into the turn, dispensed some more chaff to defeat any unseen radars and selected a Sidewinder missile that would hopefully lock onto their exhaust plumes before we had even completed our turn.

'Magpie 2, tally 2, sorted side.' Slime said.

Fantastic—he could now see both jets and was targeting his weapons onto the righthand man. I targeted mine to the left and had a quick look for the other pair that were out there somewhere, like sharks circling for survivors. Then, like a spanner hitting me in the back of the head, my RWR burst to life. '*Beep beep beep beep beep beep*'.

I had been locked up by the untargeted bandits and a weapon was being slaved onto me at that exact moment. The adrenaline surged through my veins like lightning and the art of war started.

'Magpie 1 spiked, 2 press.' I performed an 8G break away from the enemy radar, dispensed more chaff, watched Slime flash above me as he headed to engage the first pair, while trying to get my eyes onto the second pair.

'Magpie 2, Fox 2 eastern bandit, Fox 2 western.' Slime had a heat-seeker enroute to each of the first two aircraft. Awesome—first beer is on me, Slime, once I get my eyes on these other two pricks . . . SHIT!

'Magpie 1, engaged defensive.' I had lost spatial awareness during the turn away from the untargeted pair and wasn't looking in the right piece of sky. Instead of turning up off my wingtip where I had been looking, I detected a slight movement out of the corner of my eye that caused me to crank my head around 180 degrees only to find two large jet intakes pointing at me like fangs on a wolf. Looking backwards at high G is physically difficult because your head and helmet weigh up to eight times their normal weight, which is literally equivalent to someone sitting on your head. You struggle to keep your head up but to lose sight means to lose the fight. And I wasn't about to let that happen.

I unloaded the G to zero, such that I was briefly floating in my seat against my lap straps with my helmet pinned to the canopy. This would momentarily break his gun line by upsetting the lead calculations on his weapons computer which feed his gunsight. It would also allow me to perform a maximum-rate aileron roll onto my back. I selected idle thrust and punched out some flares to prevent a heat-seeking missile being shot up my date and then slammed the stick straight back into my guts in order to fly under him. With my tailpipe pointing away from him again, I lit the burners and felt the punch in my lower back as they both ignited.

'Magpie 2, shot lost western. Kill on the eastern.' Slime was on fire. He had killed one of the first pair but probably had his second shot defeated by flares.

'Magpie 2, yo-yo', I called, meaning 'you're on your own', as I could no longer see nor support Slime. Right now, I was a little busy as the wolf started following me through my bail-out manoeuvre.

It was then I got a fleeting glance of my bandit's wingman who was orbiting over the fight like a hawk waiting for some roadkill to be provided by the impending accident—dumb-arse. I could see the shot before he did. I gently eased the G off to prevent bleeding all my speed while pitching up to get a radar lock and then a good missile lock. Trigger, squeeze. Good shot.

'Magpie 1, Fox 2 free bandit, western fight. Magpie 2 status.' I had a heat-seeking shot away on the lazy hawk overhead and wanted an update on my wingman's progress. I was hoping he was being the 'Ace from Aerospace' in the east as I needed some help—the engaged bandit had followed me neatly through my aggressive bail-out manoeuvre, matched my flight path, and I had given away some advantage to him by pitching up to shoot his wingman. This bandit was on his game—it was TVH or Simmo for sure. OK, this fight just got a little more personal.

'Magpie 2, engaged offensive in the east.' Slime was manoeuvring for guns on his remaining bandit.

We can still recover from this, I thought. I just need to survive a little longer until my wingman dispenses his justice in the east and gets his arse over here to save me. My bandit was positioning for guns and his fangs were out again. The loafing hawk had seen me late, but not late enough, and dispensed a flare while pitching down and into me to drive the range inside of the minimum range of my Sidewinder. Damn!

'Magpie 1, shot lost on free fighter in the west.'

I couldn't continue uphill towards the hawk any longer with the wolf about to shoot. The hawk had now flown down at me but I was too close to shoot him with a missile in the face. I performed another bail-out manoeuvre which drove the wolf off, and then delayed my pull-down until the dumb hawk had passed me in the vertical and flown into my gunsight. I was now offensive on the free fighter in a daisy chain across the bottom of the loop: free fighter (not so free now, dumb-arse), then me and then the wolf. This was getting ridiculous and the hard deck of 1500 metres, the imaginary ground level that we used for safety, was fast approaching; not to mention the fact that I only had one missile left, few flares and not much fuel.

'Magpie 1, daisy chain in the west—defensive.'

'Magpie 2, guns kill F-18, righthand turn, 11 000 (3400 metres).'

'Blackbird 1 acknowledges.'

Awesome—Slime had just cleaned up both bandits in the east. Unfortunately I wasn't having as much luck in the west. At 1200 metres I started to ease out of loop so I wouldn't hit the hard deck— 1499 metres in the HUD would be a hard-deck kill, something else I wasn't going to give TVH or Simmo the pleasure of doing to me.

The bandit, however, was not about to let me ease out of my turn and started to again bear his fangs for a gun attack. With an ability to shoot 6000 high-explosive supersonic grenades per minute, he only required half a second of 'pipper on' to kill me (50 rounds). I had to keep moving my jet until my wingman got here.

'Magpie 2 status,' I transmitted to Slime, asking him to tell me how far away he was.

'Magpie 2 just inside eastern gate, 17000 (5000 metres), joker.' That was not good. He was at least 90 seconds away and I wasn't going to last that long. He was also approaching his minimum recovery fuel.

I sprayed some rounds in the direction of the hawk in front of me but with the wolf behind me I couldn't stabilise long enough for the weapons computers to provide a high probability of kill. Then Betty, my onboard computer, started bitching at me.

'Bingo, bingo.' Bitching Betty was letting me know I was less than one minute from reaching my minimum fuel to return to base (RTB). I deselected afterburner to reduce my fuel flow—and increase my time of survival—and reached in to reset the fuel bug to my minimum RTB fuel. Quickly scanning between the wolf behind me, my altitude of 1800 metres and airspeed of 500 kilometres per hour in the HUD, and the fuel bug near my left knee, I was starting to run out of ideas. Like Goose said to Maverick in *Top Gun*, it was 'time to do some of that pilot shit.'

The wolf must have also been getting close to minimum fuel as he had matched me so closely through the fight. My wingman couldn't save me, he was too far away. I needed to survive for the next 60 seconds by myself with no fuel, no flares, no altitude or airspeed. It was then I saw it . . . a thin layer of stratus cloud just below me.

With hope that the cloud was not below the hard deck of 1500 metres, I eased the jet down and started to sink into the soup. This was easy to do flying at 300 kilometres per hour and 35 degrees angle of attack. Losing sight of both the bandits behind and in front, my RWR went silent, telling me the wolf had lost his lock on me. At the minimum flying speed of 300 kilometres per hour, I performed the best turn I could through 90 degrees from the direction the bandit last saw me heading into the cloud and set full military power.

'Magpie 2, bingo.'

'Magpie, Blackbird, Condor, knock it off.' I transmitted to end the fight.

'Magpie 2, knock it off.'

'Blackbird 1, knock it off.'

'Blackbird 2, knock it off.'

'Condor 1, knock it off.'

'Condor 2, knock it off.'

We'd done it. I had survived the octagon of death but with no kills. Slime had survived with two kills—legend!

In the debrief it turned out that it had indeed been TVH on my tail. He said all sorts of things in an attempt to claim a hard-deck kill on me. Simmo later critically reviewed Slime's tape into the evening hours, claiming he had flared appropriately to defeat Slime's shot. In the end, like always, we went to the bar as mates and continued our tactical discussions on how to approach the octagon of death.

So that's what I mean by fighting hard. Fighting to the limits of your body. Fighting to the limits of the airframe. Fighting to the limits of your air-combat knowledge. Fighting for your wingman like he's your brother.

Continual practice, discipline, grit and determination was how we honed our skills. By constantly throwing ourselves at each other and at the ground, living up to each other's expectations but never our own, we formed a unique and tight bond. Only a few years later these bonds would serve our fighter pilots well when 75SQN deployed to Iraq and the surface-to-air missiles (SAMs) were no longer simulated. To paraphrase Bruce Willis in *Die hard*, YKYMF Magpies!

That year I won the 75SQN weapons prize and my inadequacies finally started to die—I was starting to believe in myself. It was thanks to guys like TVH and Simmo, who pushed me beyond my limits and enabled me to develop my skills to the level I did. And over the course of that same year, the lemons were eventually exposed and quietly moved out of the unit. To this day the weapons competition continues at 75SQN and the squadron, along with Australia's submarine and Special Forces units, remains one of Australia's top-three strategic capabilities.

13
The Cannonball Run

Spook was our exchange pilot from the United States Marine Corps (USMC). Every two years Australia would send an F-18 pilot to the USMC and they would reciprocate. For a marine the 75SQN and the home of the Magpies was a good gig. For single Marines, however, the middle of the Northern Territory could take some getting used to.

Spook and I formed a close bond early on and shared a common interest in practical jokes and generally elevating squadron morale—the difference between Spook and I, though, was that he had diplomatic immunity and I didn't.

I think Spook's issue was that he was highly intelligent and a little bored just hanging out in Tindal—so he would do things to keep himself entertained. On one occasion Spook used an ink pad to paint the inside of Duck's oxygen mask, so that Duck came back from a flight with a giant red stain around his nose and chin. Duck walked into the squadron unable to see what the rest of the unit was in hysterics about, but soon worked it out.

Spook also had the executive officer (XO) firmly in his sights. JP had previously completed the USMC exchange which we believed had fucked him up and caused him to become anally retentive—a trait I admired but it really got under Spook's skin. Spook started out with little things like tampering with JP's email when he wasn't in his office. I remember well when an email hit the inbox of every individual in the entire squadron—1500 of JP's subordinates:

From: SQNLDR JP Conlan, XO75SQN
Subject: I'm coming out of the closet

Fellow Magpies,

I can no longer hide my true feelings and wish to inform you all that I am gay. I look forward to your continued support.

JP

This got the reaction Spook anticipated but, like an attention-seeking child, he didn't let up; in fact, the practical jokes escalated. He got a handful of small prawns, removed the ends of the curtain rod in JP's office and filled the rod with prawns. Needless to say, a week later the XO couldn't work in his office nor could he find the source of the smell. Assuming some sort of land-walking desert prawn infestation, he called the pest removalist who soon found the cause.

Next was 'upside-down day' for the XO. Spook spent an entire weekend rearranging JP's office so that everything was upside-down. Pictures were rehung, filing cabinets, desks and computers turned over—the lot. It was having to spend his next weekend re-filing all his paperwork that had fallen out when the filing cabinet was turned upside-down that really ticked JP off.

With the XO in a foul mood, Spook could no longer own up to his escapades for fear of being deported back to the States. He thought it best to lay low for a couple of days, so we signed out the CO's new red V6 Commodore and headed to Darwin for the weekend.

Until recently the Northern Territory of Australia was the last great bastion for red-blooded rev heads. With long (1000-kilometre) straight roads and no speed limit, the Territory was a fantastic place for straight line speed and was briefly home to Australia's Cannonball Run. Sheiks, sportstars and billionaires from all around the world would converge on Darwin for one week a year, bringing with them some of the world's most expensive sportscars: Dodge Vipers, Porsche GTs, Ferraris and Lambos would all be paraded on the Stokes Wharf early Sunday morning before the race.

Spook and I thought we would watch the start of the race before we headed back to Tindal. We met some of the drivers and had a lengthy drool over the cars before the pits were closed and the vehicles prepared to depart. The competitors departed at two-minute intervals and after about half an hour Spook had seen enough, so we went back to our car and started heading south ourselves. What we didn't realise was that the Cannonball route was not closed to other vehicles and competitors were bound by the normal city speed limits until they got out of town where speed was unlimited. As such, we unintentionally ended up with a Dodge Viper in front of us and a Ferrari behind. Spook was driving and took one look at me with his big shit-eating grin and I knew what he was thinking.

As soon as we were out of the city, Spook floored it. He wound the CO's car out to 220 kilometres per hour, which was as high as the speedo read.

'I'm sure we can win this first leg of the Cannonball to Katherine, Serge—what do you say?' he asked in his Detroit accent.

Gripping the sides of my seat with white knuckles, and the middle of my seat with my seriously puckered arse, I agreed—we would either win it or die. It was that simple.

Spook was overtaking cars like they were standing still. I'm not sure if it was because the drivers weren't professional, or possibly because they weren't maniac fighter pilots like Spook, but we were taking a lot of places and no-one had yet passed us. Then we saw a police car that was acting as a safety car for the race. I looked at Spook and he grinned back.

We screamed past the police car in excess of 220 kilometres per hour and I took a photo of the stunned officer. Spook checked the mirrors for flashing lights. Nothing.

'Dude, he thinks we're one of them,' he said. And that was it—we were in the race we weren't officially competing in.

Darwin to Katherine is about 350 kilometres. A Commodore can normally achieve about 500–600 kilometres per tank. Less than an hour into the race, we were nearly out of gas—although we had travelled 200 kilometres in that hour. We briefed for the pit stop and Spook screamed into the petrol station, locking up the wheels as we arrived. I was out first, running to the pump. Spook had already popped the fuel lid. I had the nozzle in and was pumping as Spook went in and threw some cash on the counter. He grabbed a couple of drinks, told the attendant to keep the change, got back into the car, started the engine and revved the shit out of it as I was hanging up the hose. As I stepped into the car he floored it—almost leaving me on my arse. We had done our pit stop in under three minutes and only lost one position in the race.

Spook left a trail of dirt and stones as he fishtailed the CO's car back out on to the Stuart Highway. He soon locked onto the car in front of us—it was the police car again. Surely we couldn't do this again and get away . . . *Vrooooom*—we passed that cop car like it was standing still.

Then Spook started to reel in more of the competitors. Porsches, Lambos, muscle cars—you name it, we passed it. We lost count of how many we overtook—but nothing passed us between Darwin and Katherine.

Coming into Katherine it was like driving down the Bathurst straight—hundreds of people lined both sides of the highway. Spook kept his foot on the gas and the CO's Commodore screamed its head off at red-line. As we hit the 100-kilometre per hour zone Spook stayed on the gas. People were leaning out with video cameras as Spook manoeuvred so that we were travelling down the centre of the road. We could see the people cheering but could hear nothing other than the V6 whining its head off. We hit the 80-kilometre per hour zone before Spook started to back off below 220. Up ahead we saw lights flashing and shit ourselves. Cops, we thought; if they had a radar gun Spook would have been over three times the speed limit—he'd lose his licence for sure. And then we saw what the lights were all about.

It was a marshal point where cars were being herded to the competitors' paddock and the media was waiting with beers and grid girls. We were wishing aloud that we could get into the VIP area to continue our racing careers when the marshal's hand went up and he directed us straight to the competitors' paddock. We played it as cool as we could, but with all the adrenaline still flowing in our veins we couldn't hold back our chuckles.

We were actually being marshalled to the podium where the first five place-getters were to be awarded a prize. We had left Darwin 30 minutes into the race and had placed fifth on the Darwin-to-Katherine leg. We were so stoked until the judge asked us for our number. Shit. Spook tried his best to use his diplomatic immunity, but we were quietly ushered out of the competitors' paddock.

Oh well. Spook and I might not have the piece of paper, but we were satisfied we were the true fifth place-getters in that leg of the Cannonball Run.

Monday morning was just another day and the XO seemed to have settled down a bit over the weekend. At the end of the morning brief the CO made a few comments and finished off with a request: 'That's all I have, thanks. If I can just see Ayrton Senna and his navigator in my office after brief, please.'

The CO called us into his office where we remained standing in front of his desk. 'Unit' was a wildcard. He could be a great guy one day and an absolute gun-toting cowboy the next. We just hoped he was in a good mood.

'OK, boys. I have a report from the military police here stating that my car was in the Cannonball Run over the weekend. Is that true?'

Spook and I looked at each other and I searched my mind nervously for what the ramifications of our little unscheduled international motor race might be. Spook just looked like a smug diplomat about to claim immunity.

'Serge,' the CO continued, 'you seem to be the most lost for words—spit it out.'

'Well, Sir,' I replied cautiously, 'Spook and I drove back from Darwin at the same time as the Cannonball Run and unfortunately got caught up in the race traffic. We definitely did not enter your car in the race, Sir.'

'Right, good answer. Because the military police have a video of a red Commodore that looks a lot like my car which was filmed racing yesterday.'

This is not good, I thought—we were fucked.

The CO went on: 'I asked to see the tape and could not read the numberplate due to the speed of the car so I told them to go fuck themselves unless they've got some proof. OK?'

'Yes, Sir,' we both said.

'Now, can either of you dickheads tell me the maximum speed for a service vehicle?'

'The signed speed?' I hesitantly answered.

'No. It's 120 kilometres per hour regardless of the maximum stated speed. So, in future, don't be racing my fucking car in the Cannonball Run . . . and I hope you filled it up.'

'Yes, Sir. Three times actually,' Spook stated proudly.

'Right, get out of here, you two, and don't talk about this to anyone.'

'Yes, Sir,' we replied and promptly marched out of his office.

The boss had stood by us. Without knowing the who, the what or the why, he went into bat for his boys. He endeared himself immensely to both Spook and I that day, and in the future I always did my best to look out for him. True loyalty is earned, not bestowed by rank.

14

On steel horses
we ride

WHEN YOU GET around at 2000 kilometres per hour for your day job, it can become just a little frustrating jumping into your Hyundai at the end of the day and trying to be patient in traffic. Most knuckle-heads will go through a phase of fast cars or motorbikes and lose a significant amount of their income to speeding fines.

I had wanted a motorcycle for years and while I trusted myself to ride safely, I was worried about the other morons who I was forced to share the road with, not to mention the wildlife in the Northern Territory such as cattle and donkeys. Eventually I compromised and settled for a limited edition 1981 Harley Davidson Sturgis.

Spook also had a 'hog' and we would enjoy riding to and from work together as well as along the Adelaide River Road to Darwin on weekends—a rider's dream with long, gently winding scenic roads. Flange soon arrived at 75 Squadron with his custom-painted Harley and we had three bad-arse road warriors in our outlaw motorcycle club. Soon we were sporting skeleton face masks, ridiculous German army helmets and leather jackets with all of our squadron colours. We figured it wouldn't be long before the local Hell's Angels chapter got wind of our Marauding Magpies.

Honko joined the squadron not long after and for the first time in ages I had a shit-magnet with a stronger magnetic field than myself. Honko was a great guy and remains a good friend after all these years. He never really fit the fighter pilot mould, being short, chubby and incredibly relaxed, with a great sense of humour. He had been at the squadron for only two days when the CO stormed into the operations room.

'Who the fuck has the keys to the other crew van?' he bellowed at the operations officer (OPSO).

'Ahh, it's, umm, the new guy, sir—Honko.'

'Well, that prick just ran me off the road on my way here. He was on my side of the road, driving way too fast with two wheels off the ground—I thought he was going to roll into me. Tell that little shit I want to see him as soon as he gets back!'

I couldn't believe it—finally I was no longer in the boss's sights. And things just got better.

Only a week after the CO had dressed Honko down for his stunt driving, the OPSO received a call from the motor transport section.

'G'day, Sir, this is Sergeant Anal Retentive from motor transport. When your crew van arrives back at 75 Squadron, would you kindly have the driver return our refuelling hose? He drove off with it still in the tank and tore it straight out of our bowser.'

Sure enough, ten minutes later, Honko arrived back at the squadron and proudly signed in the keys to the crew van. 'Hey, Serge. The crew van is back and full of gas.'

He had driven right through base squadron, around the base and into 75 Squadron with 5 metres of refuelling hose dragging behind the van.

I was loving it. Honko was resetting the CO's bullshit tolerance for us all, which meant we'd all be able to fly below the CO's radar.

Honko went on to miss a squadron redeployment because he was on a beach with his girlfriend. Due to redeploy with the squadron from Perth to Tindal after a gunnery camp, Honko was late for brief and no-one had seen him all weekend. Meanwhile, back on Cottesloe Beach . . .

'Honko, I'm really going to miss you when you go.'

'Sorry, babe, but my country needs me.'

'You must really need to be on the ball to fly those amazing jets.'

'Pretty much, babe—comes naturally to the Honk.'

'When did you say you were leaving me again?'

'Not until Monday. You have until then to enjoy all that the Honk has to offer.'

'But today is Monday, Honko, my studmuffin.'

'Faaaaaaaark!' Honko missed the redeployment and was forced to pay for his own commercial flight back to Tindal a couple of days later.

Honko's pièce de résistance, however, was crashing the crew van directly out the front of the Darwin Base. The police were called first, and then the HAZMAT team when they found fuel leaking from the vehicle. They cordoned off the area which left Honko standing on the side of the road in his flying suit while all the Darwin emergency services teams attempted to get the situation under control.

Eventually an observant fireman walked up to the dripping fuel, removed his glove, cupped his hand under the flow, lifted the fluid to his mouth and took a sip.

'Crown Lager, boys. No problems.'

Honko had been ferrying beer around in the crew van which had smashed during the accident and was now leaking out through the floor. The Northern Territory newspaper reported the incident exactly as it occurred, which made the CO even more furious.

At the end of a Darwin deployment, Spook, Flange and I were planning on riding our hogs back to Tindal when Honko waded in for a piece of the action.

'Hey, guys, I was thinking of buying a bike while we're in Darwin, and riding back with you.'

'Do you even have a bike licence, Honko?' asked Spook.

'No, but I was hoping you could run me through it a bit before we go,' Honko replied, without batting an eyelid.

'Mate, I take it you have ridden a bike before?' I asked.

'No, but if you can just run me through the basics . . .'

Honko was serious and when we asked what type of bike he had in mind he straightaway replied that he wanted a Hog. We knew our Tindal chapter of the Marauding Magpies was gaining momentum, with my over-rich carby that could throw 8-foot flames out the exhaust, but Honko was risking his body, his bike, possibly his job and not to mention his life if the CO found out that he had joined an outlaw motorcycle gang as bad as ours without a licence—well, they do call them 'outlaw' for a reason, I guess.

On the Saturday at the end of the deployment we rode our hogs to the Darwin Harley store with Honko on the pillion of Spook's bike. We swaggered into the showroom in all our leathers, like four of the baddest arses the store owner had ever seen, right up until Honko opened his mouth.

'Mate, I like that blue one—what sort of bike is that?' Honko asked, pointing at the brand new Fatboy that was positioned centrally in the store under the spotlight and labelled 'limited edition don't buy me unless you have a shitload of cash'. The salesman's eyes lit up. Clearly here were four Hell's Angels wannabes who didn't even know what a Fatboy was. I could see the dollar signs on his eyeballs.

Without any further ado, Honko handed over his car driver's licence (not sure how that worked) and credit card, and 30 minutes later he was pulling on his brand new Screaming Eagle leather gloves, jacket, helmet and mirrored sunglasses. We asked the salesman if he knew where the nearest tattoo parlour was for our latest gang member and he smiled with a 'I don't give a shit how fucking stupid you all are, I just sold a twenty-grand bike' look.

After checking the fluids and pressures, the salesman wheeled the bike out the front of the store. I think it was here that I had to leave and get on my bike as Honko started asking questions like, 'Where's the brake?', 'Which pedal is for the gears?' and, worst of all, 'How do I start it?'

The salesman started to look seriously concerned despite the afterglow of the greatest sale he'd ever made. 'You have ridden before, haven't you?' he asked.

'Yeah, sure, it's just been a while,' replied Honko with a sufficient coating of bullshit to convince the guy.

With his Motorcycle 101 class complete, the salesman stood to one side as Honko mounted his trusty steed. Honko looked so awkward I felt sorry for him but, you've got to admit, he had balls—walking into a Harley store, buying the best bike there, getting on it and riding away into the sunset, all without ever having ridden a bike before.

We all mounted our steel horses and, with that thousand-yard stare that marks true outlaws, we released our clutches and let the 1000-decibel symphony erupt. I headed off first with Spook right behind me, then Flange and finally . . .

In my rear-view mirror I watched painfully as Honko turned onto the road far too slowly, had an attack of the death wobbles, and dropped his brand new bike on its side and his leg.

We all turned around and got back in time to see the salesman wiping away a tear and helping Honko up. He had broken a mirror, bent the clutch, dented his tank and smashed his indicator. Other than that there was hardly a scratch on it.

The ride back to Tindal was awesome. Four good mates silently enjoying each other's company, and Honko's near-death experiences, riding through one of the most picturesque parts of the planet.

Sadly, our outlaw gang only remained together for about one more year before the despised RAAF posting cycle disrupted it and I was sent back to Williamtown. I reluctantly sold my bike before my departure, convinced there would be too many loonies on the road in Newcastle, even though I knew Honko was staying in Tindal.

15

Flying guinea pigs

EVERY FEW YEARS, pilots are required to undergo an Aviation Medicine Refresher Course (AVMED), which is essentially a course in bleeding—sometimes literally. The course is held at RAAF Base Edinburgh in Adelaide and consists of both theory and practical classes in hypoxia, fatigue, drugs and ejection-seat training. The course hurt more people than real-life incidents ever did, and was subsequently drastically altered; however, I was unfortunate enough to complete a number of 'old school' courses.

One year, the course attendees consisted of two COs from competing fighter squadrons, and about eight pilots from both fighter and non-fighter squadrons. The course ran for a week and was treated with disdain by fighter pilots. For us, the course was just another obstacle that kept us from flying. However, those who weren't fighter pilots tended to take the course very seriously.

During the mandatory lecture on non-prescription drugs, the lecturer outlined the dangers of flying under the influence of different kinds of drugs. Aspirin thins the blood. Aspartane (diet cola) can give you grand mal seizures. Hayfever tablets can act like speed and increase your alertness (funny how a lot of fighter pilots suffered from hay fever).

The doc then went on to explain the risks associated with taking a particular drug which was used in the treatment of mental health patients: 'I'm sure none of you would be familiar with this drug. It is generally used with mental health patients, but you would never want to fly with it as it can cause psychotic episodes, hallucinations and . . .'

'That's bullshit,' interjected one of the fighter COs. 'I've been using that stuff for years and it's never affected me.'

'Sir, you must be mistaken. This drug is not widely prescribed . . .'

'No, he's right,' said the CO of another fighter squadron. 'I've been taking it for years as well, and I've never had a problem. Your slide's in error, boy.'

The junior pilots all glanced at each other with that 'now that explains everything' look on our faces. Both of these COs were known to be at least half-crazy. Perhaps we'd underestimated them.

A day later the doc was lecturing on the dangers of sensory illusions, where the sensory inputs of a pilot do not match the actual flight conditions of the aircraft. The most common of these illusions is 'the leans', where the vestibular system in the inner ear which we use for balance disagrees with what we see. It is often experienced by junior pilots when first flying on instruments and has been the cause of many aviation accidents right throughout history.

'Who can tell me what the leans is?' asked the doc.

A conscientious Hercules copilot down the front, who really felt this course was the highlight of his year, waved his hand around like he was on a game show: 'It's when there is a mismatch between the somatogyral canals and the optic nerve, the result of which can be the pilot incorrectly relying on his vestibular system to fly the aircraft, whereby he ends up in an unusual attitude which can result in an accident.'

'Very good [suckhole]. Now, has anyone here experienced a sensory illusion we haven't mentioned here today?' asked the doc.

'Yeah, I have,' said one of the fighter COs in his normally gruff voice. 'One night when I was flying Mirages, I felt like I was flying around upside-down.'

The junior guys looked at each other as if to say, 'Idiot, the doc has just mentioned the leans.'

'Well, Sir, that would be a case of the leans, which we discussed earlier,' said the doc, doing his best to hide his frustration.

'No, it wasn't the leans. I was flying around and I felt like I was upside-down in the aircraft with my head down near the rudder pedals and my feet up near the canopy. I then felt like I was outside the aircraft, looking in at myself flying the aircraft.'

We all just sat silently, embarrassed for the CO. You could hear a pin drop until one of the Bograts piped up.

'Doc, what was that you were saying about the side-effects of those drugs prescribed for mental health patients?'

The room cracked up.

The ejection seat trainer was literally a pain in the arse. The AVMED staff would place a bloody big explosive charge in an ejection seat that was attached to a rail and tell you how to position yourself so you didn't crack your vertebrae. Each course member would then pull the handle and gamble his career away—getting a cracked vertebra meant the end of your flying days. After years of ruining pilots' careers through these practice runs, the blunts finally figured that they were losing good men for no reason and did away with that part of the training. Let's face it, ejection is just not that hard: you catch on fire, pucker your arse and pull a handle.

The other part of the course that had some risk associated with it was the hypobaric chamber. Here the Dr Strangeloves would peer in at us through a small window as they raised the altitude of the chamber and conducted experiments on us. We were required to take off our masks at 20 000 feet and perform a series of coordination and mental tasks. At the first sign of hypoxia you were meant to put on your oxygen mask before you succumbed to the hypoxia and could no longer fit your own mask. This was always amusing as a peron's response in an oxygen-depleted environment is almost identical to how they behave under the influence of alcohol. Some guys want to fight, some go to sleep, some get randy and some find everything hilarious. I generally just sit in the corner with a shit-eating grin before going to sleep.

Another experiment the blunts do on the aircrew is the C Run, where they simulate an ejection and subsequent freefall. One year I had a slight head cold and brought it to the attention of the doc before entering the chamber. The doc checked my ears and said I'd be fine, so I entered the chamber and started the C run. The explosive depressurisation to 35 000 feet was easy—air can exit your sinuses and ears easily. It is getting the air back in when you can have a problem.

Halfway through the 10 000 feet per minute rapid descent I raised my hand to stop the descent, complaining of strong sinus pain. The doc entered the airlock, equalised the pressure and then opened the door to the main chamber to allow me into the airlock where he could check me. He closed the door to the main chamber where the rest of the guys continued their rapid descent. The doc then grabbed a large airbag that resembled an oversized air horn which had a probe attached to it. He promptly stuffed it into my nose and squeezed the rubber ball in an attempt to reinflate my sinus. He kept us at altitude while he wrestled with the head-inflator. The pain was bearable; however, he was unable to clear it.

When the main chamber was almost to sea level, an over-pressure relief valve, designed to prevent the wall between the airlock and the main chamber imploding, gave way. This had the effect of descending me instantaneously from 20 000 feet to sea level where the main chamber was. My sinus ruptured immediately, which relieved the pain but took me off work for a couple of weeks. Needless to say, like the ejection seat, the C Run is no longer performed at AVMED.

I revisited my chamber experience a few years later while instructing a student who had a head cold. He, too had gone to the doctor to have his cold checked before flying. The doc had given him the all-clear and so off we went.

During the supersonic mach runs my student started to complain about sinus pain, so I took over and climbed the aircraft back up to where the pressure equalised. I restarted the descent and his sinus blocked again, and so we repeated the climb back up. Every time we descended, his pain returned. We continued doing this until we were at an emergency fuel level and had no choice but to descend.

I felt awful listening to my young student scream in pain as his sinus ruptured and blood flooded his oxygen mask. There was nothing I could do, though, as we had to descend because we were running out of fuel. I had the ambulance meet us at the end of the runway and take my student off to medical. He was back-coursed but thankfully graduated six months later.

16
Mining in Townsville

Aerial mining is a highly effective tactic of seeding harbours, rivers and maritime choke points with high-explosive air-dropped bombs to disrupt or destroy opposing maritime forces. The mines are dropped in a checkerboard pattern and fuses can be set to detonate on noise, magnetic detection, seismic disturbance or time—including random times. The effectiveness of aerial mining lies in the psychology of this type of warfare as much as it does in the actual effectiveness of the weapons themselves—the thought of a mine sinking a ship with thousands of sailors onboard can disrupt an opponent's maritime campaign just as much as the weapons actually destroying a ship or two. When dropped across a harbour entrance by low-flying F-18s, 33-pound 'Blue Death' practice bombs can shut a harbour down for as much time as dropping real high-explosive mines—it would be a brave maritime commander who would sail his ships through a minefield, either apparent or real.

Establishing the checkerboard pattern of mines, without GPS guidance, is not as easy as it sounds. Essentially, multiple aircraft must be flown along parallel or perpendicular lines, with the trajectory of the mine accounting for aircraft G, velocity, weapon type, side and vertical ejection velocities of the mine, temperature, humidity, aircraft configuration and a whole range of other things that some geek wearing Coke-bottle glasses has worked out to accurately place the mine. Fortunately for knuckleheads those same weapons geeks designed a really fast calculator for us that tells us where to fly and when the mines should be released—it was called 'mission computer number 2' or the weapons computer. All we had to do was press a few buttons to program it . . . and then hang on.

Despite its effectiveness, aerial mining is rarely practised in the F-18 community, and this form of combat is generally left to the experts in aerial mining—the P-3 Orion community in Adelaide. Trouble was, we were never quite sure how the P-3 would perform in a shooting match against enemy fighters and ground defences that would be defending the same maritime chokepoints. I'm sure there was an expert analyst somewhere in Canberra who had an answer for that one. Probably something like, 'The F-18s will neutralise the enemy fighter base and then the P-3s will mine the harbour.' Not a bad plan, really, I reckon the air combat group could probably give that one a good crack—however, it didn't account for surface-to-air missiles or anti-aircraft artillery on ships nor shore. A slow-flying P-3 was not going to fend too well in this environment, so once the shooting match started the same analyst who said F-18s don't need to mine would probably complete an operational risk management plan to determine that 'the threat environment at the harbour is too high a risk for the P-3 so we had better send the Hornets after all'. I guess the analyst wouldn't have seen that one coming. Well, our squadron fighter combat instructor (FCI), Robbo, could, and so over the next two weeks 75 Squadron set about learning the finer arts of aerial mine laying.

We started by critically assessing the types of boats we were attempting to disrupt or destroy. Essentially, the larger the ship, the greater the size of the squares on your mine checkerboard you could afford and still ensure that the ship couldn't sail through the checker pattern without hitting a mine. We then learnt about different fusing methods employed by the mines and the effective radius of the Mk 82-based mine against different ships. We analysed real-world harbours and ports while preparing mining plans that would be used and stored in the vault for future 'possibilities' that our Canberra-based analyst had not foreseen. We looked at the effects of tide on the depth of the harbours and the subsequent weapon effects we could achieve—sometimes deeper water does more damage than shallow. We studied the acoustic, magnetic and seismic signatures of the ships and how these changed with variations in temperature, salinity and tides. A few of us spent time considering the psychological effects of the mining and how this could be optimised, while others reviewed the Laws of Armed Conflict (LOAC) concerning the mining of waterways and minimising civilian casualties. After a week of preparation it was time to put our theory to the test.

JP set the stage with an operational mission brief that he and Robbo had prepared. Under the guise of supposed real-world operational tasking that he had been warned about two weeks prior, we were to fly a long-range mining mission to Country X and mine their two most strategic harbours. With his impressive briefing style, JP made it appear very real . . . our hearts notched up a beat and we started to wonder whether he was jerking our chains.

Robbo then clarified the situation with the mission brief which was a mining mission to Townsville. The flight would be 1600 kilometres each way (about two hours) and would require an aerial refuel in and out. We would be flying the mission as a twelve-ship formation (three four-ships), releasing twelve bombs each to enable a twelve-by-twelve checkerboard. The enemy harbour was simulated by a weapons range east of Townsville, not far from the Great Barrier Reef. Due to the high number of recreational vessels in the area, the range had been gazetted in the local papers and our airborne range safety officer would ensure no boats were inside the bombing site.

So for the next twelve hours we set about planning the mining mission in fine detail. Duties were divided between the twelve knuckleheads in the mission: navigation data, fuel plan, air-to-air refuelling (AAR) plan, intelligence, weapon plan, air-to-air combat plan, electronic counter measures plan, communications plan, etc. With the mission pack and briefing slides complete, we knocked off for the night and headed home. We needed our beauty sleep before flying our five-hour mission—we rarely flew for more than 1.5 hours in a single stint.

Robbo briefed the mission to his expected high standard—we all knew our roles and responsibilities based on our callsigns. Magpie was the first four-ship, Blackbird the second, and I was in the last four-ship Condor. As Condor 4 I would be last through the target area—the worst place to be. Magpie would wake up the enemy, Blackbird would give them something to tighten their systems on and Condor would be shot. Fortunately Robbo had a good gameplan, and would use Magpie to cover us during our run into the target. I might make it yet, I thought.

With the briefing complete we signed our authorisation book, picked up our safety equipment, and headed for the jets. Our config-uration included two jugs (770-litre fuel tanks), a targeting pod and two SUU-5003 bomb racks with six Blue Death bombs per side. These 15-kilogram bombs replicated the ballistic freefall profile of the Mk 82 mines we were simulating; however, as they weighed only one-fifteenth the weight of the real mines, the performance of the jets was going to be well above what they would be if we were carrying the real thing. In order for us to learn real-world lessons, Robbo had limited us to military power only—that meant no afterburner. This would limit our thrust from 14 500 kilograms back to 9000 kilo-grams, and would replicate the performance of the aircraft as if we were carrying the real weapons that weighed 2700 kilograms more.

We launched from RAAF Tindal at 1000 local time with each four-ship launching in a five-minute trail. This meant that Condor was 300 kilometres behind Magpie en route to the tanker. The tanker had already launched 10 minutes ahead of Magpie and was climbing to FL290 (flight level 290, or 8500 metres) where it would cruise at 500 kilometres per hour. The tanker plan was designed such that the F-18s would chase the tanker down at our higher speed of 800 kilometres per hour and rendezvous at the planned refuel start point. Ten minutes after the first four-ship had topped up their tanks, the second four-ship would arrive and commence refuelling. This would then be completed for Condor, and all twelve would depart together to commence the tactical ingress.

Air-to-air refuelling is probably the single most intimidating action for a fighter pilot. As you are by now no doubt aware, fighter pilots have an overdeveloped sense of bravado, which enables them to comfortably perform nudie runs through the most public of nightspots, but AAR puts the one thing fighter pilots cherish more than their manhood on public display: their flying ability. Dogfighting also puts their flying skills on display; however, only one other person (the person flying the other aircraft) ever gets to see their skills—or lack thereof. AAR, on the other hand, usually involves 'plugging' behind a tanker that is full of mechanics, flight attendants, media and any other hangers-on that want a free flight with a frozen meal. Add to this the fact that it's a very difficult flight manoeuvre to perform well, and you have a situation that makes most of these over-confident killers turn into nervous girls.

When AAR goes really wrong, it usually involves lots of pieces of metal violently departing the jet, the probe or the drogue at 600 kilometres per hour. This then causes loss of fuel for every other guy behind you, as you've wrecked their moving refuel bowser, resulting in jets landing at every other airfield except their intended destination. The repercussions of this, depending on which countries your mates end up in, can mean your mates sleeping with their jet, diplomatic incidents, foreign military police and a lot of pissed-off people—hence the pressure to not fuck up the plug. On this instance I would be last through the tanker. The problem was, we still needed the flying gas station to plug us on the way home.

Thankfully, refuelling on the way across was uneventful, and I broke formation from the tanker to join back on Condor 3's wing. With all jets full of weapons and fuel, we departed the tanker as a twelve-ship and climbed to FL390 (12 000 metres) where we started contrailing. With a tight formation and twelve white vapour tails behind us, we accelerated towards fighting speed, did a final check of our weapons and sensors, and deployed into our tactical formation.

Despite common misperceptions, fighters rarely fly in close formation. We generally do it on departure, landing and bad weather to facilitate maximum airfield movements and at NRL/AFL grand finals to impress the public. The rest of the time, if you ever see two fighters together, the wingman deserves a rap on the knuckles. The idea of a tactical formation is for each member to be close enough to see a bandit attacking his wingman from the other side, while being far enough apart for the bandit to not see you. It varies with visibility, sun angle, day/night and night vision goggles; however, if a bad hat turns up on your buddy's arse, you have a contract to keep: kill the bandit.

On this mission, we would be flying an eight-ship wall spread wingtip-to-wingtip about 3 kilometres apart with another four-ship wall 40 kilometres behind. This provided an additional layer of protection to the lead eight-ship, as Condor down the back would be able to shoot any bandits that came from behind them.

With the tactical formation set, we checked in on our fighting frequency:

'Magpie Combine, check.'

'Magpie 2.'

'Three.'

'Four.'

'Blackbird 1.'

'Two.'

'Three.'

'Four.'

'Condor 1.'

'Two.'

'Three.'

'Four.'

'Range control, this is Magpie Combine, flight of twelve for single pass on Cordelia Range, twelve by BDU-33 each.'

'Roger, Magpie Combine, this is Dagger 15, you are cleared onto the range. Be advised we have an interloper on the southern edge of the range and you will need to ensure all ordnance remains 1 kilometre north of southern border.'

Our mine checkerboard was designed on a west-to-east pass by all aircraft, with myself carrying out the southernmost attack—the one that was currently in conflict with some fuckin' rubbernecker. Faaark!

Robbo then swallowed a giant pill of harden-the-fuck-up and transmitted: 'Magpie Combine copied. Magpie Combine offset all attacks 1 kilometre north, acknowledge.'

Sounds easy, doesn't it? Well, by this stage we were passing 300 metres AMSL at 900 kilometres per hour in a steep descent, trying to scan the sky visually and with radar, flying formation, not hitting the ground, and now reprogramming a mining attack that had taken twelve hours to plan and a good five minutes to program into my weapons computer. I looked at my distance to run—60 kilometres. At 11 kilometres per minute I would be dropping bombs in less than four minutes.

The attack run was designed to start from a point in space that was to be referenced to a distinct radar/forward-looking infrared (FLIR) update point. Prior to GPS in the F-18 we would update the inertial navigation system (INS) by pointing a sensor to a known geographical feature. The navigation computer would then compare the radar/laser range with the INS position and update the INS to match the more accurate radar/laser position. To offset my run north by 1 kilometre, all I had to do was increase the offset in my target waypoint. I quickly scanned the sky and my radar before going heads down into the navigation computer to find my target waypoint, edit it, increase the offset by 1000 metres, enter it, save it, exit it, select it, designate it, select the FLIR, move the designation, arm the laser, fire the laser, accept the designation, update the INS, accept the update. It was times like these I wished I had an office job.

With my navigation system adjusted and designated, it was time to turn the autopilot on. This, like close formation, was something we rarely used as fighter pilots but was necessary to achieve the very fine tolerances in our mine checkerboard. At 900 kilometres per hour, 60 metres off the water, even knucklehead reflexes are not fast enough to accurately pickle twelve bombs off in quick succession and ensure the checkerboard is square. With the autopilot engaged, and hearing the lead aircraft coming off the target and covering our ingress, I held onto the canopy rail handles. I had never used these handles prior, nor did I ever use them again, but with the autopilot flying low-level high-G manoeuvres, you needed to hold on to stop your head hitting the canopy—the autopilot was rougher than any student I would ever teach.

I watched expectantly as my lead's belly appeared and he peeled off on his final attack heading.

'Condor 3 and 4, in live,' called my lead.

'Condor 3 and 4, you are cleared live,' replied the range safety officer.

I flicked my master arm switch—the bombs were now live. I nervously awaited the five seconds to my planned turn-in direction. This would be the litmus test whether my Mach 1 mathematics and data entry were correct, or not. On cue the jet banked left into an 80-degree angle of bank turn and pulled 4Gs. Off cue, however, my bombs started automatically rippling off in the turn.

I was not on the attack heading and I was still in a 4G turn as I felt the *thump, thump, thump* of the bombs dropping off at about one-second intervals. We are taught in Bombing 101 to never drop in a turn because the mission computer cannot accurately predict the centrifugal velocities combined with the ejection velocities that would normally be exerted on the bombs in the vertical plane. Additionally, the high G puts a lot of disturbed air over the bombs on separation, causing them not to fly as predicted by the weapons computer. Lastly, and of most concern, I had seen the interloping sailing yacht disappear under my belly in the turn just prior to the bombs starting to eject.

I disengaged the autopilot, made the master arm safe and rolled out of the turn to plot my own bombs—again, something you are taught never to do in Bombing 101. Many fighter pilots have flown into the ground looking over their shoulder at 900 kilometres at low altitude. In this instance I felt the relative consequences of what was about to happen were possibly comparable. While the mines were delivered from a low-level delivery with a ten-second time of fall, it felt more like a 15 000 metre delivery as I waited for the string of twelve bombs to impact . . . and then the first one hit.

As I looked over my right shoulder a sequence of events unfolded that had me crapping in my G suit. The first bomb hit approximately 1000 metres on the far side of the yacht and then over the next ten seconds I watched as the remainder drew a line across the ocean—a line like a slowly drawn scalpel cut across the skin of the sea. A line that was homing in on the yacht. Bombs two, three, four, five, six—all at perfect 150-metre intervals. The yacht was next. I tensed.

Miraculously, bomb number seven went over the top of the yacht, missing it by about 100 metres, and then the remainder of the bombs continued in a line.

'Check fire, check fire, check fire. Condor 4, you have dropped outside the template area. Make switches safe and return to base.'

'Urrr, arrrr . . . Roger. Condor 4, check switches safe.'

Faaark! I must have cocked up the data entry. I spent the next two and a half hours flying back to Tindal trying to convince myself that flying a brown bomber (a desk) in Canberra really wouldn't be that bad. I'd get lunch every day and possibly be home before 8 p.m. to have some sort of social life.

Back on deck we reviewed our weapons videos, with the entire squadron wanting to watch mine—I think KP, the janitor, might have even got a piece of my action. After the debrief Robbo sat with me going through every switch selection and data entry I had made. He rang the flight line and had the cockpit data recorder file pulled and I went home feeling like shit—certain I would be down in Canberra before the week was out, working alongside the analyst who knew fuck-all about mining (though I certainly wouldn't have been coming from a position of strength to argue the nuances of aerial mining with him).

The subsequent investigation ended up taking months and ultimately even included Boeing. It turned out there was a minimum range to engage the autopilot for mine laying that was equal to twice your turn radius, and I had engaged the autopilot inside of this range. The limitation hadn't been previously published by Boeing—I guess the nerd with Coke-bottle glasses failed to mention that bit when he was cutting the code. I had, in fact, been the unintended test pilot for Boeing on this one and they wrote up a new procedure. Fortunately for the mining analyst, I avoided being posted to Canberra to fly a 'brown bomber'.

17

Houston, we have a problem

I THINK MOST fighter pilots wish they could be astronauts at some stage in their careers. It is the pinnacle of aviation training after all, with stringent entry criteria requiring your country to be a participant in the space lab program, and you to be a fast-jet pilot who holds instructional or test pilot experience and a minimum of six science degrees. I think it must be out of immense frustration that some pilots try to fast-track their way into the space program—though most generally come unstuck.

Spook was our maintenance test pilot, which meant that when Hornets came out of the workshop after repairs he would take the aircraft flying and check its serviceability. It requires a special qualification to perform these tests and generally the job is given to pilots with high levels of experience, which Spook, as our USMC exchange pilot, had.

It was after such a test flight that I bumped into Spook in the corridor at 75SQN. He had an uncomfortable smile on his face and took me into one of the pilot debrief rooms. With the door secure he put his HUD tape into the video player, fiddled around until he found what he was after and paused it to freeze the frame. There before me was a sight I never thought possible in an F-18.

The HUD indicated Mach 1.94 and 20 000 metres. Spook had

somehow got his aircraft to twice the altitude of airliners and almost twice the speed of sound. This was a breach of our flying orders, which limited aircrew to 15 000 metres when not wearing a pressure suit. A pressure suit is what astronauts wear in space and it stops the gases in your blood, like oxygen and nitrogen, from coming out of solution into gas and lodging in your brain or spine. This is what happens to divers who get the bends when they surface too quickly, like opening a can of Coke. Space radiation is also dangerous and another reason for a space suit. They all sounded like good reasons not to go above 15 000 metres to me; however, Spook hadn't read the memo.

I asked Spook how the hell he had done it—I had never been anywhere near that altitude or speed. Apparently, as part of the engine air test, you were required to climb to 9000 metres and accelerate through the sound barrier—Spook had just been a little overzealous about testing those engines. Using up nearly all his fuel he had spent 30 minutes getting the jet as high and as fast as he could. I complimented him for his achievement, understanding that he was not aware of the high-altitude flying limit. He looked a little sheepish when he asked me to press play. With a heavy feeling in my stomach I started the tape.

The jet was smoothly flying at almost twice the speed of sound on the edge of outer space when the mission computer, 'Bitching Betty', went off: '*Deedle deedle*. Bleed air left, bleed air left.'

That was not good. The Hornet uses high-pressure air from the engine compressor to pressurise the cockpit and seal the canopy. Spook had just lost half of his pressurisation system, threatening to turn him into a human Coke can.

Before I could finish my expletive, the bitch let rip again: 'Bleed air right. Bleed air right.'

You have got to be shitting me. Spook was above the Armstrong Line of 19 000 metres and he had just lost his entire pressurisation system. The Armstrong Line could also be called the Coca-Cola Line because, above this line, gases come out of your blood if you lose pressurisation. It seemed that the supersonic air entering the engines was so hot that the fire sensors surrounding the bleed air lines had heated up to the point that they were falsely indicating a fire. On the good–bad scale of Hornet flying, this was way, way up the righthand side.

As I watched the tape the insanity continued to unfold before my eyes, drawing me closer towards the screen like a horror movie— you don't really want to watch, but can't stop yourself from looking. Spook rolled inverted and attempted to pull down to descend at maximum rate. Trouble was, aircraft need air over their wings to fly and Spook was barely inside the earth's atmosphere.

The jet was at nearly twice the speed of sound, but the air was so thin that he was indicating only 300 kilometres per hour, which is about as slow as a Hornet can fly. When he rolled and pulled, the aircraft went straight to 90 degrees angle of attack—the jet's nose was pointing at the ground but it was still moving horizontally through the atmosphere. This situation was now about to get a hell of a lot worse.

'*Deedle deedle*. Engine left, engine left. Engine right, engine right.' Betty was now singing an entire opera.

With the air flowing across the front of the engine inlets, and not into them, both engines had compressor-stalled and flamed out. Spook was now on the edge of space, without a pressure suit, with a failed pressurisation system and no engine power—he was essentially a sub-orbital glider pilot with his body about to froth over like a shaken can of Coke. I was terrified watching the tape—this couldn't get any worse, I thought—and then it did.

'*Beep beep beep beep*.'

Oh god no—it was the spin tone. This sound is very rarely heard in the Hornet because the jet does not play nicely in a spin—many ejections have been made from Hornets in spins. Spook's enthusiasm to hang up his astronaut's wings and become a pilot again had caused him to overcontrol the Mach 2.0 split S manoeuvre he was attempting. The lack of airflow over the wings and tails meant the aircraft had stalled, rolled and yawed, and there was nothing Spook could do to fix it—he needed to let the jet spin back down to where the air was thicker and then he might have a chance to recover it. Once he got the jet flying again, then he could worry about some of the other issues—like not having any hydraulic pressure for his flight controls.

In losing both engines Spook had lost the two hydraulic systems that power his flight controls. Without the hydraulic pumps he only had a small amount of pressure stored in his hydraulic accumulators. As he was starting to have just a mild panic attack, his pumping on the joystick and rudders to recover from the spin was quickly draining the remaining pressure. With the air so thin, and the airflow so disturbed in the spin, he couldn't even get the wind to blow through his engines and drive the hydraulic pumps—what we call 'windmilling the engines'.

Spook's electrical generators had gone offline when the engines failed. His electrics, including his fly-by-wire controls, were now being fed by the battery. So now he was an out of control, battery-powered, sub-orbital glider with no cabin pressure and soon to lose all flight controls.

With one eye on the spin arrows, one eye on the altimeter, one eye on the hydraulic gauge and one eye on the engine rpm, Spook started praying for something to go right as the yellow and black tiger-striped handle between his legs started to look pretty inviting—this is the ejection handle, a fighter pilot's last resort. By now, I think few pilots would have called Spook's predicament anything other than a last resort. Except, of course, the dickhead who put himself in the predicament and knew his career would be over if he banged out. Spook had to stay with the jet and get it under control.

The first thing to recover was the aircraft flight path. With Spook's assistance, and some thicker air, the spin tone disappeared and Spook nosed forwards to dive for speed. The speed, in turn, increased his hydraulic pressure so he would not lose control of the jet. OK, things were looking up.

The oxygen system had automatically switched to 100 per cent when he lost cabin pressure so he wasn't about to lose consciousness —oh, how the little things in life can seem so important at times! The dive also brought the jet back below the Armstrong Line and reduced the risk of Spook's blood boiling. All that was left now was to start the engines.

The engines need to be below 7500 metres to start so Spook continued his dive all the while talking quietly into his oxygen mask: 'Light, you bitch. Come on. Light, you bitch.'

Passing through 7500 metres the engines relit, the generators came back online and Spook flew a normal return to base.

Walking with unsteady legs into the flight-line hut after his engine air test, Spook was greeted by the engineers.

'How did she hold up in the test, Spook?' they innocently asked.

'Couldn't be better—great jet,' he replied.

And that was the truth. There are few aircraft on the planet that you can take to the edge of space and back again safely, but she was one of them.

18
Diplomatic immunity

DIPLOMATIC IMMUNITY IS the legal protection afforded to consulate officials while working overseas. Somehow the true meaning of this term would get 'lost in translation' whenever we deployed a squadron overseas, with junior pilots truly believing that they could do nuddie runs through police states like Singapore, drink beer walking down the main street of Muslim cities, or sink jet-skis in Thailand while doing their best impersonations of the Blue Angels. Generally the embassy staff would be prepared for our deployments, with multiple phonelines, contact officers and briefcases full of cash to sort things out. On one occasion, however, the consular assistance never came through and I was forced to operate alone behind hostile lines.

I had finished my B Category upgrade at 75SQN which licensed me to now lead a squadron to war. I was then posted to 77 Squadron at RAAF Base Williamtown to work as an understudy to Proudy—a fantastic fighter combat instructor who was going to groom me for my own FCI course the following year. We deployed 77SQN to Kuantan, Malaysia, to participate in high-level strategic exercises which, on this occasion, included the opportunity to fight the Russian MiG-29 Fulcrum—and we would be the first Western nation to have this opportunity. To date we had only read intelligence reports and 'jet porn' magazine articles about the aircraft, but it all read bad. The hysteria culminated with our pre-deployment intelligence briefings at RAAF Williamtown which was run by the Defence Intelligence Organisation. I know, I know—I shouldn't use those terms together, and this was an excellent example of why.

A young intelligence officer (Intelo) from Canberra had flown up to Williamtown with his secret briefcase handcuffed to his wrist. All the pilots sat expectantly in the main briefing room in the hope the 'spy' would have some gouge on how we weren't going to get our arses handed to us when we deployed. Oh, how fragile is thy fighter pilot ego?

Most of his babble went in one ear and out the other, then I heard him say: 'The MiG-29 is fitted with a helmet-mounted sight, and he will be able to achieve an AA-11 Archer lock on you far sooner than you will achieve an AIM-9 Sidewinder lock on him, and once he does there's nothing you can do . . .' and the twelve-year-old continued on like there was nothing significant in his last statement.

What the? Proudy and I exchanged raised eyebrows as if to say 'you must be shitting me'.

'Spy, just back up a second,' I said. 'Are you saying that our flares don't work against this threat?'

'That is correct. The MiG's missile will go into memory mode and just wait for you to stop flaring.'

'And what happens if we change our flight path while it's in memory mode? How will it know where we've gone?'

'It will just track your flares and follow you. Trust me, there's nothing you can do,' he snapped, as if to say, 'Who the fuck are you, pilot, to dare question the Holy Grail of intelligence'.

'Mate, what's your source on this information?' I fired back at him.

'I can't say,' he replied curtly. 'You do not have a need to know.'

Of course I didn't. I was just one of the first twelve Western guys ever to train against this threat. Why the fuck might I possibly have a need to know the reliability of the information he was regurgitating?

After the brief, the FCI and I went back to his office, closed the door, opened the safe and started going through all the 'top secret' intelligence we had, both on our weapons systems and the information on the MiG that the propellerhead had extracted from flight international, or wherever the hell he'd got it from. We stayed back late after work, calculating our radar cross-section, chaff blooms and the MiG's radar resolution cell to find a way to defeat it. That bit was the easy part.

For the next week we worked on the flare issue: releasing a string of flares, leaving large gaps between flares, small gaps—we tried everything, until finally we found a tactic that would work. I reflected that the intelo was quite right in the end—we didn't have a need to know which Weeties box he got his data from, we could calculate our own intelligence.

We deployed to Malaysia and Proudy briefed the squadron on the back-of-the-beer-coaster flare program that he and I had calculated. By the end of week one we had a 21 to 1 kill ratio against the MiGs. Sure, they were less experienced than us; however, we were pretty sure that the intelligence assessment we'd received had been totally flawed. This is not completely new, I know. In fact, it's something that I have now seen repeated over and over again in the last 25 years. Intelligence has to be one of the only jobs in the world where you can completely screw up and then just hide behind some vague statement like 'Intelligence is never 100 per cent reliable'. Imagine if soldiers, airmen and sailors took the same approach to their jobs. I could crash the jet on landing, roll it into a ball of fire, eject and land next to my burning stallion, then explain to my commanding officer (CO) that 'my piloting skills are never 100 per cent reliable'. The 'weapons of mass destruction' debacle in Iraq was no surprise to me at all.

The exercise continued until the final week, when the large-force employment phase kicked off. This phase was when us Aussies came into our own, with our ability to mass force well and, conversely, break up large forces well. The exercise was held over the South China Sea and we were required to hold an Alert 3 posture at the end of the runway with one engine shutdown while awaiting the scramble order.

Schlopps was my wingman for the exercise as he had just arrived at the squadron and was one of our new Bograts. He fitted in well and was learning the ropes quickly.

By the Thursday of the last week Schlopps and I hadn't had a single scramble but had simply taxied out to the runway for three hours and then returned—over and over. I was filthy. I was in the middle of a large exercise and Schlopps was a sponge—I wanted to get him out there among the shit to start training him. His taxiing was very nice, however—which was good because it was about the only thing we did for the first three days of the five-day exercise. I'd had enough and so I'd started flicking through all the fighting frequencies that the airborne aircraft were using, trying to find a fight anywhere over South-East Asia that we could go and get into. Eventually I found one . . . sort of.

'Hermes, Viper, bingo fuel, departing for the tanker.' Viper were a pair of Singaporean F-16s who had been airborne long enough to run out of fuel and were now heading to the tanker. This was bullshit. I was sitting here in my 60-degree Celsius cockpit, wearing plastic jeans, life jacket, helmet and gloves, while the F-16s were swanning around doing nothing but filling up their logbooks. Not if I had anything to do with it. I pushed my radio across to the scramble net.

'Hermes, Despot, request scramble.'

'Negative, negative. Despot remain Alert 3,' came the reply. The role of Hermes was to efficiently manage resources so that we always had aircraft up and aircraft on alert. They would manage the assets like grand champions of chess. Trouble was, today one of the pawns was a little froggy.

'Hermes, Viper have departed CAP [combat air patrol] Bravo 3 for the tanker leaving the eastern sector exposed. Suggest strike will ingress via eastern sector. Request immediate scramble.'

I could imagine the controller, Pause. Think. Does Despot know what he's talking about? He's an Aussie. They generally know what they are talking about.

'Roger, Despot, scramble, scramble, scramble. Vector 090. Make angels 30.' We had our scramble order to head east and climb to 9000 metres (30 000 feet).

'Roger, Despot, scramble,' I replied and gave Schlopps the wind-up signal.

We lined up, with Schlopps on my right wing, and I nodded my head, signalling him to release the brakes. Slowly lighting the burners, I made all movements as smoothly as I could to help Schlopps stay in close formation. Once airborne, we checked our weapons systems and were vectored out over the South China Sea. There were huge isolated thunderstorms that stood tall and vertical over the water, making it feel like we were flying through a mega-city of massive cloud skyscrapers. We jumped onto the Viper CAP point which probably required them to return to base (RTB). I wasn't concerned for them—we hadn't flown all week. Schlopps and I sat CAP for two hours without any activity before we headed to the tanker to refuel.

There are two types of air-to-air refuelling: a probe and drogue, or boom refuelling. Boom refuelling is simple. You just fly in close formation behind an airliner travelling at 500 kilometres per hour and an operator onboard the airliner flies the refuel boom down to your aircraft and plugs in. Probe and drogue refuelling is an entirely different animal. With this type of refuelling the fighter pilot has to steer his refuel probe into the centre of a giant shuttlecock, like a modern day knight jousting at 500 kilometres per hour. To compli-cate the issue, the brainiac engineers who modified the RAAF Boeing 707s decided to mount the drogues out near the wingtips—right next to the wingtip vortices. Now without getting too bogged down in Aerodynamics 101, wingtip vortices are very strong eddies which come off the wingtip of all aircraft. The larger the aircraft, the stronger these eddies. With the B707, the eddies are strong enough to flip an F-18 on its back—something that has happened on more than one occasion, with the Hornet missing the tail of the B707 by only inches.

The other difficulty with the probe and drogue refuel system is that the drogue (or 'basket') seems to have a mind of its own and knows when you're starting to move in close to it. It will sit there not moving, solid as rock in free space, until your probe is just about to enter the basket, at which time the basket moves up and to the right, resulting in a 'missed plug'. It was the weirdest thing, but it really did seem to know the best time to move and cause us to miss. The pilot then had to back out slowly so as to not damage the aircraft in any way—and believe me, there are lots of ways it can be damaged: ripping the drogue off and having to return to base like an Olympian carrying the flame with pride; ripping off the drogue so that every other guy that's waiting behind you has to divert to an airport to get fuel; ripping off an angle of attack indicator or air data probe and losing your flight instruments; ripping off the probes and having them go down the right engine intake, resulting in a catastrophic engine failure and/or fire; ripping the entire 30-metre 2-inch hose out of the B707 like an enraged Lorena Bobbit; or cracking your windshield with the drogue. The odds were always against you when performing air-to-air refuelling—especially when 150 of your fellow squadron members were onboard the B707 watching you attempt to plug.

We picked up our gas and returned to CAP where we sat for another hour waiting—something you get very good at in air defence exercises. Eventually the tanker returned to base out of fuel and we started to run low on fuel when Hermes called us to advise that our airfield had closed due to unforecast bad weather. I immediately went across to the tower frequency and could hear a C-130 conducting a missed approach due to low cloud. I then contacted our operations (ops) desk and had the weather reports of all the diversion airfields read to me. While we still had enough fuel to fly to our base at Kuantan and fly an instrument approach, we didn't have enough fuel to attempt an instrument approach and then divert to Kuala Lumpur, which was our nearest airfield with suitable weather.

I explained to our operations desk that we would immediately divert to KL, the capital of Malaysia. Suddenly the voice changed and my flight commander was on the ops radio.

'Despot, this is A Flight. You will RTB to Kuantan immediately.'

'Copied ops. I just heard a C-130 go around—we don't have the fuel for that. We need to have the field open now or we have to divert.'

'The weather is improving and should be fine by the time you get here,' replied my boss, and I could hear a slight irritation in his voice.

'They said that before we left, and now the field is closed. I think the weatherman is having a bad day and I'm not going to risk it.'

'Despot, this is a direct order. You will land at Kuantan. You do not have diplomatic clearance for KL.'

While I sympathised with my boss, knowing the amount of paperwork that Schlopps and I were about to generate, I really didn't feel it was worth throwing a couple of jets away for.

'Copied ops and understand. However, as captain of this aircraft and the formation lead, I'm making the call. Despot, Channel 12 go' and with that we changed frequency and started our diversion to KL.

The weather was fine at KL and we flew a close-formation arrival in order to minimise our impact on the civil traffic, which there was a lot of. I had trouble concentrating on the approach, knowing that I was probably about to be demoted, kicked off FCI course, dequalified and god knows what else by the Australian embassy staff in KL.

On landing I requested an immediate refuel and advised air traffic we would be returning to Kuantan in one hour. The control tower sent out a 'follow me' car and Schlopps and I taxied into the refuel area. Not long after shutdown, the refuel truck arrived and we started refuelling Schlopps' jet.

We noticed some Thai F-16s parked a little further along the ramp, and so I wandered down to develop the Thai–Australian military relationship. I broke into my best Thai.

'Sar wah dee cup, mate,' I said, reaching out to shake the hand of one of the pilots as I said hello in my strong Aussie accent.

The Thais are extremely friendly, and we have good aircrew relationships with them. It wasn't long before I had swapped some of my flying suit patches for Mekong whisky and returned to Schlopps with arms full of bottles of the addictive rice spirit. I opened the gun bay of my jet and was filling it with my Golden Triangle contraband when the Malaysian MPs turned up, lights flashing, and circled our jets. This didn't look good, I thought, and started wondering if ejecting in the missed approach at Kuantan might have been a better option—I had heard some bad stories about Malaysian prisons.

The senior MP approached me, asking for ID, papers, flight plan and diplomatic papers—none of which I had. What about this Kangaroo roundel and Australian flag on the jet? I thought.

'Our embassy has all the paperwork. They didn't send you a copy? I'm sure the paperwork is at your office right now,' I said in my best 'you'd better have your facts straight, mate, or you'll be in the shit' voice.

The MP told me not to go anywhere and promptly led his convey back off the ramp, no doubt to check out my story.

As soon as they had driven off, I disconnected the fuel hose from Schlopps's jet.

'Mate, strap in and start—be ready to move ASAP. You have 200 litres—that's enough to get us out of here.'

I then attached the hose to my jet, asked the driver to increase the pressure and started putting on my G suit and Secumar as quickly as I could. I raced over to Schlopps' jet, stowed his ladder and gave him the wind-up signal. I then disconnected the fuel hose, signed for the fuel, telling the driver that the MP would be back with the authorisation shortly, and then climbed into my jet.

I immediately cranked the engine and lowered the canopy to make it look like we were a lot closer to taxiing than we actually were. Then I got a glimpse of the MPs coming back along the taxiway with their lights flashing. I pushed up the throttles, released the park brake and started to taxi—not even strapped into the jet yet. I called up the ground controller, asking for permission to taxi, and somehow had both Schlopps and I moving when the MPs arrived. They pulled alongside us and I kept my eyes looking forwards as if oblivious to the guards waving their arms and guns around.

It was a long taxi to the far end of the runway, during which I had ample time to complete my strap-in and after-start checks. I checked with Schlopps and gave him a look-over to make sure his canopy, flaps and trim were set correctly. By now the weather had improved back at Kuantan and we were soon airborne and on our way back to our base.

I think the boss was more upset at me transporting Mekong whisky than disobeying his order, as the mechanics had started a rumour about me, that I was running some sort of contraband trade across South-East Asia. And I never did hear from the Australian Embassy—seemed those diplomatic clearances were overrated.

19
Mission impossible

MILLIONS OF DOLLARS and hundreds of studies have been funded by militaries all around the world in an attempt to recruit people with the right make-up to be fighter pilots. It costs so much to train one that the last thing the bean counters want is a pilot to flunk out after spending all that money on him. One study indicated that mathematical agility and mechanical skills were key prerequisites—both true in my case, but not true in a lot of others. A key ingredient I believe is an almost self-delusional belief in ourselves—a deep knowledge that we can do what is asked, no matter what the odds, and never, ever give up. This was certainly the case on one of the most complex missions I've ever flown—a sixteen-ship maritime strike using live rockets off the coast of Nowra in New South Wales.

I was midway through my fighter combat instructor (FCI) course—a six-month course that cost $25 million per student. The course was to train six of us in the art of killing from the air, and the ADF were supplying a lot of assets to support the course: jets, tankers, transport, SAS soldiers, ships, US assets, satellites—you name it and there was a good chance we would be working with it at some stage during the course. For this mission we would be flying against other F-18s and ships that could shoot us as we crossed the horizon.

Nowra is where the navy do the majority of their anti-aircraft training. F-18s launch out of Williamtown and practise shooting the ships with harpoon missiles, bombs, rockets and guns, while the navy practises their defence against these attacks. I was grateful that I was at our end of the stoush and not theirs—particularly when it comes to hot bunking with a couple of hundred blokes and no beer.

On our FCI course I was required to plan and lead a sixteen-ship strike utilising twelve Hornets and four F-111s (Pigs), as well as a P-3 maritime surveillance aircraft. We would be shooting at a small boat being towed behind a Navy frigate. The challenge was that we were not allowed to use our Harpoon anti-ship missiles but had to fly into the threat envelope of the SM-1 SAM (surface-to-air missile) and the ship's guns in order to shoot our Vietnam-era rockets—it was not a fair fight. As soon as we popped above the horizon at 50 kilometres, the ship would start shooting us and we would have to continue in to 6 kilometres—the maximum range of our rockets—in order to attack them. This was a deliberately difficult task designed by the instructors to frustrate the students. However, it had the opposite effect on me. In my mind there is always a way to win—I just have to find it.

We started with an in-depth analysis of our capabilities. At what range would the P-3 be able to detect the ship? What range could the Pigs see the ship in their targeting pod? What was our radar cross-section in our planned configuration? We then moved onto the threat capabilities. What range would they see us head-on? How close did we have to fly to each other to hide our true numbers? What effect would our chaff have on their radars? Where were their blind spots?

We scoured all available intelligence in an attempt to find the ship's Achilles' heel, as well as other operational information such as weather. Weather plays a critical part in almost all military operations and is often overlooked in the world of GPS, satellite communications and robotic vehicles. Temperature differences in the atmosphere can form layers that reflect radar waves and increase their detection ranges. Thermal sights do not work looking directly at the sun. A radar has a finite number of aircraft it can lock onto and shoot. It has a limited number of missiles. Somewhere we would find the critical capability to exploit.

Deception is a fundamental principle of war and is another aspect that can be utilised, particularly in those cases where technological supremacy can lull an aggressor into a false sense of security. For example, F-22 stealth fighters can be seen at 160 kilometres by the human eye, but only if they are flown too high and produce contrails. Deception was where we found our answer in solving the tactical dilemma.

Ships have an incredibly difficult job when operating close to land in what we call the 'littoral environment'. In this environment their radar pulses are bounced back at them from land obstacles which reduce the sensitivity of their radars. Additionally, because of civilian air traffic, the rules of engagement (ROE) are very restrictive so that they don't shoot down a civilian airliner (which has happened in the past[6]). In this case, the ship was 80 kilometres off the shore from Nowra and 240 kilometres from Williamtown. A normal departure from Williamtown would allow the crew to start working through their rules of engagment with lots of time, so much so that by the time we were at 50 kilometres they would be able to start shooting.

Our thinking was, if we could somehow sneak up on the ship we could prevent them meeting their ROE in time, which would allow one of our aircraft to deliver its rockets and knock out the towed target which was being used to simulate the fire control radar on the ship. Additionally, the ship could not target all sixteen of us at the same time. Once the ship had targeted its maximum number of aircraft, the untargeted aircraft would be able to continue in without being shot. It sounded like a plan, albeit high risk, and we started plotting and briefing accordingly. It was during this planning that I would make a simple but grave error.

Planning a multi-mission strike takes significant effort from all formation members. Data cards must be prepared, weapons programs calculated, navigation data printed out, maps prepared, electronic countermeasures calculated and flight plans submitted. We were time-compressed for the planning phase, another artificially imposed stress on us, and I asked our duty air traffic control (ATC) officer if she would file the flight plan for us. The flight plan was needed as we would be going out of Williamtown's airspace and into uncontrolled airspace. It would alert all low-level civilian traffic that high-speed military traffic was in their area so they could avoid us and/or communicate their location to us. This effort was made in order to avoid midair collisions and it was illegal to fly without one.

With the planning and briefing done, we went to our aircraft for a no communication (NOCOM) and emission controlled (EMCON) departure. These practices ensured we didn't trigger any of the ships' onboard electronic support measures (ESM), mechanisms which had an ability to detect our emissions from a very long range, thereby enabling them to commence targeting activity against us—we didn't want to alert them any more than we had to.

We lined up all sixteen aircraft adjacent to the end of the runway and at exactly the planned time I pulled out and flashed my landing light—my NOCOM signal to request take-off clearance. I now waited for a green light from the air traffic control tower to indicate we were cleared for take-off and track in accordance with our flight plan. Unexpectedly I got a red light. This was very unusual and had never happened to me previously. I was now required to break radio silence and contact the tower to clarify the situation—something I was reluctant to do with a giant vacuum cleaner sitting off Nowra ready to suck up all my transmissions.

I disguised my radio call as a civilian transmission: 'Williamtown tower, this is Alpha Bravo Charlie.'

Thankfully, the tower controller wised up to my intent and didn't use my real callsign 'Ford 11'.

'Alpha Bravo Charlie, it appears we have no flight plan for you. Confirm you lodged a flight plan?'

Then it hit me between the eyes like an axe—the ATC officer I had asked to lodge the flight plan hadn't lodged it. I was leading a sixteen-ship and she had to go to lunch—or whatever reason, I didn't care. Fucking blunt!

Ultimately it was my fault, but the situation really had me questioning what the fuck those oxygen bandits did to help us. Time ticked on as I ran through my options. My wingman, who was also my instructor, was looking at me through his black visor—I knew he was smiling and wondering how the fuck I was going to get myself out of this. Then it hit me.

'Willy tower, Alpha Bravo Charlie, do you have a flight plan for Papa India Golf?' Still trying to disguise my transmissions, I was hoping this ATC officer was a little brighter than the one who couldn't lodge our plan, and would know that I was referring to the P-I-Gs. I was asking if the tower had a plan for our F-111 friends coming down from RAAF Base Amberley in Queensland. We could still make the rendezvous (RV) time, but we would have to launch now.

'Alpha Bravo Charlie, affirmative, Sir, we have a plan for Papa India Golf.'

'Roger, request you amend that plan to include Alpha Bravo Charlie and request immediate take-off,' I hurriedly transmitted.

'Will do, Alpha Bravo Charlie, but you will have to wait for Sydney to approve the plan before you take off.'

This was going to take too long and we would miss our RV with the Pigs, which would mean they would probably get shot without the use of our jammers, numbers and rockets. The mission was going to shit as quickly as I could think of options.

'Alpha Bravo Charlie, request immediate take-off into William-town Airspace awaiting Sydney approval.' If I could get the jets into the air we could start tracking for the RV point, provided we got our clearance from Sydney before we left the Williamtown airspace.

'Roger, Alpha Bravo Charlie, you are cleared for take-off, make right turn.'

My afterburners were lit and we were rolling before he had finished his sentence. We joined up in tight formation after take-off and maintained our altitude below the radar horizon of the ship. Despite the ship moving at 40 kilometres per hour, we had a tight fix on the ship's location courtesy of our friendly P-3 that was shadow-ing the fleet and reporting to us by long-range high-frequency radio. I could still recover this if I could just find the Pigs. Without radar and a radio it can be hard to find something travelling at 1000 kilo-metres per hour—that is, unless you've planned the mission well.

I accelerated the formation to make good our RV time and rolled upside-down to look. There 3000 metres below us, were the Piggies. 'Sooowwweeee!' On time and on target. We descended to join into the pre-briefed formation. With the mission back on the rails, it was time to start getting sneaky.

The Sydney airspace was going to help us achieve the level of deception necessary to sneak up on a bunch of floating big-arse SAMs. Underneath the Sydney control zone, running right along the beaches, is a little-known flight corridor called Victor 1 (V1) which is used by small Cessna-type aircraft when they want to fly past Sydney airport without an air traffic control clearance. This corridor would allow us to fly right down the coast hiding under the airliners operat-ing within Australia's busiest airport control zone.

At our closest point of approach we all lit the burners and turned to point directly at the ship. Wingmen were flying nice and tight to hide our true numbers from the ship. Jammers went on and chaff was dispensed on our 80-kilometre run at the ship—we were less than four minutes out and would not break their radar horizon until we were two and a half minutes from them. They would then have to find us on their radar through all the background traffic, positively identify us as hostile, run through their crew coordination and weapons checks and then start shooting. We were betting on them not being able to do all that in time, and even if they did, not all of us could possibly be targeted. The targeted aircraft would turn around and outrun any weapons fired at them, while our untargeted fighters would continue in for the rocket attack. That was the plan, at least, though I couldn't get too confident, as air combat rarely goes according to plan.

We got to 50 kilometres and broke their radar horizon. I nervously waited for the first formation members to start bleating and the formation to totally disintegrate as targeted fighters went in every direction. What I didn't expect was what I heard next.

Nothing. Silence. No radio calls. Just the reassuring drone of the two engines in full afterburner as we screamed across the ocean in perfect formation at the speed of sound. It was surreal. I looked down to check the status of my radar warning receiver—I was 'naked' or untargeted. The silence on the radio indicated the rest of the formation was the same.

I looked into the heads-up display (HUD) and watched the miles to run racing down: twenty, nineteen, eighteen, seventeen . . . We were covering 2 kilometres every six seconds. I looked out at the formation—it was perfect. It was a rare moment to sit back and admire Australia's best: the intensive planning, the lengthy briefs, years of air combat knowledge all came together at this brief moment of near-perfection—I know every pilot had a big smile on his face at that moment as they foresaw what was about to happen.

At 30 kilometres I got tally of the ship and gently manoeuvred the formation on a direct path for the target which was about 2 kilometres behind the ship. At 20 kilometres I was still undetected. Master arm to safe. Simulated mode deselected. Air-to-ground selected. Master arm to arm. Rockets selected. The checks rolled off in rapid fire and on cue—and I knew that the same was occurring inside the cockpits of the other jets. With checks completed, I broke radio silence for the first time in the mission.

'Ford Combine, check.'

'Ford 12.'

'One-three.'

'One-four.'

'Holden 21.'

'Twenty-two.'

'Twenty-three.'

'Twenty-four.'

'Nissan 31.'

'Thirty-two.'

'Thirty-three.'

'Thirty-four.'

'Buick 41.'

'Forty-two.'

'Forty-three.'

'Forty-four.'

After 90 minutes of taxiing and flying in formation without talking once, the entire team checked in without missing a beat—the boys were on fire.

'Range safety, this is Ford Combine, in live,' I transmitted with the slightest suggestion of satisfaction in my voice.

We were still untargeted as we received our clearance to fire. At 14 kilometres the first four-ship split outwards into two pairs and conducted opposing rocket attacks, unloading twelve rockets from each aircraft. With the first rockets hitting the target, the fire control system was now deemed destroyed and the visual guns were the highest threat. We continued jinking and turning away from the ship as the remainder of the jets conducted their rocket attacks. All twelve Hornets had delivered their rockets in under twenty seconds, allowing the Pigs to close in for a laser guided bomb attack. With all aircraft off target we rejoined and climbed enroute back to Williamtown.

It was a good recovery of the mission from a really bad start. It was also an example of one of the few missions I can remember where we had almost total air-combat perfection—something that I never achieved in thirteen years.

The Defence Science Technology Organisation (DSTO) had an observer team in the operations room of the ship during our attack in order to conduct an operational analysis of our maritime strike tactics. A debrief from one of the scientists later revealed that the first time the navy had been aware of our impending attack was when our shock waves hit them as we flew over the top. Hot bunking, 500 blokes, no beer, no chicks, no pubs and those Hornet guys flying missions against you—you can keep that.

20
The learning curve

Top Gun DID wonders for RAAF recruiting—and Ray-Bans. Trouble is, fighter flying is nothing like the movie. The topguns of the US navy, the weapons officers of the US air force and fighter combat instructors (FCIs) of the Royal Australian Air Force all represent the same thing—the epitome of tactical air-combat employment. In Australia only six FCIs undergo training every two years. The six-month course takes a minimum of six years to prepare for, costs $25 million per student to run, and one or two students will usually fail. In 1997 I was selected for No. 25 FCI course. This was what I had worked towards since I was eighteen—this was going to be fun.

It seemed no matter how experienced I became the next challenge only made me feel as inadequate as that first day at Point Cook. The FCI course was run only by FCIs who had a serious reputation to protect. Their mark was a distinctive blue shield worn on their right shoulder—they would put me through some serious trials emotionally and psychologically before they would deem me to have earned the right to wear the patch. By this stage of my career I had pretty much perfected the art of channelling my nervousness into performance—and I had never been so nervous.

The course is run at Williamtown and consists of a two-month instructional technique phase, a one-month airborne instructional technique phase, a one-month air-to-air phase and a one-month war phase. With visits, exams and projects thrown in, the course was the culmination of nine years training for me—the PhD in the art and science of air warfare that I had wondered about as a kid when Dad wanted me to be a doctor.

The instructional technique course was a crock of shit and only conducted because a blunt somewhere didn't like the fact that these smart-arse fighter pilots could actually learn to train someone without having to undergo the mandatory lobotomy from RAAF training command. This command consisted almost entirely of education officers (EDOs) who were schoolteachers in uniform that insisted that the sharp end had to get on board with their blunt methods. No credit was given to the fact that we had been observing and delivering training in flying for nine years and were considered in the top percentile of intelligence in the population. Nope, us clowns knew nothing and would have to complete the course.

So there I was. Nine years to get there and I was sitting in the room with five other warriors ready to train in the finer points of aerial combat and we were being asked moronic questions.

'So, 25 FCI course, who can tell me what an instructor is?'

Isn't that what you're meant to be, dickhead?

'Who can tell me how we learn?'

What the fuck has this got to do with learning how to take out a Su-27 Flanker base in bad weather at night? I was so furious I went and saw my brand new commanding officer (CO) of less than half a day.

'Sir, can I speak with you, please?'

'Yes, Serge. What is it?'

'Sir, I have just spent the last six months reading every F-18 ops manual, tactical manual, weapons manual, intelligence report and standard operating procedure to best prepare myself for this course. Do you have any idea what's going on in our classroom right now?

Honestly, we're learning nothing and the blunts they've sent from training command are fucking idiots.'

'Yes, I know your frustration, Serge, but that's what we must do to keep the blunts happy in order that you guys can legally instruct students.'

'Who's running this fucking air force, Sir—the sword swingers or the sword polishers? Can't you put them back in their box and let us get on with what we came here to do?'

'No, Serge, I can't. Just go back in there, bite your tongue for a few weeks and you'll be through it before you know. If you want my honest opinion, you'll look back at this phase and long for it once the flying starts.'

'Copied, Sir. Thanks.'

What is fucking wrong with this outfit? I thought. Now the teachers are telling the pilots what they can and can't do. While I may have been the only one to approach the CO, the frustration was being felt by all six of us. We made a pact to fight stupidity with stupidity.

The first project we had to work on was a ten-minute demonstration. The idea was that these brainwaves could teach us how to demonstrate an activity to a student, direct him through the activity and then monitor him performing it alone.

Grubby started off with his presentation on how to make a caesar salad. I really thought he had overstepped the mark and that the EDOs were going to report him to the CO for screwing around. On the contrary—they loved it. They debriefed him in front of the whole course, complimenting him on his concise manner, deliberate method and clear communications. I was gobsmacked. Was this really happening? After nine years, is this what I had been working towards?

OK, Grubby had set the trend. It was time to ratchet the stupid-ity up a notch. I chose TVH as my student in the good knowledge that he already knew how to play guitar, and more importantly, sing 'Viva Las Vegas'. One of TVH's not-so-great secrets was his honest belief that he was Elvis Presley incarnate. It was a hangover from our 75 Squadron days when the entire squadron had Elvis suits. Well, TVH never got rid of his. Quite the opposite. He had bought other rhinestone-covered suits, visited Graceland, bought a wig, secured his own supply of female velcro for sideburns and entered himself in professional Elvis-impersonation competitions. I figured that teaching him how to play 'Viva Las Vegas' was going to be easier than making a caesar salad.

'Good morning, ladies and gentlemen. My name is Serge and today I will be teaching you how to play "Viva Las Vegas" on the guitar. I will be assisted by TVH and will be referring to the chord slides on the board. I will first demonstrate the techniques. I will then direct TVH through the techniques. And finally I will ask TVH to play the song without my assistance, after which I will provide feedback on his technique.'

I sheepishly looked at the EDOs to make sure they hadn't headed for the CO's office. To my amazement they were sitting in their normal 'carrot up the arse' position, beaming giant smiles on their faces. I couldn't believe it. I started to think that somehow they may have been subjected to presentations worse than what we were giving them—God help the RAAF if that was the case.

Sitting next to TVH on the stage, I started to demonstrate the three chords that go together to make up the song. Deliberately sticking his fingers in all the wrong places, TVH pretended to be really struggling to not drop the guitar and play a single note—let alone a chord.

Using my best instructional technique, I steadily 'encouraged and corrected' TVH, who then pretended that he was suffering stage fright and unable to perform in front of the class. I looked to the EDOs who started to appear genuinely concerned that TVH might be getting too embarrassed. With some team encouragement—'You can do it, TVH' and 'That's really good, mate'—TVH was able to pull himself together. Complimenting him on his courage I asked him if he would feel comfortable performing 'Viva Las Vegas' without my assistance.

'I'll give it a go, but I'm not sure . . .'

'You're doing really well, TVH. Now take your time. Concentrate on pressing firmly with your left hand and strumming lightly with your right,' I said.

Starting off slowly and quietly, TVH got midway through the first verse—and couldn't hold back any longer. The Elvis in him had to be released. Standing up and kicking the chair back, TVH started to shake his hips and knock his knees while increasing his volume like only TVH can.

By midway through the second verse, a few of our F-18 instructors and the CO himself had congregated at the door to our classroom to see what Australia's finest were up to. The CO looked at me standing at the podium next to Elvis, he looked at Elvis gyrating his hips and then back to me. I just smiled with the best smart-arse smile I could muster. He might think a little harder about not making the next FCI course sit through this bullshit, I quietly hoped.

With a final knee slide from TVH and a standing ovation from the crowd, the staff returned to their offices and my debrief from the EDOs commenced.

'Thank you, Serge and TVH. If you can both take a seat, please.'

I was sure I was going to be blasted for what was a blatant set-up—surely it equates to plagiarism of some sort.

'Well, Serge, without a doubt, and I think Dave here would agree [big north–souths from Dave] that would have to be one of the better instructional briefs we have ever seen. The way you . . . blah blah blah.' You've got to be shitting me—they actually bought it.

With the bullshit out of the way, we got into airborne instruction. Put simply, this is the art of flying the F-18 from the back seat regardless of what your student tries to do to you from the front seat. We would practise taxiing from the back seat, which is hard because the forward visibility is very limited with the front seat and the leading edge extension pretty much obscuring everything. We would practice all basic flying sequences, take-offs, landings, aerobatics, low flying, formation and air-to-air refuelling from the back seat. With this domestic training out of the way, the fun started.

The air-to-air phase was fundamentally about advanced dogfighting or basic fighter manoeuvres (BFM). BFM forms a key building block for a lot of fighter flying. It teaches pilots the ability to rapidly assess range, aspect and closure of an enemy aircraft, and then manoeuvre behind the bandit in minimum time and employ an offensive gun attack. These skills are then used in such manoeuvres as rejoining with friendly fighters, rejoining with air-to-air tankers, low-altitude manoeuvering and conducting pop-up attacks against ground targets. BFM is a fighter pilot's basic toolbox; however, it's among the hardest things we would ever have to teach a student.

Dogfighting imparts phenomenal fatigue on the F-18's wings, fuselage and tails. As such, the cost of dogfighting is so expensive that limited hours are available to teach students. The FCI course taught us to squeeze the maximum amount of learning into the inherently short flights—generally less than 50 minutes due to fuel limitations. There's no room for floundering with such little time to train, so this phase can be tough. I loved learning how to put the jet into places I had never previously seen. Full rudder, high-alpha spins and 60-degree high-alpha 'cobra' manoeuvres allowed an FCI to move from a defensive position to an offensive position in 40 seconds, or maintain an offensive position regardless of the defender's manoeuvres. With our tactical skills now as sharp as a samurai's sword, it was time to practise swinging it.

Exercise Aces North is the final phase of the FCI course, otherwise known as the war phase. The phase is treated as a real-world deployment to an overseas base and includes pre-deployment isolated personnel training, real-world country briefs and real-world threats. The missions are the most complex that FCIs ever get to fly—even for those FCIs who went to Iraq.

The last flight of the FCI course is a dawn strike from RAAF Base Tindal back to Williamtown. Dawn is chosen for a couple of reasons: one is that the enemy is the least prepared from a circadian rhythm perspective, and for the same reason it's difficult for us to operate at this time of day so it is something that FCIs are expected to be able to do well. The other thing about the dawn strike is that it's traditionally led by the dux of the course who no-one has any idea about until the day before the strike.

I was amazed when our course 'mum' called me in to ask if I would lead the dawn strike. I couldn't believe that after all my nerves, all my sleepless nights during which I had visualised every manoeuvre, every attack, every radio call . . . I had topped the class. I didn't feel deserving and in some way continued to deny myself any satisfaction from the personal achievement—the mission was my focus and it was not about me . . . it was about the force.

The mission was a twelve-aircraft strike versus everything that Williamtown and Nowra could launch at us, with a high-explosive drop onto Singleton Range at 0600. We put together a simple plan that we felt we could execute well at that time of day before we took some Temazepam sleeping tablets and went to sleep at midday.

I woke a couple of hours later and was unable to get back to sleep no matter how many sleeping tablets I took. I had quadrupled the maximum dose before I gave up and got up to do some more mission planning. I woke up when my alarm went off, with my maps soaked in drool and feeling like I was really hungover.

I dragged my sorry arse into the crew van and managed to wake up enough to give my last brief of the course. Our three four-ships were given the callsigns 'Superior', 'Marginal' and 'Unsat'—the grades that we had grown used to throughout the course . . . particularly the last two.

The flight would require two 'plugs' into the tanker to get us from one side of Australia to the other. The night tanking went well, with numerous UFO reports being issued throughout central Australia as twelve jets and one tanker flew in relative formation for three hours en route to the western airspace that lies west of Newcastle. We fought through the seemingly endless line of MiGs, got our bombs off and, afterwards, conducted some approved low fly-pasts of the base on arrival.

We were greeted at our aircraft by family, friends and a host of senior officers. I appreciated the congratulations from our instructors, now peers, the most. I had truly loved the course and was grateful for the effort that each one of them had made to get us through— instructing is a very selfless act.

Within 30 minutes of landing we were at the back bar and the fun began. Patches were presented and shot glasses filled with Jeremiah Weed—an entirely putrid paint-stripping whisky renowned to fighter pilots the world over. I was just getting into the swing of things when a senior knucklehead thought he would rain on our parade.

'Trouble with you FCIs,' he announced loudly, 'is that you think that the entire wing revolves around you—you're really not that important in the big scheme of things.'

He was probably right, but it was our day and we had all sacrificed a hell of a lot to get there—and not so some cheese dick could piss on us. I couldn't let it go.

'Tell me, mate, were you born a fuckwit or did you just grow into one?' I asked, glaring at the idiot with a lot more bars on his shoulder than me. This incident would haunt me for the next two year as I was charged for insubordination before being posted to work for the guy where he was my executive officer (XO). I was really getting to love the RAAF posting cycle.

At the end of FCI course we were sent to the US for two weeks of instructional visits including Topgun, Nellis Air Force Base and numerous other fighter combat training institutions. After what was effectively nine years of study, most of the trip was spent with some sort of blood alcohol level.

Nellis Air Force Base was 'Home of the Thunderbirds'—the US display team—and the biggest fighter base in the world. We had a series of lectures and courses to complete on the AMRAAM (advanced medium-range air-to-air) missile, NVGs (night vision goggles) and Datalink, which allows me to see exactly where friendly aircraft are and what they're doing—precisely the sort of stuff no-one should have to endure in the City of Sin.

We hired out some rooms at the Las Vegas Hilton to re-create our own Tailhook convention. Tailhook had been an infamous US naval aviator party that was held annually in Las Vegas prior to it being shut down in the early 90s due to accusations of inappropriate behaviour and politics. Not bound by the same rules as the US navy, our night turned into an endless blur of strippers, casinos, Elvis suits and limousines which would lead me to have a serious case of deja vu a few years later when the movie *The Hangover* was released.

The next morning I convinced our Intelo 'Spy' and Grubby to come with me to Area 51 to see if we could chance a UFO sighting. I had to work on Spy to get him to go as he was due for his deep background security check. I convinced him it would all be harmless and we would just drive the crew van out to the alien town of Rachel to have lunch at the Little Ale Inn. For three years prior to visiting Nellis I had been corresponding via email with the 'Groom Lake Desert Rat'. The rat had more than one screw loose as he had been penetrating the Groom Lake Area 51 UFO Base for years and posting the results of his 'surveillance reconnaissance' missions on the internet. I had to hand it to him; he was either totally fucking stupid or incredibly brave.

'The box', as we called it when flying around Area 51, was a designated restricted area that even US air force aircraft were not allowed to fly into without special authorisation. During an exercise one year a US F-15 pilot had a fire warning light illuminate which he could not extinguish. Assuming he had an uncontrollable fire, he landed on the runway at Area 51—at 12 kilometres, it was three times the length of the longest military runway in Australia. Whatever they were flying out there was either really fast, very heavy or flown by really bad pilots who had difficulty landing on a runway of normal length. The F-15 pilot was given a 'Guantanamo beanie' and marched to an isolated holding facility where he remained for a day while someone (or something) who knew a lot about F-15s repaired his jet. The next day when they removed his hood he was standing next to his running jet in the middle of the runway. The security personnel told him to get in, take off and keep his eyes looking forwards.

I figured if they treated a US military pilot with a top-secret clearance that way, then my little desert rodent friend was probably going to end up 'disappeared' if he was ever caught commando-crawling around the base in his army surplus uniform—either that or with an alien probe up his date. The other thing that made me question the mental state of the Rat was the fact that he was publishing the results of his suicide missions on the internet. That was how I had come in contact with him originally—I had found some pictures of aircraft that looked a hell of a lot like the B2 stealth bomber, plus other things that weren't yet public. From a military aviator's perspective I became fascinated with these futuristic aircraft that were being developed and the potential I may have to be involved with them years down the track.

Once I knew my trip to Nellis was confirmed, I contacted the Rat in order to meet him in person after so many years of email. And, of course, I was keen to do some 'sightseeing'. The Rat provided me with access to satellite imagery of the site well before Google Earth was invented as well as maps and, most importantly, a schematic diagram of the seismic movement detection sensors. The Rat had worked out how to disarm these sensors, which were placed along all access roads surrounding ET's home.

I received my final 'instructions' from the Rat, who was unable to meet with me because 'it was too hot'. He warned me not to leave the bitumen as there had been an unusual number of 'black helicopters' patrolling the perimeter of Area 51 and we would be sure to be detained for questioning if we left the road.

Disappointed that I wouldn't get to meet the former alien abductee, we headed off to Rachel for lunch. The town was in the middle of nowhere and I assumed most of the locals to be aliens or very closely aligned. We ate at the Little Ale Inn where I informed the publican we were all UFOligists from Australia. He then reached under the counter and pulled out his 'special album' which contained photographs of all sorts of aircraft that I had never seen before, including aircraft without tails nor wings. I started to believe that maybe Fox Mulder and Dana Scully were telling the truth.

We left the diner and were heading back to Vegas when we came upon the infamous 'black mailbox' that the Rat had told me marked the dirt road that led to the alien base. Despite protests from Spy and Grubby I turned off the bitumen and started the one-hour dirt drive towards the base. We were now officially 'off the reservation' so Grubby and Spy started scanning the sky for the 'black helicopters'. I was sure the whole thing was nothing but an out-of-control rumour spurred on by Hollywood. Then the radio went dead.

And not much longer after that Grubby and Spy fell asleep. Now I couldn't be sure whether the previous late night of strippers and blackjack was the cause of their altered state of consciousness, or the hypnotic ruts in the dirt road—surely there was no such thing as an alien mind-control device and, if there was, why wasn't it working on me? Maybe they were saving me for the anal probe?

Eventually I saw a small wooden stump on the side of the road with an orange reflector on it—the sign of a seismic detector according to the Rat. It was now death or glory and so I floored it. I figured the response time was going to be based on the average speed of an average vehicle on this average road. We were fighter pilots in a hire car that I was sure could cover the ground in half the time. I thought, if we can just get there before they load up their choppers we might stand a chance to spot a three-fingered grey man and make the ensuing interrogation a little easier to get through.

Spy and Grubby woke when the hire van started to get airborne over some of the dirt mounds.

'Mate, what are we hauling the mail for?' asked Grubby.

'We just passed one of these,' I said, handing Grubby the graphic of the seismic movement detector. 'They now know we're here.'

'Serge, stop!' pleaded Spy.

'We'll be fine. They're not going to pop a couple of Aussie military folk—we have diplomatic immunity. Could you imagine the shit-fight?'

'You're wearing thongs and a Hawaiian shirt, Serge, and you're driving a rental car,' pointed out Grubby.

'Yeah, but surely they won't shoot without asking who we are first—will they?' I replied, hoping Grubby's three-year US residency might be able to shed some light on the matter.

'Yes, they will.'

By this stage Spy had put a towel over his head to hide his face so that the electro-optical surveillance system they were sure to be using wouldn't be able to identify him and create a headache for him when he got to his security interview. Convinced that they were both overreacting, I kept my foot to the floor as we approached the narrow pass that acted as an entry through the crater-like mountain range surrounding the base. We were almost there.

As I slowed to negotiate the bends through the pass, a large sign appeared on the side of the road: 'Access Prohibited—Use of Lethal Force Authorized.'

'Do you reckon that's serious, mate, or just put there to spook you and Spy?' I asked Grubby.

'No, mate, that is deadly serious,' said Grubby. 'I strongly suggest we get the fuck out of here now.'

As I started to debate the seriousness of the sign, and my constitutional 'right' to legal representation, a tan Humvee came into sight less than 100 metres from where we had stopped next to the sign. I could make out a gun on the top and some big boys in the front seats wearing black sunglasses. The Desert Rat had warned me that these guys would be ex–special forces with a shoot-to-kill mandate.

'Serge, turn the fucking car around now!' growled Grubby.

Spy was having some sort of conniption in the back seat under his towel which, along with my copy of the disarmament procedure for the seismic detection sensors, wasn't helping my cover story that we were lost tourists. I had now passed my critical sphincter level and immediately turned the van around to sprint away, looking even less like tourists.

We made it back to the highway without being intercepted by any black helicopters, the radio signal returned and we again traversed the alien mind-control field which I was immune to. We never did get any confirmation on the presence of aliens. Spy passed his security upgrade. I have experienced unexplained pains in the arse ever since.

Grubby had his chance to reciprocate my alien adventure a week later when we visited a training establishment on the east coast of the US. We stayed at Virginia Beach and had another party promoting 'international relations'. Very early the next morning I was woken by Grubby.

'Serge, wake up. Let's go or we'll be late.'

'Late for what?' I asked, believing we had a day off.

'The Pentagon. I think I can get us in.'

With that we threw on our flying suits and drove three hours to Washington. Grubby had previously completed an exchange to the United States Marine Corp (USMC) to fly F-18s and had made contact with some of his marine corp mates who were now assigned to the 'five-sided wind tunnel'. The drive hurt as we were seriously hungover and sweating out pure tequila—by the time we arrived we stank.

We parked the hire car and walked straight into the main entrance.

'Aren't we going to have to get some visitors passes or something, mate?' I asked as I looked around and saw every military officer staring at our flying suits. I then noticed the complete absence of any other flying suits in the area. 'No-one else is wearing flying suits. Are you sure you've got this covered, mate?'

'Stick with me and look like you own the place, Serge,' Grubby insisted. He then walked straight up to the head security guard and pulled out a fake USMC military ID card that he carried around with him. It read 'Colonel Grubby Grub'.

'Morning, sergeant. Colonel Grime and Flight Lieutenant Serge from Australia, if we could have some passes, please?'

The head of security asked for my ID, looked at it and then smiled. 'OK. You guys are from Australia. You guys are like brothers. Here you go,' and promptly handed us two 'no escort required' badges.

YGTBSM! We were in.

Grubby kept walking around like he owned the place and soon we were standing outside the 'Balkans War Room' from where Operation Allied Force in Bosnia was being run. Surely this was not good, I thought to myself. Right next door was an office signed 'William Cohen—Secretary of Defence'.

'Mate, what the fuck are you doing? You're going to get us killed.'

'Stop worrying, Serge. We have diplomatic immunity,' he replied and proceeded to walk straight in.

'Can I help you, Sir?' asked the secretary's secretary.

'Morning, Ma'am. Is Bill in?' asked Grubby without batting an eyelid.

I was finding it very hard to keep from blushing with embarrassment. Surely we were going to be made—we were the only guys wearing flying suits for fuck's sake.

'I'm sorry, Sir, Secretary Cohen is out right now. Would you like to leave a message?'

'Yes, please. Could you just let him know that Serge and Grubby dropped in to see him and we'll catch up with him later on.'

'Certainly, Sir. I'll get the message to him as soon as he returns.'

From there Grubby was somehow able to find the only bar in the Pentagon, which was hidden inside a navy vault that looked like a giant bank vault. The local navy guys poured us cold beers all afternoon and were amazed that we'd been able to walk around the Pentagon in flying suits—let alone get in without any official ID.

Two years after graduating as an FCI, I was fortunate enough to run the war phase for the next FCI course. I was the Aces North phase commander and pretty keen to use my overdeveloped imagination and passion for fighter flying to dream up some great scenarios. For this FCI course the ground scenarios involved Special Forces (SF) integration. We were all about to learn a thing or two about training for war.

With the squadron deployed to RAAF Tindal, and operating out of the secure underground bunker, the atmosphere was controlled by the instructors to create a very realistic wartime environment for the students. Intelligence feeds, bomb damage assessments, insecure base procedures were all used to stress the students to a level that would prepare them for the real thing—including resistance to inter-rogation training.

The SF missions centred around supporting the SF team to conduct a special recovery operation of a downed pilot that was behind enemy lines. The scenario wasn't known to the students and was initiated by myself coming off target on a night-strike mission. I had specifically chosen Slime as my wingman because he'd been having some difficulties and I was hoping that the change in mission type might help him to lift his game.

We were number eleven and twelve in a twelve-ship laser-guided bomb (LGB) strike—not the safest place to be. 'Tail End Charlie' means you rarely arrive with surprise and you are always the last out. We had fought through eight Su-27 Flankers which were flown by 75 Squadron pilots flying F-18s in a manner that replicates the weapon capabilities of the Su-27. Slime and I had shot a couple en route to the target and now focused our attention on identifying the correct target through our targeting pods and making sure the weapons program and switches were correctly made to get the bombs off the jets. After we gently moved the targeting hairs onto the targets, our lasers ensured two direct hits from our LGBs.

'Warhound 3, off safe.' Slime had got his bombs off.

Looks like he might pass this ride, I thought. Let's see how he handles this next bit . . .

'Warhound 4, off safe, mud 6 defending . . . I'm hit, I'm hit . . . ejecting.' I was simulating that an SA-6 SAM had hit me. I turned off my lights, my transponder and departed at low level out the civilian side of the airspace. Still listening in on our fighting frequency, I could monitor Slime as he initiated combat search and rescue (SAR). This is a very challenging task with Su-27 Flankers trying to shoot you and ground forces trying to pick up your ejected mate.

Then, like a man possessed, Slime went into action: 'Dark Angel Combine, this is Warhound 3. Warhound 4 is down in the target area. I am established as on-scene SAR commander 31 000 feet (9500 metres). Dark Angel, request you establish a barrier cap between the target area and touchline [code word for the enemy airfield]. Vengence 1 and 2, track now to the tanker for 4000-pound (1400-litre) onload. Expect to replace me on station ASAP. Vengence 3 and 4, request you recommit hard left now to assist Warhound 3. Fox 3 southern group recommitting for the target area.'

Slime wasn't just handling it—he was eating it up. Within 30 seconds he had correctly assessed the friendly/enemy disposition with full consideration of fuel states, weapons, safe altitudes, the downed pilot and the surface threats. He had then issued immediate orders that would ensure all eleven aircraft could work together to survive and hopefully help me survive on the ground.

After five minutes, the simulated time of fall for my chute, the radio came alive on the international emergency frequency.

'Warhound 3, this is Warhound 4. I've touched down south of the target area and can see headlights south of my position. Get me out of here.' The downed aircrew was now being simulated by another instructor, Westy, who had been choppered out earlier and dropped in the middle of nowhere with nothing more than his survival vest. I think I giggled in my oxygen mask as Westy was about the most unlikely guy to survive a night in the jungle—or the 'J', as we called it.

In the middle of his air-to-air engagement with two Su-27s, Slime still had the brainspace to talk to Westy. I was impressed.

'Warhound 4, authenticate Alpha.' Slime was confirming that this was indeed Westy on the radio and not the enemy trying to lure us into a trap.

Westy replied, 'Warhound 4, I authenticate Golf.'

I knew it was Westy's voice but he had screwed up the authentication. The authentication phrase of the day was 'lazydog' and he should have authenticated with Zulu—one letter to the right of Alpha. This was not going well.

'Warhound 4, authenticate Golf,' Slime transmitted, hoping Westy would get it right this time.

'Warhound 4, I authenticate Alpha. Get me out of here.'

Shit, Westy had screwed it up again. I couldn't let the exercise get off the rails so I intervened on the radio: 'Warhound 3, authentication complete. Continue.'

Through a series of challenges and responses, Warhound 3 was then able to locate Warhound 4 before he reached his return to base (RTB) fuel state.

'Warhound 4. Sit tight. Conserve your batteries. Continue to listen on the hour for five minutes. We are RTB this time and will have you out tomorrow.'

The formation then returned to Tindal and entered the debrief room for a quick overview of the incident. Once we were seated I introduced Tool to the course. He was a former F-18 pilot and most of the guys knew him. Thing was, Tool had not flown F-18s for a couple of years now—he had transferred to the Special Forces and was the SF team leader for the exercise. He was a very unique SAS cat indeed. Together with the rest of his team, they all wore very casual clothes, probably could have done with a haircut and seemed far too meek and mild. While their manner may not have oozed 'hardened killers', they each looked like they could have taken out our entire FCI course with one hand tied behind their back. I quietly wondered how they would hold up in a dogfight.

The next day we started work at noon. After a quick capability overview from each member of the team, the intelligence officer (Intelo) gave us an update on the status of our unlikely jungle man— Westy.

During the night Westy had moved in accordance with his escape and evasion plan and continued his radio calls—well, at least he got that bit right. Intelligence assets had located his position in the early hours of the morning—unfortunately, so had the enemy. Westy was now being held by the enemy and the intelo flashed up some satellite imagery of a prison facility in the middle of the Northern Territory. The prison was simulated by a multi-storey compound made from shipping containers, which I had organised to be purpose-built for this specific mission. The SF team and the FCI students now went into a 48-hour planning cycle on how they would rescue our jungle man who, I was guessing, had probably had enough of the mozzies, cold, snakes and spiders about now. Knowing Westy, I was enjoying this mission a little more than I should have.

With the day's planning finished at midnight we went to the bar for a quick beer. The SF guys didn't accept our invitation. A level of focus and attention that rivalled our own became apparent in every member of Tool's team. The other aspect that became apparent was how well the two organisations worked together—I don't think I heard the word 'no' used once. It was always 'rog', 'can do', 'wilco' and 'no probs'. What a pleasure it was. I filed away a little human relations maxim: The more insecure a person is, the more likely they are to say no to you.

With the next day came the first night of what was really a three-night mission; the insertion, the direct action and the extraction. While the mission would probably occur in just one night in the real world, we segmented it in order for all the students to be able to participate in different roles, such as air-to-air lead, air-to-ground lead and helicopter escort lead.

Night one appeared simple: escort two helicopters to their intended landing zone to insert the SF team. Trouble was, there were three enemy MiG bases, 36 MiGs, numerous SAM threats and ground forces that could compromise the SF team. All the aircrew and SF team members briefed the mission for 90 minutes. The SF team were dressed in their tactical field equipment, night vision goggles, camouflage face paint and weapons—they looked like aliens of some sort.

But night one did not go too well, with numerous fighters getting shot down. The good news was the choppers made it in and out unscathed.

The next night was the prison break. By this time Westy had started to go troppo. Isolation, even for short periods of time, can do weird things to people—especially those who don't spend much time alone. Westy was getting restless, and cold, and itchy, and thirsty. It was time to get him back.

This mission commenced with the SF team walking in from their landing zone and establishing themselves in a hide outside of the simulated prison. Their progress was a little slower than normal as they had been asked to ground-laser the target for our LGBs.

With this tactic, the SF team illuminate specific targets with a large, man-portable laser that then guides our bombs accurately to where they point the laser. It is a hazardous type of delivery for numerous reasons—the main one being the team has to be close to where the bombs impact.

With their ground laser ready on time, at the planned location, the FCI students pushed in to start fighting the MiGs in order to get to the target area. The plan required the aircraft to take out the guard houses, the barracks, and breach the wall to enable the SF entry to the compound. Each aircraft would release one laser-guided training round (LGTR), which are 3-metre long steel tubes fitted with a laser guidance kit that impact the ground at around 1000 kilometres per hour. This was the first time they had been used in Australia, it was the first time any of us had used them, the first time we had ever seen the target, and the first time the team had used the laser designator. And, oh yeah, we were going to do it at night, with lights out and no communications.

Unbeknown to the students, Tool and I had spent weeks planning this mission—including how to do it without talking to the SF team. The students were naturally cautious; however, with total dedication they went out and flew the missions.

The first jet arrived overhead the prison, pushed over into a dive and transmitted: 'Ford 1, in live.'

Shortly thereafter a tone was transmitted indicating the weapon was in flight. The SF team heard the tone and started illuminating the second storey window of the high-rise building—the first guard house.

Vvvvvwwwwwwooooommmmppppaaaa. A 'shack' or direct hit.

There was no time for celebrations, the next jet was in his dive. This continued until all jets had released—twelve shacks.

It was now time for the SF team to rendezvous with Westy. This was the bit I had envisaged being the funniest.

The team approached Westy over a one-hour period using their stealth tradecraft. Unlike the team, Westy was not equipped with NVGs. So Westy just sat on a log at the pre-arranged GPS position waiting for the team to pick him up. However, the isolation had been too much for him and he had started to lose his marbles. By the time the team got to him they were shocked to find him singing.

'Seventy-one bottles of beer on the wall, 71 bottles of beer. If one of the bottles should happen to fall, there will be 70 bottles of beer on the wall . . .'

This blatant lack of professionalism in Westy riled the SF cats tremendously. The scenario called for covert procedures to be used in order not to be compromised by the simulated enemy patrols. With Westy's singing, there was a likely chance the SF team would also be discovered. The team decided to teach him a lesson and started to play games with him.

'Seventy bottles of beer on the wall, 70 . . .'

Crack. A stick snapped. The SF team had manoeuvred within a few metres of Westy but he couldn't see them.

'Who's there? Is anyone there? Sixty-nine bottles of beer on the wall . . .'

Crack crack.

'OK, guys, if you're there, come out. It's not funny anymore. I've been out here for three days and I just want to go home and have a shower and a . . . Uuuuggghhh.'

The wind was knocked out of Westy as two operators hit him from behind while picking him up and starting to run through the bush. Westy could see nothing.

'Ohh, are you guys right? Take it easy, will . . .' Westy was cut off by a tree branch in his face. And then another, and another. The operators continued to run at a pace Westy couldn't match. His flying boots scraped across the ground as he struggled to keep up.

Eventually the operators stopped running and pushed Westy to the ground, making no assumption he was friendly until his isolated personnel procedures had been authenticated. Lying on his stomach with a boot pinning his head down and a MP4 muzzle pointing at his face, Westy started to get a little off-balance.

'What type of car was your first car?' the interrogator asked gruffly.

'Umm, ahh, a Holden?' he replied with that uncertain inflection at the end—like a child trying to hide a lie.

'No, dickhead. What about your first pet?' The boot started to get heavier and the barrel was now thrust into his forehead.

'Umm, err, a dog?' It was obvious Westy was guessing. Isolated personnel reports, or ISOPREP forms, are completed prior to deployment and are used to identify persons in these isolated circumstances. Problem was, Westy had not paid any attention while completing his form and was now unable to remember his responses.

'OK, flyboy. Last chance before we take you back as captured enemy. When were you born?'

Westy finally got the correct answer and night two was complete.

The final night involved escorting choppers in to the team, conducting bombing in support of the helicopter pick-up and then escorting the choppers back out again. The mission went well and Westy's relief at getting home was only surpassed by that of the team for not having to put up with his bitching and moaning any longer.

Before the SF team left, we got them all up for a flight in the Hornets and I got to make my guy spew—not so fuckin' tough now, hey, tough guy? Upon their departure the SF team presented our squadron with one of the LGTRs we had dropped and a message of appreciation written on it. They also presented Westy with a giant dummy on a chain to help him stop whinging.

It was a great exercise with all the students graduating as FCIs— Slime went on to be one of the best FCIs Australia has ever had.

Professional relationships and procedures were developed with the generally closed SF community, and tactics were developed that only a couple of years later would be used by both 75 Squadron and our Special Forces personnel in Afghanistan and Iraq. Westy has been camping ever since.

Tool once said to me, 'What's the difference between an SF operator, operating deep behind enemy lines, and an F-18 pilot conducting a combat air patrol over the Timor Sea?'

As I was fumbling for an answer, he cut me off.

'Nothing, mate. You're on your own. You call the shots. You take your commander's guidance, rules of engagement, intelligence, whatever, and you put it all together at that split-second in time to make the right decision.'

This ability to operate autonomously is fundamental to the Australian way of warfare and something we used to hold over the Soviets, who had very centralised command and control structures. Sadly, it is something I have seen eroded terribly over the last few years. Technology now gives commanders in Florida, or Canberra, the ability to see the same radar picture, Datalink picture, weapon pod picture, unmanned aerial vehicle (UAV) feed, etc. as the dudes operating deep—air, land or sea. This technology inherently leads to the 1000-mile screwdriver effect—desk jockeys and politicians curled up safely in some bunker miles forward of enemy lines, drinking a coffee and telling you what and how to do your job. Leadership is about empowerment—letting that 21-year-old SF operator or fighter pilot do what he is trained to do best. If you don't trust him then you haven't trained him well enough.

21

Close call

After spending $25 million to train me into becoming one of Australia's most lethal aerial killers, with the knowledge and skills to take down any medium-sized country on the planet, the RAAF posting officers did what they do best and screwed things up yet again. Our entire FCI course was posted to the F-18 basic training school to teach students how to start and taxi the jet. We had to take a back seat—literally. This was going to hurt.

Teaching young fighter pilots is a true privilege—if you can call young guys continually trying to kill themselves, and you, a privilege. The first batch you teach is the hardest, and you do the worst job at it. This wasn't really our fault but the fault of the dumb-arse posting officers who took these highly skilled, tightly wound individuals and asked them to play nice with twenty-year-old kids. It takes a while to become 'conscious of your unconscious' and realise that students are not born with the ability to perform a maximum-performance split S from 700 metres above the hard deck. We had to learn to break down the most basic skills we had into their fundamentals. How did we taxi straight? How did we read a checklist while flying and not lose control of the aircraft? The majority of our FCI course no longer seemed really relevant—perhaps that 'Viva Las Vegas' stuff might actually be useful now.

The F-18 operational conversion course is a demanding six-month course consisting of one month of ground school, one month of general flying (GF), one month of instrument flying (IF), one month of air-to-air, one month of air-to-ground and then a one-month deployment to Townsville for the culminating event—Exercise High Sierra.

The ground school is a combination of lectures and computer-based training where the students learn how the Hornet works. The engines, fuel system, hydraulics, flight controls, avionics, emergency systems and a whole lot more are covered in fine detail. This then allows the students to understand their normal checklists. What is the green window on the hydraulic accumulator for? What is an accumulator? The normal checklist is then learnt verbatim using a series of cockpit photos. The patter becomes a mantra where the hands follow the eyes follow the voice. Every switch, button, lever, computer menu and program is methodically set to match the checklist. Every action has a purpose which, if not performed correctly, will most likely lead to an accident.

It was missing one of these switches during the air-to-ground phase which brought me the closest I would ever come to ejecting from the Hornet. My student, Smoogsy, had struggled through the IF phase in which we demand the highest levels of performance from the students when flying in cloud, at night and with multiple emergencies. During the air-to-ground phase, we teach the students to use these skills to find a target and bomb it in these same conditions. Normally these radar navigation exercises were the most benign missions we ever flew—not this particular night, however.

We had taken off from Williamtown shortly after sunset and tracked west towards central New South Wales at high level. During this domestic leg Smoogsy tuned up his radar and targeting pod in preparation for the descent to lower altitudes. Using his radar in the dark, Smoogsy correctly found radar-significant features we had planned and was tightening up his inertial navigation systems (INS), which formed the heart of the F-18's weapon system. Without good gyroscopes the weapon computer could throw some fairly big bombs—and just finding the target can be difficult.

Tracking over Orange and Dubbo, Smoogsy commenced his descent to low altitude. On dark nights, with no copilot to back you up, something as simple as a descent can scare you shitless. You can't see the ground or horizon. Your descent can get as high as 10 000 metres per minute, which is the equivalent of hitting the ground one minute after the flight attendant on an airliner tells you to put up your tray table. With nothing to warn you, so little time, and the requirement to be multitasking on other things like flying formation, looking at your radar, looking at your radar warning receiver (RWR), trying to get tally on the bandits or trying to find a target on the targeting pod, something that seems very simple and benign can end up killing you.

With our eyes focused on the altimeter, and our navigation system assured, we descended to the minimum safe altitude (MSA)—300 metres above the ground. This was the minimum we could safely fly at night without night vision goggles (NVGs). We were now tracking Dubbo to Tamworth at 950 kilometres per hour and everything was going to plan. Approaching Tamworth, Smoogsy again did a good job of multitasking to find a bridge on his radar and again checked our navigation system. The INS was tight. We turned the corner and climbed to our next MSA for our track to Armidale across the Northern Tablelands, where the terrain rises to 1500 metres AMSL.

Suddenly the master caution light lit up both our cockpits like bright orange floodlights and the *Deedle deedle* tone fractured the calm drone of the engines. That old adrenal gland, and I mean old by now, had just slammed another dose straight into my veins. An 'INS ATT' (insufficient attitude) caution message illuminated on both of our left displays, advising us that the navigation system Smoogsy had been doing such a great job aligning was now not playing the game—our primary attitude display was now no longer reliable. This display is projected into the heads-up display (HUD) and Smoogsy was using it to make sure we didn't descend into the ground—which, at this speed, we could hit in under ten seconds.

While the outcomes could be serious, the processes Boeing and the RAAF had put in place meant that Smoogsy was more than capable of getting out of this little jam.

'Master caution reset. HUD switch to standby [STBY].' Smoogsy was all over it and had promptly carried out the emergency checklist he was trained to do during the GF and IF phases. By moving the HUD switch from INS to STBY, Smoogsy's HUD and my back seat repeater display were now both being driven from Smoogsy's backup attitude display indicator (ADI) down by his right knee and not by the failing INS. Resetting the master caution light had plunged our cockpits back into darkness and my heart started to slow below 150 beats per minute.

'Nice one, Smoogsy,' I said to him supportively, and did a quick scan of all my primary flight instruments—which is hard in the back seat of the Hornet. There is no HUD in the back seat so as an instructor you are limited to a small 10-centimetre square display which is well off to the side, forcing you to lean left and forwards to fly accurate instruments. While I was in this uncomfortable position, I noticed a problem.

The vertical speed indicator (VSI) was indicating a 70 metre per minute rate of descent but the attitude was indicating level with a slight turn to the right—we would hit the ground in less than five minutes. But five minutes is a long time in fighters so I didn't get too excited just yet.

'Smoogsy, confirm you selected the HUD switch to STBY,' I asked him.

'Confirmed. HUD switch is set to STBY,' Smoogsy replied.

'Well, then, fly the attitude and get us back up to MSA,' I commanded in a fairly direct tone.

I felt Smoogsy pull back on the stick slightly and kept my eyes on the VSI anticipating a decrease in our rate of descent and a slight climb back up to MSA. It didn't happen, but the angle of bank increased without Smoogsy commanding it to. The fun factor of this mission was now gone. We were now 250 metres AGL with our rate of descent increasing and the compass starting to spin.

'Taking over, Smoogsy,' I called, and firmly planted my hands and feet on the controls as the adrenaline started pumping full bore—this was now fight or flight time. There must be a relationship somewhere between adrenaline and the mind's time clock, because time dilation is a phenomenon I was very used to—as well as the fact that fighter pilots' minds generally run fairly fast on a slow day. A flying lesson I had been given in Perth when learning to fly the Macchi jet trainer came flooding back into my mind like a well-aimed bullet—partial panel flying.

Partial panel flying is a degraded IF technique that used to be taught due to the relatively poor reliability of aircraft attitude indicators. Using this technique, pilots are taught to fly without reference to attitude by using secondary instruments alone—skidball to help you fly with the correct amount of rudder, the vertical speed indicator to help you fly with the correct pitch and the compass to help you fly with the correct angle of bank. It is no longer taught due to the reliability of aircraft avionics, though I decided I would give the chief flying instructor at the Central Flying School a quick call to discuss his syllabus—if I managed to get us out of the mess we were in.

'OK, Smoogsy, I'm going to give this one go and then we're out of here,' I rattled off, and started to use Tiger Moth flying techniques on our $50-million jet. With the compass spinning right I quickly rolled slightly to the left (imagining we were right wing low) and

At age 24 I was awarded the Sir Richard Williams ('Dick Bill') trophy for Fighter Pilot of the Year—RAAF Base Tindal, 1994.

'In Hot for the O's Mess'—weaving some magic on a Friday afternoon. The contrails lasted until after sunset. RAAF Base Tindal, 1995.

The Murderous Marauding Magpies of No. 75 Squadron, 1995. Some of the most capable individuals this country has ever produced (plus Spook).

'In the basket'—en route from Darwin to Singapore for Exercise Churinga, 1995. Shortly after this photo was taken another aircraft ripped the entire hose out of the jet, resulting in F-18s diverting to pretty much every airfield between Singapore and Australia.

Robbo, TVH and Marty were groomsmen at my wedding—Brisbane, 1995. TVH later went on to compete successfully in the Australian National Elvis impersonator competition.

The King and his security detail—TVH's bucks party, Pine Creek, Northern Territory, 1996.

The ejection seat trainer. More pilots had their back injured in this device than were ever injured in real ejections. RAAF Base Edinburgh, Adelaide, 1996.

Fly by Wire—RAAF Base Tindal Hang Gliding Club, 1996.

How I like to remember JP—a free spirit, living his life to the full. Byron Bay, 1996.

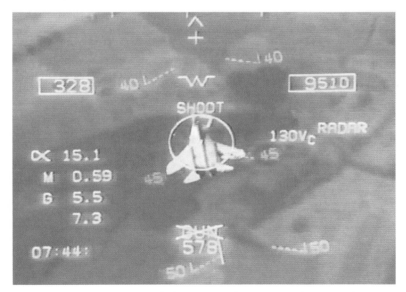

'Guns kill the loafing MiG at 9000 feet'—HUD tape from exercise Churinga, Malaysia, 1997. No. 77 Squadron were the first Western air force to fight the MiG-29, which 'intelligence' was telling us could not be beaten. Not sure the pilot of this jet had read the intelligence report. (Image found at http://upload.wikimedia.org/wikipedia/commons/3/3a/German_MiG-29_in_F-18C_gun_camera.jpg)

Fourship formation made up of jets from all four Australian Squadrons—3SQN (Southern Cross), 75SQN (Diamond Checkerboard), 77SQN (Green 'swoosh' that Nike stole) and 2 Operational Conversion Unit (Tiger)—off the coast of Newcastle, 1997.

Provisioning our C-130 Hercules for our 'survival course' in the Whitsunday Islands, 1998. These sailing trips were held at the end of every fighter course as a way to welcome the students into the fold.

View through the HUD. (Image found at http://upload.wikimedia.org/wikipedia/commons/7/79/HUD_view.jpg)

'In Hot'—a 10-degree strafe with a 'war load' of missiles and bombs, Delamere Weapons Range, 1996. Two seconds late on the pull-up and you will be transformed into a smoking hole.

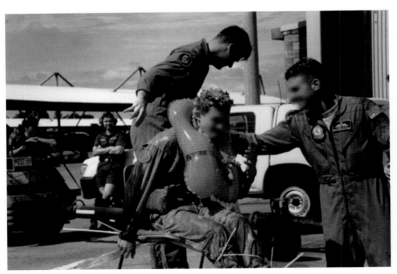

My last flight, RAAF Base Williamtown, 2000. The boys had prepared a brew of off-milk, sour yoghurt and other time-expired produce that would have made Saddam Hussein's WMD scientists proud—if they existed.

gave a slight check-back on the stick. The compass partially slowed and the VSI indicated we had stopped descending—200 metres AGL the ground. I repeated the inputs and was able to stop the turn and start a slight climb. By dead reckoning I put us at wings level and so checked back further on the stick to increase the rate of climb and lit the blowers. The rate of the climb on the VSI increased to 2000 metres per minute and we were away from the ground.

At this stage Smoogsy had determined that his standby ADI near his right knee was working fine and so I handed back over to Smoogsy. A student on his standby ADI was a far safer option than me trying to recall flying techniques I had not used in nine years. With Smoogsy shooting us back up to safety, I told him to start heading back for Williamtown. The weather forecast for Willy was bad, just as predicted. Now Smoogsy would have to try and fly an instrument approach on his standby instruments, at night, in bad weather, onto a wet runway. I had a better idea and jumped onto the squadron common radio which would put me in contact with another instructor—if there was another one airborne.

'Maple ops, this is Maple 22, any aircraft north of Willy request you come up this frequency.'

'Maple 22, this is Maple 26, go ahead.' I recognised the voice—it was Shop. He was a great operator and I started to feel a bit more comfortable about the situation.

'Schtorr, this is Serge. We've had some sort of attitude malfunction, we've run the checklist but I'm on partial panel in the back and Smoogsy is standby only in the front. Request rejoin for formation RTB [return to base].' I was going to get Schtorr to lead us home and fly a visual close formation on his wing through the thunderstorms and land with him as a pair. Sounds difficult? It is.

Schtorr asked for my bearing and distance from Willy. Then we coordinated our locations and commenced a 150 nautical mile intercept on each other. While I worked with Schtorr, Smoogsy was coordinating air traffic control clearances and getting us some priority by declaring an emergency. With our clearances sorted, I demonstrated a night rejoin to Smoogsy, flew into close echelon on Schtorr and we started our RTB 'holding hands'.

Schtorr did a great job of reassuring us and providing a nice stable platform through the bad weather. Consideration for your wingman is an essential attribute for a good fighter lead. He checked our fuel, got the weather for us, used his own radar to avoid the more turbulent parts of the storm, turned all his formation lights up and eased in and out of turns. Great flying from a great flight lead.

We flew through dark, turbulent clouds for ten minutes during our instrument approach to Willy, breaking out of the soup at around 500 feet. I drifted over to my side of the runway and we performed a perfect pairs landing onto the wet runway. Schtorr led us back to the carports where we shut down out of the rain and unstrapped.

Smoogsy climbed out first and descended down the stairs. I turned to descend after him and took a quick glance at the HUD ATT switch where I noticed it in the INS ATT position and not the STBY position as the checklist called for. I was immediately pissed off with Smoogsy, who realised his error as soon as I showed him.

The HUD ATT switch is a three-way switch. During the pre-flight check, the HUD ATT switch must have been in the INS ATT position or the middle position. If the INS fails then the switch is moved up one position to the HUD STBY position. Smoogsy had not completed his pre-flight inspection thoroughly enough and the switch was in the bottom position, HUD AUTO. When he moved the switch up one click, he thought he had made the right selection— which he would have if the switch had been in the right position to start with.

This is an example of how the smallest of errors in fighter flying can lead to the largest of consequences. Smoogsy failed the flight, but continued on to graduate and became a solid fighter pilot.

I quietly thanked my No. 2 Flying Training School instructor who went outside the basic syllabus to teach me the long-lost art of partial panel flying—supposedly no longer required in aviation.

While instructing at the Hornet school I started playing in a covers band in Newcastle. I had taught myself the guitar in Tindal on my first posting and soon auditioned for 'The Belt'. Most of the other band members were unemployed junkies who never really gave a rat's arse about anything other than their next hit—and the cost of the PA. I had my own PA so despite my musical abilities I was in.

We gigged for a year and placed second in the Newcastle 'Battle of the Bands'. I was enjoying it because I was learning more than I ever had about music and I felt like I was in my own social science experiment. Here I was flying jets by day, rubbing shoulders with some of Australia's most highly motivated and intelligent people, and by night I was working with people who would sell their own mother for their next fix—it was truly fascinating.

Eventually a photograph of the band appeared in the Newcastle paper and my cover was blown. Some of the knucks from work turned up on a couple of occasions but left as soon as they took one look at the establishment we were playing in—it was very much like the scene in *The Blues Brothers* where Jake and Elwood play behind a cage and have beer bottles thrown at them . . . except we didn't have a cage. I'd like to think my mates left for fear of losing their aircrew medicals rather than how bad we sounded. The stubby throwers seemed pretty happy, though.

We played one gig in Wauchope which was nearly the premature end of our meteoric rise to fame. We received an anonymous call from a guy who wanted to pay us top dollar for a gig but wouldn't tell us where or when until the day of the gig. We eventually loaded up our hire van and drove to Wauchope waiting for the call. Instructions were passed on and soon after we were setting up in a shearing shed in the middle of nowhere without a soul in sight.

Our host was very polite and offered us beers while we set up, tuned up and waited. Eventually the tranquillity of the idyllic valley was shattered by the 'Howl of a Hundred Harley', as we called it. It seemed we were going to be playing for the eastern Australian chapter of one of Australia's most notorious outlaw motorcycle gangs—I'm too scared to name them here. We all looked at each other. 'What the fuck are we going to play for these guys?' Our repertoire consisted of the current top 100—and Black Sabbath hadn't had a hit for at least twenty years.

The first set started off with myself on an electric acoustic and our lead singer, Adam, singing some ballads. It was only 3 p.m. so we thought that maybe they wouldn't mind a bit of Milli Vanilli.

It went over so badly that Adam called out the rest of the band and we went straight into our second set—bypassing the first 45 minutes of pop ballads we knew. This was going to be a quick gig. By the end of our original second, now first, set, we thought we were about to be dismembered by the bikies and fed to their dogs. John, the lead guitarist, and I spent the entire first break working out how to play 'Paranoid' by Black Sabbath and trying to teach it to Adam.

Set two was our normal set three and included a couple of heavy metal classics by AC/DC and Metallica—even these songs failed to lift the crowd. We started to seriously worry that the big bald guy who had been assigned to us as 'security' might in fact be packing a shotgun inside his long jacket. John then suggested we give 'Paranoid' a crack.

Our performance sounded like we had never rehearsed together as a band, which we hadn't, and Adam even forgot the words. The bikies, however, went fucking mental. They all got up off the grass and started fighting, running through the bonfire and throwing stubbies at us in appreciation. I nervously smiled at John knowing that this was it—this was all we had. As soon as we finished the bikies started yelling at us to play it again—we weren't going to argue. And so we did—six times in a row—and each time the song elicited the same response. I was thankful that bikies were a bit like goldfish and never remembered the last lap of their bowl.

22
Secrets in the desert

THE US MISSILES guru, and my idol at the time, Cliff Wiffle, had completed his two-week visit to Australia to teach us about our new missile—the AMRAAM—and returned to the land of the free and the home of the brave with his two Men in Black in close escort. His brain was deemed to be a national asset as he had 124 classified patents, and his departure left a hole somewhere inside of me. Who was I going to talk to about doppler range gates, proportional navigation and pulse repetition interval switching? Well, at least I had my 'SECRET NO CUNT Field Army Notebook, one, for the use of'.

My little green notebook was not standard issue for fighter pilots. As the NATO name suggested, it was for army guys who don't use PDAs, notebooks, laptops or even abacuses. With waterproof pages, it was the only thing I had found that I could write on that would not spoil when living inside of my sweaty flying suit sixteen hours a day for years on end. This notebook, or 'my brain' as I called it, had everything in it that your regular new-age fighter pilot could want, including my personal details. Such simple details are easily forgotten when your brain is full of minutiae such as the effective fusing radius of every enemy missile on the planet, all relevant articles of the Geneva Conventions on the Law of Armed Conflict, and the verbatim F-18 checklist to start, fly, employ and land the aircraft.

This checklist is embedded into you during training and, eighteen years on, I can still recite it. Surely that amounts to some form of brainwashing, qualifies 81 Wing as a cult, and has left me permanently scarred?[7]

With Cliff gone, it was now up to a small team of us to develop the necessary tactics to employ the new AMRAAM, or advanced medium-range air-to-air missile. With all the gouge I had written down from Cliff's 'secret' lectures stored in my notebook, we set about dreaming up tactics, practising them, refining them, documenting them and disseminating them to the wider fighter pilot community.

After six months it was time to put them to the test in Exercise Pitch Black, which is a multinational biannual exercise with participants from Australia, the United Kingdom, United States, Malaysia, Singapore, Indonesia and Thailand. The exercise is held in the Northern Territory, which permits some of the most extreme flying available on the planet—this is Schumacher's Monaco Grand Prix track. As well as great flying we might also indulge in the occasional wafer-thin tequila sunrise at the home of the Murderous Marauding Magpies—No. 75 Squadron.

The social scene in Katherine is fairly limited, with one nightclub (if it can be called that) imaginatively named 'Wings' and another two bars which were generally off-limits due to the high risk of losing your aircrew medical to some drunken cowboy or Aboriginal bloke. In the pursuit of greener pastures, most single fighter pilots would load up the crew van and drive the three hours to Darwin.

With debriefs complete by 1500, we rendezvoused at the officers mess bar for some survival rations to make the trip to Darwin. A couple for the road, an esky in the back, and our twelve merry men were on their way—still in our sweaty flying suits. With tactics discussions, mission debriefs and evening plans all mixed in together on our journey, our 'beer low' warning lights were soon illuminating.

I'm not sure if Mr Stuart, of Stuart Highway fame, had anything to do with 75SQN in the past, but his highway is perfectly designed between Katherine and Darwin, having a watering hole approximately every hour. By the first town of Pine Creek we were starting to charge and by Adelaide River we really did think we were funny, smart and good-looking. Not long after resuming our trip from Adelaide River, with the sun setting, I quickly developed the urge for a toilet break—and I mean right now.

'Stu, stop the van, mate. I've got to go.'

'Fuck, Serge, we just got in the van. Can't you wait until Darwin?'

'No, mate, I've got to take a shit,' I said.

'You can't go here—what are you going to wipe your arse with?'

'I'll be right, mate, just pull the bloody van over . . . now.'

Much to the reluctance and moaning of all the other guys, Stu pulled over and I burst out of the sliding door heading for the bushes. My flying suit was undone—beauty of a zip-up suit—before I reached the bushes. Half-expecting the engine revs to increase and the boys to leave me there as a joke, I was surprised when every single one of the moaners got out of the van for a piss.

With my urge attended to, I started to feel around the bushes for some decent-sized leaves—nothing but razor grass. Not wanting to slice my quoit, I reached into my left breast pocket and fished out my brain. Turning it over I ripped out some of the back pages as a surrogate for toilet paper.

With my problem solved we jumped back in the van and continued on to our flash digs in Darwin—the Darwin backpackers. It wasn't that we couldn't afford good hotels, it was that we generally got in less trouble at the backpackers. Plus it was a shorter distance to walk home.

Stu pulled up in front of the backpackers in the most unsubtle way he could—up onto the nature strip, knocking over a billboard and scaring some cosmopolitan diners. Getting a few disgusted looks, he crunched the gears into reverse a few times, stalled it a couple of times and then bunny-hopped the van back onto the street as if he'd never driven before. With cars behind us blocked, pedestrians standing clear, diners steadying their glasses and the backpackers in the lobby all staring at the moron driving the air force crew van, the doors burst open and twelve of Australia's finest flowed out of the van in a sea of empty cans.

Onlookers stared in disbelief at what appeared to be a bucks' night of a group of guys all attempting to look like Tom Cruise. The costumes look real. Check. The haircuts look real. Check. The numberplates look real. Check. But no, there's no way those kids could be real fighter pilots, they'd be lucky to be twenty years old.

Yes, we were—very lucky indeed.

We raced to our rooms, showered, changed and met up back in the lobby before heading to dinner. With dinner complete, the pub crawl down Mitchell Street began.

It's a sad fact that fighter pilots can't dance. I think it's a genetic maxim. Whatever it is that gives us intelligence, lightning-fast reflexes and quick minds must also prevent us from dancing with any real rhythm or grace. Except my good mates Nokka and Jerdo. I think Patrick Swayze's movie *Dirty Dancing* had been out for two weeks when these two decided to pay homage to the movie by scripting their own repertoire of 'Daggy Dancing'. The idea was to lull girls into thinking they were quite smooth dancers, get them alone on the dance floor—or part thereof—and then break into the most ferocious jerking and spasms I have ever seen. They would take turns in performing this routine, alternating from pub to pub, and usually got thrown out after their fits ended up on the floor with furniture falling on top of them.

This borderline-offensive behaviour, more often than not, attracted others with over-developed senses of humour who weren't afraid to tag along with a boistrous group of guys who lived in a permanent state of delusion that they flew fighter jets—oh well, just laugh along with them, hell, they're paying after all . . .

By 1 a.m. we would generally end up at the Victoria Hotel—the Darwin watering hole for hardened cowboys who only come into town once every couple of months for two things: Bundy rum and a fight. We generally stayed away from the bar (Daggy Dancing just wasn't appreciated by those guys) and took our moves upstairs to the dance floor. It was here that I would first feel the repercussions of my impromptu roadside stop.

With our group hitting the dance floor convinced we all looked like Pierce Brosnan and moved like Michael Jackson, I noticed a girl paying me more attention than usual—that is, she looked a second time. I started using my grooves to hide my lateral move across the dance floor in order to see if her interest was out of sympathy or desire. My radar warning receiver immediately went batshit as she locked onto me with her eyes and started to saddle up next to me. It was then I felt it.

It started as a twinge initially and quickly grew into a sharp stinging pain. With my successful engagement of the bandit on the dance floor, I was reluctant to let on that I was having any issues south of the border. It soon became apparent to me that in my haste to complete my number-two on the side of the Stuart Highway, I had given myself a nasty paper cut on the quoit. This was not good. I attempted to discreetly adjust my pants away from the area but started to lose my Jackson Five rhythm. Using all my mental strength and focusing on the wingman's creed to never, ever give up, I gritted my teeth and stayed on the dance floor. I'm not sure if it was my psychopathic frown of concentration or my unintentional Daggy Dancing that defeated the bandit's radar lock, but she bugged out leaving me to RTB (return to bathroom), where I promptly washed the damaged area and applied an emergency field dressing (paper hand towel).

Monday morning my paper cut and associated dance-of-pain became the story of the weekend among the boys. Unfortunately for me there was going to be a bigger story once we returned to Williamtown and I started preparing my AMRAAM brief for the squadron. It was then that I opened my brain only to find that what I had cut my ring with, and what was now back in the Northern Territory[8] sitting neatly on top of my turd, was not in fact the back pages of my notebook, but the front. In the dark, and perhaps after one too many brewskis, I had torn out the front pages of my brain and wiped my arse with over six months worth of nationally sensitive AMRAAM gouge.

23
Supersonic Joseph

When once you have tasted flight, you will forever walk the earth with your eyes turned skyward, for there you have been, and there you will always long to return.

Leonardo da Vinci

To SOME, FLIGHT can be a mystical thing, almost spiritual. My passion for aviation is really a passion for anything that is not subject to earthly bonds: kites, hang-gliders, astronauts, gliders, aircraft, astronomical objects, anti-gravity devices, UFOs—you name it. Climbing large gum trees, driving over the Westgate Bridge or catching elevators to the top floor of the Collins Place Building in Melbourne, I was able to bring to life the novels of my childhood. I would scramble from the Westgate in my Spitfire to take on the Hun, or lift-off in the space shuttle *Enterprise* by pressing my face against the glass of the high-speed elevators. Childhood dreams of flight is a common thread in the fabric that bonds fighter pilots together.

I have also always been an animal lover, but with my obsession for altitude, birds have often been a focus for me. As a child I had a baby mudlark, Peewee, which I raised. I would play with him for hours, fuelling my dreams that I would someday break from the heavy burden of gravity that held me.

Annual leave in a fighter squadron is usually taken over the Christmas/New Year break. It surprised me that for one month every year Australia's number-one deterrent capability would be stood down—we really are a peacetime air force. Christmas was often spent at my mother's farm in East Victoria. It was a beautiful place, a sanctuary which I visited only once a year to give my adrenal gland a little time off. Mum's farm was a little like a rehab clinic—for fighter pilots, adrenaline can be more addictive than crack, and harder to kick. If I didn't go to the farm and force myself to relax, I'd be hang-gliding, rock climbing, big-wave surfing, completing an endurance event, or chasing (or being chased by) wild pigs with pump-action shotguns and machine guns. The farm, by contrast, was a haven of peace and quiet—it did me good.

One year, I found a baby eastern rosella parrot—like the ones you see on the tomato sauce bottles—that had left the nest too early. He was a motley green with sprays of bright red and electric blue scattered across his plumage that reflected the full colours of the rainbow in the right light—a technicolour dream coat. Accordingly, I named him Joseph. He was too young to feed himself, so I raised him on a porridge-like mix and fed him through a syringe for a few weeks until he grew the strength to crack his own seed. I soaked the seed in water initially and showed him how to peel the husk from seed. At first I had grand visions of releasing him back to the wild; however, it soon became apparent he would stand little chance of survival and so I kept him as a pet and a mate. When I was at home he spent all his time on my shoulder where he would prune my hair, clean my ear and sleep in the crook of my neck. It was during the critical stage of learning to eat for himself that I was deployed to Townsville to instruct F-18 students in their final tactical employment phase on Exercise High Sierra.

High Sierra is more like an operational squadron deployment rather than a training course. By this time, you've usually weeded the chaff out from the wheat, leaving behind just the students you're pretty sure are going to make it through the course. It is during this deployment that we start to welcome them into the fighter pilot fold.

I was able to negotiate with the supply officer for Joseph and his cage to travel up to Townsville aboard the C-130 Hercules with the F-18 spare parts and tools. This was harder than it sounds, because I had welded up a birdcage that was so big it was a two-man lift, and only just made it through a doorway. I made a cover for his cage, personally loaded him onto the Herc, and told the loadmaster that there was a very important parrot (VIP) onboard who I wanted to see alive at the other end.

I flew my jet to Townsville in time to meet the Herc when it arrived. I was worried sick that Joseph might not make it through the flight. Would he handle the altitude change? Can parrots handle low oxygen environments, or are they like canaries in coalmines? I nervously unloaded the cage and opened the cover to find him as chirpy as usual, sitting on his perch—well done, mate.

Joseph spent the month living in my room at the officers mess in Townsville, which is located right next to the runway threshold for Runway 1. I positioned his cage so he could look out across the airfield towards Magnetic Island, set the air conditioner and hoped he would be comfortable watching the jets flying past his window. Wrong.

Birds, particularly parrots, and particularly eastern rosellas, are highly strung, neurotic animals who can die from fright. This is why they generally do not make good pets. After his first day in tropical paradise I found Joseph scared to death, hiding in the corner of his cage, panting his head off—he must have been cutting laps round his cage all day and was literally about to fall off the perch. It was then that one of the last jets landed for the day and the large grey bird of prey with two tails flashed past the window. Combined with the shaking of the building, it was no wonder the poor little bugger had shit himself. I took him over to the officers mess bar where the boys fed him some beer and I put him under the sprinkler, one of his favourite pastimes. He soon recovered from the trauma of being hunted by giant grey birds and went back to normal.

At the end of the deployment the supply officer brought me some bad news: 'Sorry, mate, but there's no room for the bird.'

'What am I meant to do with him? I can't just leave him here,' I pleaded.

'There'll be another Herc in a week's time. Put him on that,' he suggested.

That was never going to work—Joseph still couldn't even feed himself properly. It was then that my animal-loving instincts took over.

I found an empty box in the mess that had originally held two champagne glasses and taped up all the seals except for the top. Next I went to a hardware store and purchased some latex tubing which, after cutting a small hole in the top of the box, I poked into the box so that about 50 centimetres was left hanging out. I put Joseph in the box with some seed that I had soaked in water and headed to the jet.

The first thing we do on arrival at the jet is to check the ejection seat is safe and then secure our navigation kit, tapes and helmet bags into a very small area down the righthand side of the ejection seat. I discreetly hid Joseph in my helmet bag and placed him down by the side of the seat. I performed my pre-flight inspection of the aircraft as quickly as possible so that Joseph would not overheat in the cockpit. Like a little hothouse, the perspex canopy of the F-18 can bring the air temperature up to 60 degrees Celsius on the ground and the black surfaces are hot enough to fry an egg on. Without the engines running, and associated air coolers to air-condition the cockpit, it can be very uncomfortable and certainly hot enough to kill a bird—at least he wasn't wearing gloves, a nomex flying suit, life jacket and inflatable plastic G suit like I was.

With the inspection out of the way I climbed the ladder and strapped in. The box I had chosen for Joseph was larger than I had planned and my right elbow wouldn't sit down next to my hip, which I actually needed it to so I could hold the joystick to fly the aircraft. Keeping a straight face as if everything was normal, I rested my right elbow on top of Joseph's box and held the joystick so I looked like I had a dislocated shoulder. I pulled the end of the latex hose out of my helmet bag and inserted it under my oxygen mask. I toggled the mask to its emergency position so it would pull onto my face extra tight and hopefully seal my cheek, mask and latex hose together. I then selected 100 per cent oxygen, which provided me with an overpressure of oxygen in my mask and in doing so hopefully push some into Joseph's box.

I was not comfortable though. I had my right elbow in the air, my mask cutting into my nose and cheeks, and I was gagging against the oxygen being pushed down my throat at high pressure. I quickly cranked the engines, opened the air vents and closed the canopy to start cooling us both down. I reached over with my left hand and gently shook the box, hoping to feel Joseph's wings protesting at my poor bird handling—I felt a little flutter. Great, I've got him here alive—now it's just the altitude, cold, turbulence, speed and G that might kill him. It was starting to seem like a really dumb idea as I struggled to give my dispatcher the chocks-out signal.

I was number fifteen in the sixteen-ship formation and therefore second last to depart. Honko had egged me on for a beat-up on departure as all the bosses were ahead of me and any slight deviation I may have had on departure would be unseen. We were departing off Runway 20 which had us flying right past our flight line where all the maintainers were still packing up spares and tools. I thought it would be good for morale to give them a bit of a show after their one month of hard work. My wingman was another staff member so my departure would not be seen by a student, which was important. It would not be appropriate to be asking for nothing but perfection from them for six months, only for them to see an instructor do an unauthorised fly-past.

With all the jets ahead now airborne and departing in a 30-kilometre snake, I released the brakes and lit the burners. After weeks of carrying bombs around, the jet felt light and responsive with only two fuel tanks under the wings. I reached rotate speed of 250 kilometres per hour and lifted the nose into the air. As soon as the main wheels were off the deck I pushed over and settled the jet at about 2 metres off the runway. With the jet cleaned up and level it was adding 30 kilometres per hour per second. As I continued down the runway I could make out the maintainers standing in a group watching—no doubt courtesy of Honko. I could make out Honko standing on the roof of the crew van just off the left side of the runway. The temptation was too much.

At over 500 kilometres per hour and only a couple of metres above the runway, I cracked the wings and pulled to point the nose directly at Honko's head—and the camera. I kept the jet low and saw him jump out of the way as I hit 1000 kilometres per hour. It was right at that moment, as I was about to pull up over the highway and civilian housing, that I remembered my feathered little friend.

I was torn between pulling back at 6G to get up and over the buildings, and not cracking Joseph's spine. I compromised at about 3G and pulled up to point at the other aircraft. I felt sick again now, worrying that I may have hurt him in the pull-up. When I was steady in the climb I gave the box a another gentle shake—the little trooper was still kicking.

We joined up in two groups of eight at 10 000 metres, with my group assigned the second Boeing 707 tanker. We all took turns cycling in behind the tanker and receiving our 2000 litres of fuel. With all sixteen jets refuelled we climbed to 12 000 metres and overtook the tankers as we headed to Williamtown.

Flying straight and level does weird things to fighter pilots. Given that we're so used to high-adrenaline situations, cross-country navigation missions are among the most boring thing that we ever do—and maintainers never like fighter pilots being bored as we start to fidget with things we shouldn't. Time is a very scarce resource in fighter flying, so when you have some, you start looking around the cockpit. What does this button do? I wonder what this sub-sub-sub-menu is for on the weapons computer? On this occasion I wasn't about to find any loose rivets around the cockpit or pulled threads on the seat straps—I was worried about my mate.

In thinking about him, I started to empathise with Michael Collins on the *Apollo 11* mission when Neil and Buzz walked on the moon. Poor Mike was stuck in the lunar orbiter while Neil and Buzz became famous. Here was Joseph—probably the only bird in Australia to ever reach 12 000 metres in a Hornet—and he was stuck in a dark box like poor old Mike. It wasn't fair. I lifted his box up and bent back the lid just enough for him to stick his head out. It had been about an hour since take-off and I wasn't sure if my MacGyver-rigged avarian oxygen system was working or not. My concern was shortly answered.

A little red and green head popped out and looked around. He looked at the big black predator with a visor and oxygen mask and then looked out the window. I mean, he just stared. I'm not sure whether it was hypoxia or some sort of spiritual experience, but Joseph's little onyx eyes just stared out from 12 000 metres as if he was enjoying it. I opened the box and he stepped onto my gloved finger. I raised him to the top of the instrument panel and he stepped off next to my HUD. He then strutted back and forth, twitching his wings as if to say, 'Who's the bird?' After a minute I returned him to his box for fear of him passing out from no oxygen, and secured his 100 per cent oxygen supply.

I was relieved when I finally landed in Newcastle to find him still alive. Joseph never seemed the same after the experience, though. We were still mates, but he always seemed a little more distant. He would sit on his perch and just stare at the sky. I guessed Leonardo da Vinci was right.

24
The last flight

I STOPPED OUTSIDE the office of my commanding officer; the corridor was lined with the class photos of every course of Australian fighter pilots that had graduated from the fighter school since Vietnam. I stared at the black and white photographs closest to his office, now faded and browned with age, and recognised the joy on the kids' faces. That's all they were—kids. Most no older than 25, their youthful features were frozen in rapture as they smiled for their photographer. I was like that once, I thought, as I attempted to understand what it was that had changed about me since I graduated from the fighter school so many years ago. What had caused me to lose that child-like smile of wonder and amazement every time I went to 'work'? I deliberately pulled my eyes away from the photos, the memories just making what I had to do all that much harder. I felt like I was tortur-ing that small boy inside of me, somehow inflicting a horrifying pain on an innocent child. This was the hardest thing I had ever done in my life—and I had done some hard, hard things compared to most 30-year-olds.

I looked down at the typed letter in my hands and noticed my hands shaking with a mix of fear and anger. Fear that I was about to make the biggest mistake of my life, and anger that the 'system' had driven me to this. I had mentally pictured this moment hundreds of times over the last couple of years, as my frustration with the air force had built; however, I had never anticipated this much emotion would well up inside of me. To be honest, I had not stopped long enough during the last thirteen years to really feel more than superficial feelings. Love, friendship, grief and heartbreak—they had all been there throughout my career, momentarily disrupting my life like small whirlwinds scattering leaves across a manicured lawn. But the truth was I had always been too busy to really feel them. As I pondered what I was about to do, I felt the years of suppressed emotion fighting to come out. I knocked on the door.

'Come in, Serge,' said the CO when he looked up from his desk, or 'brown bomber' as he called it when he was unable to go flying because of his paperwork requirements.

'G'day, Sir, I wonder if I could have a quick chat?'

'Sure, mate. Come and grab a seat. What's on your mind?' My CO, Bolly, was a great guy, and always kept his door open to his pilots for just these sorts of occasions.

'Sir, I wish to tender my resignation.' I could feel the emotion rising. 'I can no longer work for the RAAF and honestly feel like I'm contributing to the defence of the country any longer.'

Tears started welling in my eyes. Tears of sadness and anger. In my mind, rehearsing for this moment, I had always been far less emotional. In these visions, the CO had pleaded with me not to leave the force and had offered me all sorts of promotions and incentives because I was indispensible. But this was different.

'No problem, Serge,' said the CO matter-of-factly, reaching out to receive my letter of resignation. 'I take it you've made up your mind?' He knew me pretty well.

'Yes, Sir.'

And then it tumbled out: 'I will never forgive the arseholes running this outfit and the way they have traded the welfare of the service and the men they are charged with leading to ensure their own fucking pensions. You have known me for a long time and know my motivations. How can these pricks be allowed to keep their jobs while they ruin the force and the motivations of guys like me?'

I'd had a gutful of the constant paperwork, the insistence on ridiculous rules and regulations, the political correctness, the hypocrisy of them demanding we be ready to serve (and die for) our country at a moment's notice, but then not letting us do what we needed to do in order to prepare for that. I had decided I couldn't prostitute myself, my standards, nor the nation's national security for my next promotion.

'Your efforts are well-acknowledged, Serge, but you can't just fly forever,' the CO stated calmly. 'You have to go to Canberra and complete a ground job if you want to get promoted and . . .'

'I don't want to get promoted—you know that, Sir. I joined to fly and I don't need stripes on my shoulder to lead men. I lead scores of men now and I do it well. Are you honestly saying that unless I get promoted, I can't fly? And that you would happily let me walk after spending $50 million training me?'

'That's pretty much it, Serge.'

I was flabbergasted. I couldn't imagine a large corporation spending that much money to train someone and then telling them, 'Sorry, mate, but unless you stop doing what we trained you to do, what you love to do so much, then you're no longer required.' The answer I had struggled to find while looking at the photos in the corridor became clear. I was now experienced enough to see through the airshows and media releases and recognise the RAAF for what it really was. Sadly it was not what I knew it could and should be, and I knew there was no way I could ever influence that. Only one thing would do that and that would be a major war—not a ground campaign like Afghanistan or Iraq, but a major conflict where the RAAF would be required to risk personnel for national security purposes, something it has done little of since Vietnam.

I left the CO's office feeling vindicated about my decision. I thought that any organisation that values its personnel, or at least its investment, so little, is probably not going to be right for me.

My last flight was a month later and the CO asked me what I would like to do. A fighter pilot's last flight in the Hornet is traditionally celebrated with a beat-up of the base, where the outgoing pilot flies as low and as fast as the bosses are willing to authorise. Over the years this custom was progressively constrained until they were so lame I really wasn't interested in showing everyone on base that I could fly an F-18 like a civilian light aircraft. I elected for something far more memorable—for me at least.

I asked the CO if he would authorise a couple of the single-seat aircraft to have all their external stores and weapon mounts removed so that Matty and I could have a 'full-up' dogfight. With the under-wing fuel tanks and bomb racks removed, the jets would fly higher, faster, turn tighter and make our fight far more aggressive—exactly what I wanted to do for my last flight. Matty had duxed his weapons instructor course, enjoyed hang-gliding on days off, and got up to a lot of mischief throughout his career—all the things I had done. He was two years junior to me, and he was snapping at my heels. My last flight wasn't going to be in front of the base, but was going to be my litmus test as to whether I was resigning at the right time or not. Would Matty be able to beat me at one of the most physically and mentally demanding activities that human beings have ever invented—the aerial dogfight? I wanted to find out.

Also known as basic fighter manoeuvres (BFM), dogfighting in an F-18 is more demanding on the human body than the most violent roller-coaster that you could ever ride. It is more like a demolition derby at 1000 kilometres per hour, where a moment's distraction will kill you—not just have you rear-ended by another car. This is where the mental challenge comes into the activity. Throughout this violent struggle between you, your jet and the bandit, you must maintain a razor-sharp mind that knows which way is up, how much fuel you have remaining, where the edge of the airspace is, your speed, what mode your radar is in, how many missile-defeating flares you have remaining, which mode your weapon is in, your angle of attack and the heat signature of your engines. This unhuman amount of information processing must be performed in split seconds and consequently young fighter pilots often use the term 'Jedi' around the more experienced pilots to describe the Force-like attributes needed to excel in dogfighting.

With our 'clean jets' approved, I asked the scheduler to put Matty and I up the following Friday, so we could go straight to the bar after my last flight. Friday and Saturday nights were the only nights we would drink. This was something that I always found amazing, that the RAAF could screen, indoctrinate and train twenty-year-old males full of testosterone into not drinking five days of the week—the National Rugby League could do with a bit of that sort of discipline. The truth was the job was so demanding that our lives were at risk every day we went to work, and most guys had lost at least one mate on the job. We all understood the realities of the job. The outcomes of flying hungover or drunk would not be the same as a rugby league player—the only consequence for him might be getting into a fight at the casino, but for us, lives could be lost and multi million-dollar aircraft crashed.

Friday came and I arrived at work as usual and walked up to the operations room to check the flying schedule. There it was: 'Matty/Serge 1v1 BFM ALL.' No-one else was flying, so Matty and I had ALL the airspace to ourselves—which we were going to need for what I had planned.

The Williamtown airspace is a circle of 200 kilometres radius centred on the base which would allow for up to a 400 kilometre intercept to be flown if we both went to opposite sides of the airspace—which we were going to do. My brief to Matty was simple. We were to merge supersonic at 15 000 metres, one fight only, guns only—we were not to use missiles. This would ensure that the fight became a dogfight and would not be over too quickly. I wanted the hardest physical and mental challenge I could have to finish my career. A normal brief for a BFM mission like ours would be one hour to walk everyone through how to miss each other, not run out of fuel, not lose control of their jet nor fly into the water. I briefed Matty in 30 seconds—he had just duxed his course and I had a bit of experience missing jets and the water by this stage of my career.

With the mission brief complete, we stepped to our aircraft via the aircraft life-support section and the flight-line maintenance section. Life support is where we would pick up our bone domes (helmets), survival vest and speed jeans (G suit). Our bone domes contained our earphones, oxygen masks with microphones and visors. Most guys would have a clear and dark visor. I used a dark visor and a laser visor that was bright yellow and made the entire world appear yellow. Similar to high-contrast shooting glasses, this visor would filter out blue light from the sky and allow me to see aircraft earlier. Additionally, I had a slight astigmatism, and by squinting against the bright yellow world I could slightly compress my eyeball into an anatomically correct sphere and improve my vision beyond 6/6.

The helmets were made from Kevlar and extremely light . . . at normal weight. However, in an 8G break turn, this 4-kilogram helmet would instantly become 32 kilograms; when combined with the weight of your head, it literally felt like someone was sitting on your head. In case you're not familiar with the physics of G force, think about how you can spin a bucketful of water and the water is pushed into the bottom of the bucket when upside-down. Your body is the water and the bucket is the F-18, except that you cannot generate 8G with your arm.

The G suit is designed to overcome this water-in-the-bucket phenomenon. It inflates under G to squeeze the blood in your legs and gut (the water in the bucket) back up into your brain (the top of the bucket). In doing so the G suit stops pilots from losing consciousness as the blood drains from their head. However, the G suit is an active system and doesn't work without the pilot's help. The pilot must physically strain as hard as he can against the inflated bladders to force the blood back up to his brain. This straining manoeuvre is similar to forcing yourself to go red in the face except it is a full body workout and very exhausting. There's a good feedback response on your fitness and straining technique; you very quickly get tunnel vision and then grey out when your technique is wrong.

Grey out, I imagine, is similar to astral projection, except you're not lying in your bed trying to contact your inner spirit, you're piloting a $50-million machine near the speed of sound. You lose your eyesight but still have your other senses so you can feel the high-G buffet and the G suit, you can smell the 100 per cent pure cool oxygen pressurise your lungs to keep them inflated, and you can hear the roar of the wind around you as the atmosphere protests about being violated by your 7-tonne supersonic machine. You just lose your eyesight. That's all. And you're only a second away from blackout where it's Good Night Irene and the fun is over. I guess that's why they call this equipment 'life support'.

With our modern-day knightly attire on, we headed over to the flight-line maintenance hut to sign for our jets. We reviewed the aircraft maintenance history, previous servicing, previous rectifications and software versions to make sure the aircraft were up for the mission. I had specifically asked maintenance to prepare two single seat F-18s for Matty and I. Our unit was No. 2 Operational Conversion Unit (2OCU), and as such had mainly two-seat aircraft for training. The two seaters, or 'tubs', had less fuel (hard to have less than little) and were more unstable than the fighters. Matty and I would need all the fuel and stability we could have for today's mission.

As we exited the hut we both smiled at each other before heading to our jets. It was a smile of mutual respect that hid an underlying insecurity that we each had about whether we were soon to have our arse handed to us by the other. Matty was the underdog, but was rising fast. He was a dynamo, and the closest thing to a bird human-kind has yet created. He could fly anything exceptionally well and would go on to win international aerobatic competitions and Red Bull air Races. I, on the other hand, had a couple of years of experience on Matty and could also fly the jet well, but I was starting to slow down a bit. It was going to be a space-age joust between two equally matched competitors. My smile was definitely hiding a little insecurity.

I quickly pre-flighted my jet and strapped her on. That is what the jet had become—an extension of myself. I was experienced enough now to feel the jet and know where she was in the flight envelope; about to spin, about to flick. I could hear the flight envelope as well; low speed roar of the wind washing around the canopy, high-G buffet on the tails. It was a great place to be as a pilot and I knew Matty was somewhere near there as well. I was about to find out just how near.

I heard the howl of Matty's auxiliary power unit (APU) come to life. This little jet howled at 56 000 rpm and provided a power source to start the main engines. I started my own jet and ran through the programming of the radar and navigation data. Ten minutes after start I was ready and checked in with Matty on the radio.

'Hunter, check.'

'Hunter 2,' Matty replied.

'Maple ops, Hunter taxies with two, Channel 1 go.' I instructed Matty to come up on the ground frequency and got our clearance for taxi. As we taxied to the far end of the runway I could feel my adrenaline level rising as I completed my take-off checks and called ready to the air traffic control tower. Even after thirteen years the little gland was still doing a great job of pumping that heart-starting drug.

We lined up on the runway as a pair. I lined up on my side of the runway, Matty on his, and gave the wind-up signal to set 80 per cent thrust. I ran my throttles up, completed a quick check of my engine instruments and then I did a quick check to see that Matty's canopy was shut, flaps were down, trim was set and he had no fluid leaks from his aircraft. Matty gave me a thumbs-up that he was ready and then I turned my head to the front, looking up, paused, and then dropped my chin to my chest—the signal for Matty to simultaneously release his brakes with me. I never enjoyed looking at my feet while releasing the brakes and lighting the afterburners. It's only for half a second, but it always felt like my head was down for minutes whenever I gave the take-off signal.

Keeping the jet centred on my side of the runway so I wouldn't run Matty off his side, I scanned my engine instruments, confirmed good power and then used my periphery to check Matt was in position—a good habit for a lead, but it was never necessary with Matty, he was never out of position. At 200 kilometres per hour I started to gently ease the joystick back to lift the nose wheel off and then we were airborne.

Good formation flying is about good leading, and good leading is doing everything in a predictable, steady manner. I slowly leant forwards in an exaggerated manner so Matt would see me moving and know I was selecting my undercarriage and flaps up. If he was late on retracting them he would fall back out of position. I sneaked another peak at Matty—he was like a decal on the inside of my canopy. Rock solid.

At 300 metres, accelerating through 600 kilometres per hour, I gave Matty a thumb-back signal to initiate his weapons system check, to which he slid back and started checking his weapons on my aircraft. I watched his radar cycle through its modes on my radar warning receiver (RWR) until he passed abeam me, allowing me to slide back and complete my weapons checks on Matty. I checked the radar modes locked his aircraft, the heat-seeking missile could lock onto Matty's hot exhaust gases, and I checked the mission computer symbology was correct. I then overtook Matty again and we deployed into tactical formation.

'Outwards turn,' I transmitted on the radio, and watched as Matty started his turn towards the far end of the airspace. I mirrored him and started heading in the opposite direction. My air-to-air TACAN (tactical air navigation) readout indicated the distance between us and I watched it as it increased towards 200 kilometres. By this time I was passing through 15 000 metres and I was indicating Mach 1.3, or 1.3 times the speed of sound.

'Hunter 1, inwards turn—fight's on.'

'Hunter 2, fight's on.'

I eased the jet into a turn to point directly at Matty, who was 200 kilometres north and also turning directly towards me. It felt like thirteen years of 70-hour weeks was culminating in this one engagement and inside I knew this would be my last dogfight. I felt a mix of sadness from the boy still inside of me and achievement from the man I had grown into. I pushed the emotion aside and focused on the small dot that was now quickly taking shape in my windscreen as Matty and I merged, canopy to canopy, at over 3600 kilometres per hour—the fight was on.

I lit the afterburners and allowed the nose to drop to 30 degrees in my 3G lefthand turn—I was flying the G by feeling as I turned around to look for Matty. I briefly lost him in the turn and had to turn my upper body 90 degrees to see him. At this altitude and speed our turn radius was so high that we were now 16 kilometres apart. Matty was holding me on the horizon, which ensured he was trading his altitude at the same rate I was—smart move, I thought.

We both continued our turns back towards each other and soon joined in another neutral merge—now at 10 000 metres. We had lost 5000 metres in the last turn and were still perfectly matched.

The next turn was almost identical to the first, except the turn radius was starting to reduce, meaning that we only flew 10 kilometres apart on opposite sides of the circle. We both matched each other in altitude and angles to merge again at 7000 metres, perfectly mirrored with Matty flying directly under me. I lost sight of him as he went under the floor of the jet and I continued in my left turn, looking for him to emerge back between my tails—this time he didn't.

I started to scan around and soon found him very nose-low and starting to pitch back up into me—he had taken the fight into a looping vertical fight. I immediately countered by rolling on my back, placing Matty at the top of my canopy and pulling straight into him. I pulled to maximise my turn rate by feeling for the airflow separation across the tails—'driving on cobblestones' is how we taught it to students. We passed in the vertical relatively neutral with Matty immediately reversing as he passed me vertically nose-high. I matched him and we were soon in a rolling scissors, stuck canopy to canopy in a series of barrel-rolling manoeuvres passing through 3000 metres. We would soon need to give away the vertical fight and go back to the horizontal fight if we were not going to loop our way through the hard deck of 1500 metres. The trouble was, whichever one of us eased out first would become immediately defensive— whoever eased out last would probably go through the hard deck. I started easing at exactly the same time as Matty and we both ended up in a flat scissors at 1500 metres, side by side, perfectly neutral.

Betty then went off in my ear, telling me that I had reached my pre-planned minimum fuel. I assessed where we were and knocked 100 litres off the minimum fuel so I could stay in the fight. Eventually I called 'knock it off' for fuel and checked Matty's fuel—we were both the same at 800 litres. After burning 2700 litres of fuel in under five minutes and descending from 15 000 to 1500 metres through a series of two circular horizontal fights, a looping scissors and a flat scissor, we had ended up equal in speed, altitude, angles and fuel.

I had done my best and I could not defeat Matty; a clear indication to me that I was leaving at the right time while still on top of my game—just. The thirteen years I spent as a jet pilot had flown by, and I had achieved more than I could have ever imagined when I was sixteen years old and first met Ross Fox at the airshow. I had enjoyed an extremely full and satisfying career working with some of the best talent Australia has to offer, I had reached the top of my professional game, flown my heart out and loved every working day—not many people can say that. But my time had come. Despite the fact that I knew it was time to leave, I was going to miss the jet like crazy—any knucklehead who says they don't is lying.

25

Where to from here?

THIS IS A tough question for most fighter pilots and in my experience, few get it right. The personality type that is screened for during recruitment, and then steered, shaped and grown during training, is not a personality that is easily employed outside of the fighter force— who else would put up with such narcissism in the workplace?

The best way I can describe this personality is by using an analogy that my long-time mate, Tool, came up with. It goes something like this:

There is a little monkey on your back and he is a cunt. He only eats danger, excitement and impossible feats. If he is not fed, he will whisper in your ear how little you are worth. Oh, you can try and trick the monkey by attempting to navigate a conventional course in life, like flying for the airlines, and deluding yourself that your job is highly challenging while watching the autopilot for sixteen hours as it flies you halfway around the world. But you will never delude the monkey. He will eventually see through your trick and start whispering in your ear again. He is a cunt because you know that to satisfy

the monkey you will have to do things that are not entirely
sane nor conducive to a long life nor a happy family. You are
a slave to the monkey.

I initially thought the airlines would be right for me but soon found
out how wrong I was. There was no challenge . . . just attendance.
There was no room for self-improvement. There was no purpose to
what I was doing other than fattening my wallet, losing my health
and enduring a twenty-year lobotomy. Rarely did I sit next to another
pilot who enjoyed his job, felt his employment package was satisfac-
tory, or inspired me to be more than I was the day I had joined the
company. In fact, the company suppressed any motivation I had to
help them, like how to save money through training efficiencies and
improvements—something I had more than a bit of experience in.

The frustration built up to the point of depression and I sought
professional help from a wonderful shrink. At our first appointment
he spent three hours running around inside my melon scared shitless
of what he found and not able to find his way out. Eventually he
handed me a story he had written for the Annual Australian Head-
shrinking Conference. To paraphrase the article:

Life is like a journey up a giant mountain. All our life we
spend looking towards the summit—a beacon of strength
that draws us towards it with unending endurance. Along the
way we encounter crevasses and avalanches, rock slides and
storms but our focus on the summit keeps us going. Eventually we reach the summit and look around to see that there
is no higher peak. This is it. We can't get any higher. We then
realise we must descend and in every direction we look down,
north, south, east and west, we see only one thing—our own

death. This is the critical moment of self-realisation when a boy can become a wise man or a fool. For the fool sees a sight so horrible he refuses to look at it and even tries to run away from it. He trades in the family wagon for a sports car, that iconic symbol of youth, or perhaps he trades his wife in for a younger model. And how good is the sex? He feels like he is eighteen again. That's it. It's working. He doesn't have to face his own mortality any longer—he is immortal! Or perhaps he takes the path of the wise man that truly accepts his fate is death and ensures his life is in order for that fateful day that may come at any moment. He looks death in the face with a confident peace that is all-consuming, knowing that all he can do he has done.

The shrink went on to tell me: 'Serge, most people reach their summit around mid-life—hence the term mid-life crisis. You, both fortunately and unfortunately, hit it when you were 27. You fighter pilots are a lot like elite sportsmen . . .'

I wasn't sure which movie he'd been watching but I never saw many elite sportsmen when I was in the RAAF.

'Take Lleyton Hewitt, for instance,' he continued. 'He was the number-one tennis player in the world at nineteen years of age. Where does he go to from there? You guys are the same. What possible career could match what you used to do in the Hornet?'

He was right. But what was I to do?

'Read this,' the doc said, handing me a self-help book written by a lesbian.

What the fuck?

The doc did nothing but hand me a book a week to read. We would discuss each book and then he would hand me another.

On my twelfth week he said he didn't have any more books for me to read.

'Well, what will we talk about next week, Doc, if I don't read a book?' I asked, slightly concerned he was going to say what he said next.

'We're done, Serge. You'll be fine.'

'What do you mean, I'll be fine? Nothing has changed,' I argued.

'Serge, your greatest asset is your mind. You're the most intelligent person I have ever counselled and feel I got more out of the last twelve weeks than you did.'

I wasn't sure whether he meant I was intelligent or he only ever saw unintelligent people. I continued to protest. 'Thanks, Doc, but I still have to spend half my life trapped in a dark closet with some geriatric I have nothing in common with, watching a test pattern on the TV for sixteen hours before getting out of the closet totally jet-lagged only to find the sun coming up. And I'm sick of the fake tits, big houses and a totally self-absorbed lifestyle that does nothing to contribute to society—all it does is make me rich.'

'I told you we were done, Serge,' he said smiling.

A few years later, somewhere over Africa . . .

'Mate, do you realise the last time we flew together we wrote off the Nomad?' I said to Tool, who was flying as captain in the left seat of our aircraft.

We had last flown together in 1991 at RAAF Tindal when the flaperon on our quality-built all-Australian aircraft snapped, sending us out of control to the point where we essentially crash-landed onto the runway—the aircraft never flew again.

'Shut the fuck up, Serge, you'll jinx us. Now, get back there,' he said, ordering me back to the sensor station of our very unique, highly modified civilian aircraft.

I stole one more snapshot of the beautiful scenery; sunset, aqua coastline and desert plains. It made me marvel every time I looked out the window.

As I climbed out of the copilot's seat, I reflected on how far we had both come together. It was 22 years after joining the RAAF on the same date in Melbourne, and we had taken incredibly different career paths. Tool had gone into the 'forward air control' world and then F-18s before transferring to the Special Air Service and completing an exchange with the Special Boat Service in the UK.

I had gone on to fighters and then weapons instruction before briefly flying jumbos for a major Australian airline. After four years I found the courage to get off the treadmill and to set up my own government-consulting firm in Canberra. I had finally sorted out my personal life by divorcing the F-18 and marrying a wonderful wife with whom I am now blessed with two children. And here we were, Tool and I, back together again, having survived years of feeding our respective monkeys . . . and tonight the little cunts were about to get a really good feed.

I drew the curtain to blackout the rear of the cabin and felt my way to the sensor station. Tool would be flying single pilot up the front while I ran 'the gear'. I tuned up the sensors, updated the navigation system, flicked the radios across into their secure mode and keyed the radio.

'Assassin 10, Assassin 10, this is Firelight 11,' I transmitted.'

'Firelight 11, this is Assassin 10, have you loud and clear. How me?' came the American voice through my headset.

Tonight Tool and I would be working with US Special Forces who were trying to 'kill or capture' a senior terrorist running a bomb-making cell—his codename was 'Objective Switchblade'. We would be the eyes and ears for the guys on the ground, tracking the objective with our targeting pod that extended from the belly of our 'low profile' aircraft. We would clear the helicopter landing zones (HLZs) prior to their insertion, provide the operators with a count of personnel in each house as they cleared the village, identify any possible threats to the guys, clear their exit routes and above all track Mr Switchblade. Assassin 10, our controller for the mission, would coordinate our tasking and make sure our information flowed through to the ground forces effectively.

'Assassin 10, Firelight 11, I read you Lima Charlie also. Call when ready for line up,' I replied.

'Assassin 10, go ahead.'

'Assassin 10, Firelight 11, on station overhead Switchblade's compound, flight level 2000, fragged on station 1800 to 2100 local, endurance until 2359 local, sensors are sweet, pushing video on frequency 5050 meg, report good handshake, we have good products for Objective Switchblade version 3.5, go ahead situation update.' I reported that we were over the objective's home at 7000 metres and we planned to support the ground forces between 6 p.m. and 9 p.m. but could extend until midnight if required. Our sensors were all operational and Assassin 10 could receive our video feed if he tuned his TV receiver into 5050 megahertz. I asked him to confirm he could see our video feed on his display and that we had the latest information for the mission.

'Roger, Firelight 11, copied you are overhead Switchblade's compound this time at flight level 200 (6000 metres). You also have below you Nightlight 21, a reaper at flight level 180 (5500 metres), pushing video on 5080 meg and Cobalt 31, a predator at flight level 160 (5000 metres). Nightlight 21 is currently IMINT locked the objective. I have a good handshake with your video. H hour remains 2030 with four chalks touching down on HLZs as planned and two Apaches in support.' Assassin 10 had advised us that we had two unmanned aerial vehicles, or drones, directly underneath—one armed, one unarmed. The armed drone was also transmitting a TV picture and was locked to the objective's home. He could see our TV picture and four helicopters with the Special Forces troops would be touching down at 8.30 p.m.

'Firelight 11 copied all, we have a good handshake and comms with Nightlight 21 and Cobalt 31 and IMINT locked the objective at this time.'

I felt the aircraft roll as Tool centred up our orbit overhead the objective's compound.

'On station, on time,' reported Tool. We were ready with two and a half hours remaining to build the picture before the boys touched down and arrived at the objective's front door. Knock knock, arsehole.

Notes

1. Words by John Gillespie Magee, Jr (9 June 1922–11 December 1941), an American aviator and poet who died as a result of a midair collision over Lincolnshire during World War II. He was serving in the Royal Canadian Air Force, which he joined before the United States officially entered the war. He is most famous for his poem 'High Flight' which appears at the front of this book.

2. Note to Chinese spies reading this. When determining your optimal time to attack Australia, ring RAAF Base Williamtown and ask to speak to the officers mess manager. Determine from him/her the date of the next 81 Wing dining-in and utilise this evening, and most of the next day, as your D-Day.

3. The irony of officers living in 'messes' and non-commissioned officers (NCOs) living in 'barracks' has always entertained me.

4. I have used the male term intentionally here, though I do not mean to discriminate against women at all. At the time of writing this book, there are no female fighter pilots in the RAAF and as such the Australian Fighter Force possibly stands as the last bastion of male chauvinism left in this world.

5. Conning is short for contrails, which are the vapour lines left by aircraft when at high altitude. Generally fighters do not like

being seen by eyeballs before they are seen on radar and so do not fly high enough to contrail. A contrailing formation can be seen out to 160 kilometres, as distinct from 30 kilometres where the eyeball can first detect the actual aircraft.

6   Iran Air Flight 655 was a civilian jet airliner shot down by US missiles on 3 July 1988, over the Strait of Hormuz, towards the end of the Iran–Iraq War. The aircraft, an Airbus A300B2-203 operated by Iran Air, was flying from Bandar Abbas, Iran, to Dubai, United Arab Emirates, over Iran's territorial waters in the Persian Gulf on its usual flight path when it was destroyed by the United States Navy's guided-missile cruiser USS *Vincennes* (CG-49), killing all 290 passengers and crew aboard, ranking it twelfth among the deadliest disasters in aviation history. Wikipedia, http://enwikipedia.org/wiki/Iran_Air_Flight_655.

7   Quite the opposite! Having flown airliners for some of the world's best-known airlines and seen 'world's best practice', I can honestly state that this drilling of perfection into pilots makes the Australian fighter pilot stand out on the world stage. It does fill your brain up, though, so don't ask me for my parents' birthdays, when my medical is due, or where I last parked my car.

8   For the benefit of any Chinese spies reading this, I suggest you start looking on the west side of the Stuart Highway, about ten minutes north of Adelaide River—there you will find all the answers you seek.

Acknowledgements

I WISH TO thank my Dad for planting the seed and Ross Fox for nurturing it. To all the knuckleheads who pushed me further than I could ever have pushed myself—thank you, it was an honour to serve with you. To my squadron mates who are still alive and Bograts at heart, I thank you for keeping me young. I would like to thank the Chief of the Australian Defence Force, General David Hurley, for clearing the book for publication—you are definitely not the target of my senior officer rants contained within, but rather one of the few senior officers who places 'country before self'. A big thank you to Paul Carter keeping me motivated and sending my first couple of chicken-scratchings off to Allen & Unwin (without telling me). Thanks also to the team at Allen & Unwin for their encouragement and for teaching me how to tell a joke properly, particularly my publicist Amy Milne, publisher Claire Kingston and editors Kathryn Knight and Susin Chow—I still can't believe all three of you suffer from Tourette's and feel you must continually insert f-bombs and c-bombs whenever you complete an edit. Lastly, to my unbelievably patient wife Mezza for everything you do, including raising two of the best girls a dad could ask for—I thank God for every day we are together.

About the author

SERGE IS A farmer in the highlands of New South Wales, Australia, where he lives a self-sustainable lifestyle with his wife and two children on their property 'Bovarna' (heaven for cows). When not mending fences he can be found attempting to herd cattle back through previously mended fences. Serge holds a master's degree in Aviation Industry Management and manages a consulting and training company in Canberra, Australia that provides specialist services to government organisations in Australia and overseas. Serge flies anything he can get his hands on, from hang-gliders to jumbos, and enjoys participating in extreme sports. In 1991, Serge was the proud recipient of the weekly Broome 'Roebuck Inn' male handle bar competition.

This is Not a Drill: Just another glorious day in the oilfield

'Carter writes as if he has ADD, careering through his life on oil rigs in exotic locations. He won't win the Booker, but his yarns burn with anarchic energy . . . in a word, irrepressible.'—*Herald Sun*

He's back on the rigs and back in trouble.

Picking up right where he left off, Paul Carter pulls out more tall tales of a mad, bad and dangerous life in the international oil trade. Starting with action and mayhem galore, *This Is Not A Drill* sets an unrelenting pace that just doesn't let up, as Paul almost drowns when the Russian rig he's working on begins to capsize; is reunited with his Dad—another adrenaline junkie; gets married; hangs out with his rig pig buddies in exotic locations; gets hammered on vodka in Sakhalin; and spends a couple of interesting weeks in Afghanistan with some mates who run an outfit that just happens to contract out mercenaries for hire . . . this is the next fast, furious and very funny book from Paul Carter.

*Is That Thing Diesel?: One man, one bike and the first lap around
Australia on used cooking oil*

At forty years old, a successful writer, husband and father, no longer
toiling on offshore drilling rigs, was Paul Carter happily nestled in
the cotton wool of suburban life enjoying the fruits of his labour?
Was he fuck!

With his manic life left far behind and the perfect opportunity to
take it easy stretched before him what else would a middle-aged, bike
obsessed, man want?

Yes, that's right, he'd want to be the first guy to ride around Australia
on an underpowered experimental motorcycle that runs on used
cooking oil, wouldn't he? Preferably without getting hit by a semi-
trailer full of bridge parts. Is he out of his mind? Quite possibly.

Embark on a rollickingly, downright dangerous and often unhinged
quest that starts on an environmentally friendly motorcycle built on
a shoestring budget by students, and ends with a plan to break the
motorcycle land speed record for bio fuel.

Carter is back to his old balls-to-the-wall style of writing, prepare to
laugh out loud.

*Smoking Monkeys, Drilling Rigs, Bio-diesel Bikes and Other Stories:
The complete Paul Carter*

Fighter pilots call it 'task saturation'. Does it make you mental? After reading this compendium of all three Paul Carter books you will know the answer.

Life is never simple for Paul. Exhilarating and crazed? Yes. And sometimes terrifying? Often.

Strap yourselves in for a bloody funny ride through one man's adventures in the oil trade and beyond with his bestselling books *Don't Tell Mum I Work on the Rigs, She Thinks I'm a Piano Player in a Whorehouse* and *This is Not a Drill*. Death and toothache, dysentery and gambling, madness and a cocktail-serving orangutan are all part of a day's work.

Then, when you thought he'd grown up and settled down to a calm life, he signs up to be the first guy to ride around Australia on an underpowered experimental motorcycle that runs on used cooking oil.

Is he out of his mind? Quite possibly.

Smoking Monkeys, Drilling Rigs, Bio-diesel Bikes and Other Stories combines Paul Carter's phenomenally successful books into one handsome volume.